PI

Pontus

Bithynia

• TROAS

PERGAMUS

Galatia

• THYATIRA   Asia

SARDIS   • ANTIOCH   Cappadocia

• SMYRNA   • PHILADELPHIA   • ICONIUM

EPHESUS   HIERAPOLIS   trade road

              • COLOSSAE   LYSTRA•

              LAODICEA   • TARSUS

PATMOS •   • MILETUS

                                        Cilicia

                                                    Syria

                                                    DAMASCUS

                                                    Judea

                                                    • JERUSALEM

APOCALYPSE

SCRIPTURE TEXTBOOKS FOR CATHOLIC SCHOOLS

VOLUME VI

SAINT PAUL
AND APOSTOLIC WRITINGS

SCRIPTURE TEXTBOOKS FOR CATHOLIC SCHOOLS

General Editor:

The Very Reverend Monsignor John M. T. BARTON, D.D., L.S.S., F.S.A.
English Consultor of the Pontifical Biblical Commission

SAINT PAUL
AND
APOSTOLIC WRITINGS

by the Reverend Father
SEBASTIAN BULLOUGH, O.P.,
M.A.(Cantab.), S.T.L.
Scripture Master at Blackfriars School, Laxton

With a Foreword by His Eminence
THE CARDINAL ARCHBISHOP OF WESTMINSTER

THE NEWMAN PRESS   Westminster, Maryland

1950

NIHIL OBSTAT:

FR. RICARDUS KEHOE, O.P., S.T.L., L.S.S.
FR. ROLANDUS D. POTTER, O.P., S.T.L., L.S.S., M.A.

IMPRIMI POTEST:

FR. ANTONINUS MAGUIRE, O.P.
Vicarius Provincialis Provinciae Angliae.
LONDINI, *die 23a Februarii 1948*

NIHIL OBSTAT:

JOANNES P. CAN. ARENDZEN, D.D., PH.D., M.A.
Censor deputatus.

IMPRIMATUR:

E. MORROGH BERNARD
Vicarius Generalis.
WESTMONASTERII, *die 10a Martii 1949.*

First published 1950

PRINTED IN THE UNITED STATES OF AMERICA

Lithographed By WICKLAND NALLEY - INC. Westminster, Maryland.

FOREWORD

THE present series of Scripture textbooks for schools is both welcome and opportune. The books ought to arouse a more intelligent interest in the minds of the children in the unspeakable treasures which God unfolds in His written word to mankind.

It is our fervent hope that through the study of the books the children will be encouraged to read the Scriptures themselves. So many people are taught all about the Scriptures but few are taught to read them. St Jerome tells us that to be ignorant of the Scriptures means to be ignorant of Christ. This point is stressed by our Holy Father in his encyclical letter on the Bible. His Holiness explains that our Divine Lord will be better known, more ardently loved and more faithfully imitated, in as far as men know and meditate on the sacred Scriptures, and especially the New Testament.

Scripture lessons should teach children not only about the Scriptures, not only about the facts of our Lord's life, but about our Lord Himself. They should be taught to know our Lord through the reading of the New Testament. "Everything in the Scripture", says St Paul, "has been divinely inspired, and has its uses; to instruct us, to expose our errors, to correct our faults, to educate us in holy living" (II Tim. 3. 16).

May the devout and frequent reading of the Scriptures inspire us to a greater love of our Blessed Lord.

✠ BERNARD CARDINAL GRIFFIN
Archbishop of Westminster

INTRODUCTION

BY THE GENERAL EDITOR

THE readers of the present volume (and they will, I am positive, be many) will not take long to discover why I am delighted once more to welcome Fr Bullough to the series that I am privileged to edit. His earlier volume on *The Church in the New Testament* has been generally acclaimed as a masterly summary of the main events and teaching in a book (*The Acts of the Apostles*) that has had the distinction, probably unshared by any other book of the Bible, of being made the subject of a five-volume commentary. It is a testimony to Fr Bullough's very marked gift for synthesis and compression that he has been able to include in his work so much that is of value from the older writers.

Now, in the latest volume of the series, he has attempted, again with success, what might well be thought the hardest task of all. Some years ago I received a letter from a great authority on the Bible, in the course of which he remarked: "I am working hard at St Paul just now. He is not easy." Earlier on he had written: "What students need most is perfectly definite information—not general statements or theorizing." Without minimizing the difficulties in St Paul's epistles, Fr Bullough has been inspired to make many things plain that would otherwise remain obscure, and he has throughout conveyed a maximum of "perfectly definite information" of the sort that any pupil of ordinary ability can grasp. I commend his work particularly to all those who already love St Paul and the other apostolic writings, and who will love them better still after a study of these wise and luminous pages.

JOHN M. T. BARTON

ST CATHERINE THE MARTYR, WEST DRAYTON,
Feast of St Elphege, Archbp. and Martyr,
April 19, 1948.

AUTHOR'S PREFACE

In the course of education at a Catholic Secondary School a boy or girl should receive a training in Scripture that provides a general familiarity with the whole of the inspired Word. This, the sixth volume of the series, deals with the latter part of the New Testament, that is, with the Epistles of St Paul, the seven Catholic Epistles (of James, Peter, John and Jude), and the Apocalypse.

The series has been so arranged that, after a foundation has been laid in the Lower Forms of the Gospel Story and the outline of the Story of the Old Testament (Vols. I–II), in the Middle School the Gospels are studied again and followed by 'the Acts (Vols. III–IV), and work in the Upper Forms returns once more to the Gospels, now seen in connexion with the Bible as a whole (Vol. V), leading to Sixth Form work on the Epistles.

The material of the present volume has so far merely been touched upon (in the volume on the Acts), and a detailed study has been reserved for the Sixth Form, when boys and girls are usually aged 16–18 and capable of advanced work. This has been done not least because the Epistles are by far the most difficult part of the New Testament, and even St Peter said that therein are certain things hard to be understood.

The Epistles and Apocalypse are, as it were, the crown and conclusion of the whole Scriptural Revelation; for they contain not only St John's mysterious view into the future (both in heaven and on earth), and include the very last echo of God's direct Revelation to the Apostles (the Epistles of St John), with which the "deposit of Faith" is completed, but they represent the labours of the Apostles in establishing Christ's Church on earth and in teaching Christ's new commandment to the world; they contain some of the sublimest

teaching in the Bible and lie behind so much of the normal
teaching of the Catholic Church on Faith and Morals.

THIS BOOK

Although we have aimed in this book, written for a Sixth
Form, at a much more detailed study of the text than has been
attempted in any of the previous volumes, it remains impossible to include in the curriculum a complete study of the
Epistles. We have therefore adopted the following plan:

After the Geographical and Historical Introductions (Part
I) to set the stage, we study the principal character, which is
St Paul (Part II), and then proceed to his Epistles (Part III),
and certain typical Epistles from each period have been
selected for a full exegesis: I Cor. for the Missionary period,
Eph. for the Captivity, II Tim. for the Pastorals. Much time
is deliberately spent on I Cor. since it is desirable that the
student should have experience of something of a full-scale
commentary. In the other Epistles either a short exegesis of
the salient passages is made, or else, after a study of the
general argument, certain important texts are noted. In this
way one may feel fairly confident that no passage of vital
importance will be missed. The Epistle to the Hebrews,
however, owing to its peculiar circumstances, its intrinsic
difficulty, and the deep familiarity with the Old Testament
which a full exegesis would require (and which cannot be
presupposed or here provided), has received a special treatment, textually superficial, but with some explanation of the
problems and the main theses of the Epistle. Part IV deals
in a similar way with the Catholic Epistles. Part V is devoted
to the Apocalypse, where again, owing to the great difficulty
of detailed interpretation, we have had to confine ourselves
to a general understanding of the whole and to the study of
certain passages in more detail. Frequent notice is taken of
the connexions of the Sacred Text with the doctrinal deci-
sions and liturgical practice of the Church.

AUTHOR'S PREFACE

USE AT SCHOOL

We have, as in the volume on the Acts, given number-
headings, e.g. (46–50), at the beginning of each main section,
which are intended to give to the teacher a feeling of some
guarantee that he will be able to marshal his material through
the year. But these must be taken with the greatest latitude,
since of course he will want to expand the study of some Epistles
and compress that of others. We are assuming two Scripture
periods a week, which means about fifty in a school year.

It cannot be too much emphasised that in a Sixth Form
much of the study must be done by the students themselves.
Classes will be more in the nature of discussion groups than
of lectures or of classes to Lower Forms where the teacher
talks most of the time. The material put down for one class
(e.g. II Tim.) or two classes (e.g. Gal.) is often much more
than can be got through in the period without previous or
subsequent study by the class, or else the supposition of
previous acquaintance with that Epistle. These notes are
intended as a stimulus to, and guidance in, private study and
as a basis for discussion, the field of which would be enlarged
by wider reading (especially on the part of the teacher) in
relevant literature.

The very nature of this Sixth Form work makes a book of
this kind to be of possible use to study-circles or to the solitary adult student—quite apart from school use.

It is to be hoped that many Sixth Form students have
some knowledge of Greek. An ability to read the characters,
and so at least to recognise a Greek word when it recurs, is
taken for granted, since a careful exegesis often requires an
examination of the original text. Some knowledge of Latin is
assumed.

TEXTS

We take as a basis the standard Rheims-Challoner text,
since it follows for the most part literally the Greek text

A2

(through the medium of the literal Latin of the Vulgate). Other modern versions are used throughout in explanation of that text. Of especial value is the American Revision of that text made in 1941, which frequently arrives closer still to the original Greek. It is widely used by the Catholics of America, and is known in this country chiefly through Fr Stedman's Missals and "Daily Readings". The most exact rendering of the Greek among Catholic texts in English is, of course, the Westminster Version, which we refer to very often. Mgr Knox's well-known version of 1945, which is becoming familiar to so many from the pulpit, has its particular value in elucidating the meaning of a passage when the literal translation is obscure. Fairly frequent use has been made of the admirable Paraphrase by Dr Wand, Anglican Bishop of London (1946), on account of its vivid language and the faithful transfer of the exact ideas (and often of the exact words) of the Greek into an entirely modern medium. Other non-Catholic versions are quoted but rarely.

Students who have even an elementary knowledge of Greek should be urged to have a Greek Testament by them, for with the Rheims as a "crib" it is surprising how much profit even the beginner can derive from a study of the original.

BOOKS

We have deliberately avoided too formidable a bibliography, feeling that a few key-books (for the most part easily accessible) will be more valuable than an attempt to present a complete array of all available works.

Footnote references to commentaries, etc., are only given when it would be desirable to be able to track down certain particular opinions. Otherwise it can be assumed that the notes represent the ordinary *consensus* of standard works.

We have usually restricted ourselves to Catholic works, or to those generally trustworthy from the point of view of orthodoxy. Much time can be wasted if too many books are consulted. There are many good books, e.g. on St Paul, that have not been listed, for of making many books there is no end, and much study is an affliction of the flesh (Ecclesiastes 12. 12), but any sound books or commentaries which the teacher or the school library may possess will no doubt help to a better understanding of the text.

It is worth emphasising here that the main thing in this year's work is the careful study of the *text*—for it is the inspired Word of God. Introductions and histories and commentaries only exist to illuminate its obscurities and to define the circumstances of writing. Indeed the text alone will so often be plain when it is studied in the light of the "supernatural mother-wit" that every Catholic possesses from the doctrinal and moral teaching of the Church and the daily partaking in her worship.

A closer knowledge of the Apostolic writings, derived from an assiduous and prayerful study, can only serve to bring us to a closer knowledge of Christ himself, and to a better understanding of his teaching as he gave it to the Apostles, and as they give it to us, especially in the "Epistle" during the Mass, for the Mass is Christ's own prayer. After all, the whole New Testament is simply about Christ, and the knowledge and contemplation of him is really the one thing necessary in the whole world.

LAXTON,
Feast of SS Peter and Paul, 1947.

I want here to add a word of gratitude to one of my senior pupils here at Laxton, Robin Cutler, who has given me valuable assistance during the correction of the proofs and the compilation of the indices.

A SELECT BIBLIOGRAPHY

Note.—Many other books might have been added to this list, but these books certainly are of especial value. Most of them have been used so constantly while commenting, that footnote reference to them has only been made when the solution to a particular problem is thereby acknowledged.

Non-Catholic authors are marked with an asterisk; the books included are all quite trustworthy.

Numerous other books have been consulted, which are referred to in the footnotes. The authors' names appear in the General Index.

I. General Works

HUGH POPE, O.P.[1]: *The Catholic Student's Aids to the Study of the Bible*, Vol. V (Acts–Apoc.), B.O.W. 1926, 1937 (in the older edition of 1923 this volume was numbered III). A quite invaluable work.

The Westminster Version N.T. Vols. III–IV (Epp.–Apoc.), Longmans, 1921–1931. A new translation from the Greek, with important introductions and notes. Under the editorship of the late Fr Keating (†1939) and Fr Cuthbert Lattey, s.j.[2] Contributors to the relevant parts are Fr Lattey, s.j. (*Thess., I Cor., Rom.*), Abp Goodier, s.j. (*Philipp., Philem.*), Fr Keating, s.j. (*II Cor.,* with Fr Lattey), Fr Keogh, s.j. (*Gal.*), Fr Rickaby, s.j. (*Eph., Col.*), Canon Boylan (*Heb.*), Dr Gigot (*Pastorals, Jn's Epp., Apoc.*), Fr Kent, o.s.c. (*Peter, James, Jude*).

MARCO SALES, O.P. (†1936): *La Sacra Bibbia Commentata,* N.T. Vol. II, Turin, 1914. The Vulgate text with what is virtually a new Italian translation, accompanied by introductions and most useful commentary.

HILDEBRANDUS HÖPFL, O.S.B.: *Introductionis Compendium* (new ed. by Benno Gut, o.s.b.), Vol. III, Rome, 1938.

---

[1] This assiduous scholar, apostolic priest and exemplary friar died on November 23rd, 1946. Generations of students, including the present writer, looked up to him.

[2] Fr Cuthbert Lattey is the foremost Catholic biblical scholar in England today, having been one of the pioneers. For many years past he has given guidance and encouragement to younger men, and the present writer is greatly indebted to him.

MARGARET MONRO: *Enjoying the New Testament*, Longmans, 1945. A very delightful popular introduction.

II. BOOKS ON ST PAUL

JOSEF HOLZNER: *Paulus*, Herder, Freiburg i/B, 1937. (Eng. Tr. *Paul of Tarsus*, Herder, U.S.A., 1946.) Without doubt the most outstanding recent book on St Paul. A most complete and erudite (yet very readable) study, from the point of view of Biography, History and Archaeology, Exegesis and Theology.

FERNAND PRAT, S.J.: *La Théologie de S. Paul*, Paris (Vol. I) 1908, (II) 1912. (Eng. Tr. *The Theology of St Paul*, B.O.W., 1926.) A standard work; of permanent value.

C. FOUARD: *S. Paul, ses Missions*, Paris, 1892; *S. Paul, ses dernières années*, Paris, 1897. (Eng. Tr. of the former, U.S.A., 1894.)

CUTHBERT LATTEY, S.J.: *Paul*, Bruce, U.S.A., 1939.

C. C. MARTINDALE, S.J.: *Princes of his People—II: St Paul*, B.O.W., 1924.

*SIR WILLIAM RAMSAY: *St Paul the Traveller and Roman Citizen*, Hodder & Stoughton, 1895.

*H. V. MORTON: *In the Steps of St Paul*, Rich & Cowan, 1936.

III. COMMENTARIES

Note.—The two great series of commentaries, the *Études Bibliques* (in French) of the Dominicans, and the *Cursus Sacrae Scripturae* (in Latin) of the Jesuits (both published in Paris) will be indicated by the usual abbreviations EB and CSS respectively.

I–II Thess.   J. Knabenbauer, S.J.,[1] CSS, 1913

                  J. M. Vosté, O.P.,[2] Rome, 1917

                  F. Amiot, Paris, Beauchesne, 1947

I–II Cor.   R. Cornely, S.J.,[1] CSS, 1892

[1] Frs Cornely, S.J. (†1908) and Knabenbauer, S.J. (†1911) were the great pioneers of modern Catholic biblical scholarship, and their work lives in the CSS.

[2] Fr Vosté died on February 24th, 1949. He was a very well-known figure in Rome, having lectured there on Scripture for over thirty years, and having held the important post of Secretary of the Biblical Commission since 1939.

	E. B. Allo, O.P., EB, 1934 and 1937
	J. Huby, S.J., Paris, Beauchesne, 1946
Romans	R. Cornely, S.J., CSS, 1896
	M. J. Lagrange, O.P.,[1] EB, 1914
	P. Boylan, Dublin, 1934
	J. Huby, S.J., Paris, Beauchesne, 1940
Galatians	*J. B. Lightfoot, London, 1865, 1866
	R. Cornely, S.J., CSS, 1892
	M. J. Lagrange, O.P., EB, 1918, 1926
	F. Amiot, Paris, Beauchesne, 1947
Captivity	*J. B. Lightfoot (*Phil.*), London, 1865
	*J. B. Lightfoot (*Col., Philem.*), London, 1875
	*B. F. Westcott (*Eph.*), London, 1906
	J. Knabenbauer and F. Zorell, S.J., (*Eph., Phil., Col.*), CSS, 1912
	J. Knabenbauer, S.J. (*Philem.* with Past.) CSS, 1913
	J. M. Vosté, O.P. (*Eph.*), Rome, 1921
	J. Huby, Paris, Beauchesne, 1935
Pastorals	J. Knabenbauer, S.J., CSS, 1913
	C. Spicq, O.P., EB, 1947
Hebrews	*B. F. Westcott, London, 1889
	P. Boylan, Dublin, 1922
	J. Bonsirven, S.J., Paris, 1943
Catholic Epp.	J. Chaine, EB, 1927 (omits *I Peter*)
I Peter	U. Holzmeister, S.J., CSS, 1937
	*E. G. Selwyn, London, 1946
Epp. of John	*B. F. Westcott, London, 1883
	J. Bonsirven, S.J., Paris, 1935
Apoc.	E. B. Allo, O.P., EB, 1921 (abridged ed. 1930), 3rd ed., 1933

To these many others might be added, especially the third great Catholic series the *Bonner Bibel* (in German), published at Bonn, 1918–1935, which is not listed here in detail merely because it is not so often or so easily found in this country.

---

[1] Fr Lagrange, O.P. (†1938) founded the biblical school at Jerusalem and began the series EB. He was the champion of the "historical method" among Catholics, and one of the greatest modern Catholic exegetes.

All these are full-scale commentaries with the full apparatus of scholarship.
Mention should be also made of Fr Martindale's little book on the
Apocalypse, *Princes of his People—I: St John*, B.O.W. 1922, and that of
Fr R. Loenertz, O.P. *The Apocalypse*, S. & W., 1947, which follows Allo's
exegesis, and a plan similar to Gigot's in WV.

The following Versions of the New Testament are referred
to throughout this book as follows:

Rh   : Rheims Version in the current editions of Dr
        Challoner's revision (1749). If the original text
        of 1582 is quoted, this is expressly stated.

WV   : Westminster Version (1913–1935)

USA : The American (Catholic) Revision of the Chal-
        loner-Rheims Version (1941)

RAK : The Version of Mgr R. A. Knox (1945)

AV   : Authorised Version (1611)

RV   : Revised Version (1881)

Wand: *The New Testament Letters, prefaced and para-
        phrased* by Dr. J. W. C. Wand, Bishop of
        London (1946)

The following works are referred to by the author's name
only. If another work by the same author is intended, this is
expressly stated.

Pope: *The Catholic Student's Aids to the Study of the Bible*
   (2nd or 3rd ed., 1926–1938)

Prat: *The Theology of St Paul* (Eng. Tr., 1926)

Morton: *In the Steps of St Paul* (1936)

Denzinger or Denz.: *Enchiridion Symbolorum* (18/20th ed.,
   1932)

Eusebius: *Historia Ecclesiastica* (311–325)

St Thomas: *Summa Theologica* (1266–1273)

Otherwise the simple name of an author indicates a commentary on the passage in question.

Reference is generally made by volume (roman figure) and
page (arabic). To Josephus, Ireneus and Eusebius reference
is by book, chapter and (sometimes, in a long chapter)
paragraph. Reference to Denziger is by marginal number, and
to St Thomas, of course, by part, question and article.

CONTENTS

APPENDICES

INDICES

PART I. INTRODUCTORY

1. GENERAL

The part of the New Testament that stands after the Acts of the Apostles consists of the Epistles and the Apocalypse. It is this part that is the object of our study during this year's work. The "books" of this part of the New Testament are not concerned (except in chance remarks made in passing) with history, but with Christian teaching, dogmatic, moral and disciplinary. The number of chapters can be taken as some indication of bulk, and on this reckoning we find that these "books" represent the greater part of the New Testament, containing 143 out of the 260 chapters of the New Testament. Of these 143 chapters, 121 are contained in the various Epistles or Letters of the Apostles, and of these in turn exactly 100 chapters are to be found in the Epistles of St Paul, who is thus by far the most prolific writer in the New Testament. (St Luke comes second with fifty-two chapters, twenty-four in his Gospel and twenty-eight in the Acts; St John comes third with fifty, twenty-one in his Gospel, seven in his three Epistles and twenty-two in the Apocalypse.) It will not therefore be out of place that we devote more than half of this year's work to a direct study of St Paul.

The above statistical information can be tabulated as follows:

Gospels   89 chapters
Acts   28
Epistles of Paul   100 } total 121   } total N.T.: 260 chapters
Other Epistles   21 }
Apocalypse   22

Another statistical aspect of this part of the New Testament may be gathered from the information in Appendix A,

where is set out the liturgical use made in the Roman Missal
of the Epistles and Apocalypse for the "Epistle" at Mass.
So general is the practice of selecting the biblical passage to
be read before the Gospel at Mass from one of the Epistles,
that even when the reading is from the Old Testament or
the Acts or the Apocalypse, it is commonly referred to as the
"Epistle" (though the more correct term for such readings is
the "Lesson"), and that side of the altar where it is read is
known as the "Epistle side". From the above-mentioned
Appendix it appears that there are 125 excerpts from the
Epistles (101 from St Paul) used for the "Epistle" at Mass,[1]
and 10 from the Apocalypse.

Of the fifty-two or fifty-three Sunday Masses in the Roman
Missal[2], fifty-one have the reading from one of the Epistles
(forty-four from St Paul), the exceptions being Whit Sunday
and the Feast of the Holy Name, when the reading is from
the Acts. (The modern feasts of the Holy Family and of
Christ the King, instituted in 1921 and 1925 respectively,
replace a Sunday, but in any case both the Feast-Day and
Sunday Epistle is from St Paul.) On the eight Holidays of
Obligation which do not necessarily fall on on a Sunday the
reading is taken three times from the Epistles of St Paul (on
Christmas—at all three Masses, the Circumcision and Corpus
Christi), once from the Apocalypse (on All Saints'), twice
from the Acts (on Ascension-day and SS Peter and Paul) and
twice from the Old Testament (Isaias on the Epiphany, and
Ecclesiasticus on the Assumption). Out of a maximum, therefore, of sixty or sixty-one Sundays and Holidays in the year
(though, of course, certain Holidays may occur on a Sunday)
in fifty-four cases the reading is from an Epistle (forty-seven
times from St Paul).

With regard to Daily Mass (i.e. not Sundays or Holidays)

[1] These figures do not reckon with occasional overlapping.
[2] The odd Sunday, which may or may not occur, is that between the
Circumcision and the Epiphany, when is celebrated the Feast of the Holy
Name. If no Sunday occurs, the Feast is celebrated on January 2nd.

the proportion of readings from the Old Testament is much higher: the Ferial Masses of Lent provide forty-two and the other Ember Days twenty-one. In the Proper and Common of the Saints and in the Votive Masses there are forty-nine excerpts from the Old Testament used as Lessons at Mass: a total of 112. Passages from the Epistles number seventy-one (St Paul fifty-four). Nine passages of the Apocalypse are selected and eighteen from the Acts.

The information yielded by an examination of the Roman Missal shows the selection of biblical passages for the Epistle or Lesson to be as follows:

	Sundays and Holidays	*Daily Mass*
Epistles of Paul	47 } total 54	54 } total 71
Other Epistles	7	17
Apocalypse	1	9
Acts	3/4	18/19
Old Testament	2	112

From these figures it emerges that the writings of St Paul are used more frequently than those of any other biblical writer, and it is probably true to say that St Paul's presentation of Christian teaching has had a greater influence on Christian thought than that of any other single writer in the New Testament.

There are twenty-one Epistles in the New Testament. They vary in length from elaborate treatises of thirteen or sixteen chapters to short occasional letters of a mere thirteen, fourteen or twenty-five verses. Five authors are represented: *St Paul* and four of the original twelve Apostles, *St James* (the Less, the "brother of the Lord", Mt. 13. 55, Mk. 6. 3, Bishop of Jerusalem; *not* James the Great, son of Zebedee and brother of John the Evangelist, who was killed by Herod in A.D. 42, Acts 12. 2), *St Peter*, *St John the Evangelist*, and *St Jude* (called thus by himself, by St Luke in the Acts, 1. 13, and by the other Evangelists, though Mt. and Mk. in their lists of the Apostles, Mt. 10. 3, Mk. 3. 18, give his name as Thaddaeus—probably his surname; he calls himself the "brother of James" (the Less), Jude 1, and in Acts 1. 13 is listed as "Jude of James"; John specially distinguishes: "Judas (Rheims text has this form here only for this person), *not* the Iscariot", 14. 22—indeed the latter had already gone out, 13. 30).

Of these twenty-one Epistles, fourteen are by St Paul, one by St James, two by St Peter, three by St John and one by St Jude. They stand in the New Testament grouped under their authors. The seven that follow those of St Paul are called the "Catholic" Epistles, since their destination is more general than those of St Paul. The Epistles of Peter and John probably stand in their series in chronological order, but this is not so in the case of Paul. St Paul's Epistles stand in a group-order, and within the groups in a length-order.

The groups of St Paul's Epistles as they stand in the Bible are as follows:—

> *Epistles to the Churches* (written to various Christian communities—more often those he had already visited).
>> 1. Romans (the Christian community in Rome).
>> 2. I Corinthians (Corinth in Greece).
>> 3. II Corinthians.
>> 4. Galatians (Galatia, a province in Asia Minor).[1]
>> 5. Ephesians (Ephesus, a city in Asia Minor).
>> 6. Philippians (Philippi, a city in Macedonia).
>> 7. Colossians (Colossae, a city near Ephesus).
>> 8. I Thessalonians (Thessalonica, now Salonika, in Macedonia, now Greece).
>> 9. II Thessalonians.
> *Pastoral Epistles* (written to individual bishops, to teach them how to be good pastors or shepherds of their flocks).

[1] We shall reserve for later the discussion about the precise area in question.

10. I Timothy (Timothy was St Paul's great friend and companion; he joins Paul in writing Rom., II Cor., Phil., Col. and Philem.; he was made bishop of Ephesus, I Tim. 1. 3[1]).
11. II Timothy.
12. Titus (appointed by St Paul to be bishop in Crete, Titus 1. 5[1]).

Other Epistles (not written to a particular community, nor to an individual bishop).
13. Philemon (a purely personal letter to a convert gentleman at Colossae, about a private matter).
14. Hebrews (an Epistle that stands by itself in matter, treatment and style. The destination is not obvious, and the problems involved will be treated later).

There is evidence for the acceptance of all the Epistles in the second century, although the recognition of all of them as canonical was not universal at that date. The Books about which there was doubt have been called "deutero-canonical" and they are seven: Hebrews, James, II Peter, II and III John, Jude and the Apocalypse. This hesitation persisted in certain quarters until the fourth century, when we find the list complete in the Decree of Pope Damasus in A.D. 382 (with, however, the peculiarity of the statement that II and III John are "alterius Joannis presbyteri", which was corrected in the list made at the Council of Carthage in 397, and in the letter of Pope Innocent I in 405 to an attribution of all three Epistles to St John the Apostle). The earliest unofficial list (i.e. apart from passing references to various Epistles) is the "Muratorian Canon" of about A.D. 200, which does not include Heb., I–II Pet. or III Jn. The famous Chester

---

[1] These appointments are given as recorded by Eusebius (III, 4, 6) and not merely deduced from the Epistles.

Beatty Papyrus (P. 46)[1] of about the same date includes all the Epistles to the Churches, with Hebrews in second place.

(2)   2. GEOGRAPHICAL

On the first map are marked the places which St. Paul mentions in his Epistles, together with the few mentioned by St Peter at the heading of his First Epistle and those named in the first vision of the Apocalypse.

It will be observed that all the cities mentioned lie on or near the coast of the Mediterranean Sea or one of its reaches, such as the Aegean or Ionian Sea. All the land in question was Roman territory, and was divided into Provinces which had gradually during the two centuries preceding our period been merged into the Roman Empire. The system of absorption of kingdoms into the Empire, first as vassal-kingdoms and finally as provinces was described in Vol. IV (Historical Background, 1). By the time of St Paul's correspondence, every one of these areas was an established province of the Empire. In 27 B.C., when Augustus founded the Empire, he divided the provinces into Senatorial and Imperial provinces. The Senatorial Provinces were governed on a civilian basis by the Senate, and were the older and established provinces. The more recently absorbed areas were governed on a military basis by governors directly responsible to the Emperor himself. Of the provinces which are our concern here, Achaia (or Greece), Macedonia, Epirus, Crete, Asia and Bithynia were Senatorial Provinces governed by a Proconsul; while Galatia, Pontus, and Cappadocia (all in what is now called Asia Minor), as well as Dalmatia and Palestine were Imperial Provinces under a Governor, having all been only recently (e.g. Galatia in 25 B.C.) established as provinces within the Empire.

It should be noted that the "world" in which St Paul lived and worked was almost entirely bounded by sea, mountain or

[1] Discovered in 1930. One of the oldest MSS. of the New Testament.

desert. Asia Minor, the centre of his activities, is surrounded by sea except in the East, where it meets the wild Armenian mountains. Similarly, Greece is surrounded on three sides by sea, and in the North has the barrier of the Macedonian mountains. St Paul's most extended plan reached Spain, still on the Mediterranean seaboard.

The following list of places is arranged according to the provinces. When a province is named, it is in italics. Capitals are used for the destinations of the Epistles.

ROME (Rom. 1. 7, 15 destination; II Tim. 1. 17 provenance; covert mention in I Pet. 5. 13 under pseudonym "Babylon").
Italy (Heb. 13. 24 "the brethren from Italy salute you").

Achaia or *Greece* (Rom. 15. 26, I Cor. 16. 15, II Cor. 1.1, 9. 2, 11. 10, I Thess. 1. 7, 8).
Athens (ref. to his visit I Thess. 3. 1).
CORINTH was one of the biggest cities of the world at this time. The Greek city had been destroyed by the Romans in 146 B.C., but in 44 B.C. an entirely new Roman city was founded there by Julius Caesar and soon grew to great prosperity. Its geographical position on the narrow isthmus connecting the Peloponnese with the Greek mainland made it unsuitable for the pursuit of agriculture, and the inhabitants therefore lived on commerce and seafaring. Corinth had two ports, Lechaeum, facing the Adriatic westwards, and Cenchrae, facing the Aegean eastwards, and the trans-shipment of goods across the isthmus on the short sea-route from Italy to Asia (the long voyage round the Peloponnese was often difficult) brought much trade to Corinth in addition to the internal trade north and south in Greece itself. Most of the population consisted of freedmen and a hetero-

geneous mass of people attracted thither by trade.[1] St
Paul stayed twice at Corinth, the first time for 1½ years
(Acts 18. 11). (I Cor. 1.2, II Cor. 1. 23, II Tim. 4. 20.)
Cenchrae (Κεγχρεαί in Greek) was the eastern port of Corinth,
and the home of Phebe, a friend of St Paul's (Rom. 16. 1).

Macedonia, the province which extended right across the
northern part of the Greek peninsula, mostly now included in Greece with parts, however, in the present
territories of Albania, Jugo-Slavia and Bulgaria. (Rom.
15. 26, I Cor. 16. 5, II Cor. 2. 13, 7. 5, 8. 1, 11. 9, Phil. 4.
15, I Thess. 1. 7-8, 4. 10, I Tim. 1. 3.)

THESSALONICA, the modern Salonika in Greece, was the
capital of the Roman province of Macedonia, and the
residence of the Proconsul. The city had been founded
shortly after the time of Alexander the Great, in 315 B.C.,
and had been the naval base of the Macedonian kings.[1]
It lay on the overland route from Greece to Asia. (Phil.
4. 16, I Thess. 1. 1, II Thess. 1. 1, II Tim. 4. 9.)

PHILIPPI, also in Macedonia and about 100 miles eastwards
along the overland route, took its name from King
Philip of Macedon (the father of Alexander) who established the city there with a view to developing the gold
mines in the vicinity. This made it an important trade-
centre. The city was further glorified in the time of
Augustus, being the site of his defeat of Brutus and
Cassius in 42 B.C. Nothing remains of the city now, the
nearest town being Drama, about 15 miles to the north-
west. (Phil. 1. 1, I Thess. 2. 2.)

Nicopolis, in the province of Epirus, was the most important
Greek town on the Adriatic coast. It was founded by
Augustus to commemorate his victory (νίκη) at Actium

---

[1] Most of this information comes from Strabo, the geographer of the
time of Augustus (378 sq. for Corinth, 330 sq. for Thessalonica). Many
details are to be found in articles in the *Catholic Encyclopedia* and the
Encyclopædia Biblica.

in 31 B.C., having been the place where his forces assembled. It rapidly became a large city, the local populations being transferred to within its walls.[1] It would provide a good missionary centre. Although there were several towns of this name it is almost certain that this is the one which St Paul refers to in Titus 3. 12 when he announces his intention of spending the winter there after his release from prison. Some writers think that his second arrest took place here.

CRETE, where Titus was bishop (Tit. 1. 5).

Asia, the westernmost province of what is now called Asia Minor and the modern Turkey. Already Strabo (564) remarked that the boundaries of these provinces were uncertain. This is especially so of the inland provinces, such as Galatia (q.v. infra). Asia became a Roman province in 133–130 B.C. (Rom. 16. 5, I Cor. 16. 9, II Cor. 1. 8, II Tim. 1. 15—I Pet. 1.1—Apoc. 1. 4, 11.)

EPHESUS was the capital of Asia, and the residence of the Proconsul (cf. Acts 19. 38). It was the trade-centre for Asia Minor and the terminus on the sea of the transcontinental road through Laodicea and Colossae to Tarsus and so to Syria and Mesopotamia. Strabo (663) calls Ephesus " the gateway to the East". There was a city here from the most ancient times.[1] The port was gradually silting up and finally decayed. Nothing now remains of the city but a few abandoned ruins a couple of miles from the Turkish village of Seljuk.[2] (I Cor. 15. 32, Eph. 1. 1, I Tim. 1. 3, II Tim. 1. 18, 4. 12—Apoc. 1. 11, 2. 1.)

COLOSSAE, an ancient city, was about 150 miles along the main road east of Ephesus, which had gradually declined

[1] Strabo, 325 for Nicopolis; 540, 641, 840 for Ephesus; 578 for Laodicea.
[2] Excellent description in Morton, 320 sq.

owing to the growth of the neighbouring Laodicea. Nothing now remains, but the railway to Isparta passes near the site. (Col. 1. 1.)

Laodicea, on the same road about 11 miles west of Colossae, was founded by the Seleucid king Antiochus II about 250 B.C. and called after his wife. Nothing remains. (Col. 2. 1, 4. 13, 15—Apoc. 1. 11, 3. 14.)

Hierapolis stood about 10 miles from Laodicea, off the main road, to the north. Nothing remains. (Col. 4. 13.)

Smyrna, a very ancient city, is still there, and is the principal port of the west coast of Asia Minor (modern Izmir). Smyrna was always a rival of Ephesus, which it eventually displaced altogether. (Apoc. 1. 9, 2. 8.)

Miletus was already in St Paul's time a small port, having been entirely eclipsed by Ephesus. The harbour is entirely silted up now and nothing remains of the city. (II Tim. 4. 20.)

Sardis lay about 60 miles along the main road north-east from Ephesus. Only a few ruins remain. (Apoc. 1. 9, 3. 1, 4.)

Thyatira (near the modern town of Akhissar) lay 36 miles further north along the road. It was a great centre of the wool trade. (Apoc. 1. 9, 2. 18, 24.)

Philadelphia lay on the road from Sardis south-east to Hierapolis and Laodicea and was a prosperous city with a speciality of exporting wine. Its modern name is Ala Shehr, on the railway from Smyrna to Konia (Iconium). (Apoc. 1. 9, 3. 7.)

Troas (or, in full, Alexandria Troas), a harbour-city founded within a few miles of the site of Troy by Antigonis, one of the generals of Alexander the Great. The city was much developed by the Romans. (II Cor. 2. 12, II Tim. 4. 13.)

Pergamus (or -um, Greek Πέργαμον), the modern Bergama, is on the overland route from Ephesus to Troas. It was the capital of a flourishing independent kingdom in the third to second centuries B.C. when the temple of Zeus and the great library were made. The kingdom was bequeathed to Rome in 133 B.C. Parchment is said to have been first made here. It was the birthplace of the physician Galen (A.D. 130). (Apoc. 1. 11, 2. 12.)

Patmos, the island about 35 miles off the coast near Ephesus, where St John was exiled and where he received the vision recorded in his Apocalypse.

GALATIA was the name given to the province formed in 25 B.C. out of several ill-defined vassal-kingdoms and existing provinces or areas ruled by Rome. The principal ones were Pisidia, Lycaonia and Galatia proper, which last consisted of three Celtic (Gallic) tribes ruled by King Amyntas as a vassal of the Romans. It was at his death in 25 B.C. that the Romans had to revise their plans for the ruling of the whole district. The borders continued to be altered during most of the first century, and it is this fact that constitutes the problem about who the Galatians are, to whom the Epistle is addressed. (I Cor. 16. 1, Gal. 1. 2, II Tim. 4. 10—I Pet. 1. 1.)

Iconium (the big modern town of Konia), Antioch "in Pisidia" (the modern Yalovach), and Lystra (of which nothing remains) are cities in South Galatia (not Galatia proper), familiar from reading the Acts. St Paul refers to his visits there in II Tim. 3. 11.

Pontus, Cappadocia, Bithynia are provinces in Asia Minor (I Pet. 1. 1.)

Dalmatia (mod. Jugo-Slavia). (II Tim. 4. 10.)

Spain. (Rom. 15. 24, 28.)

Jerusalem. (I Cor. 16. 3, Gal. 2. 1.)

From the above notes we are able to see how St Paul chose carefully his mission-grounds. Christian communities were established in the most important cities of the Eastern

Mediterranean and in Rome itself. We have given some details
of the history of Corinth, Thessalonica, Philippi and Ephesus,
because not only were the Christians in those cities recipients of St Paul's Epistles, but they were key-points in the life
of the time. H. V. Morton's *In the Steps of St Paul* provides
admirable background-reading for the geographical side of
our study, and shows how these mighty cities have for the
most part left hardly a trace above ground at the present time.

(3–7)   3. HISTORICAL

There are two main elements which formed the background of the people to whom St Paul and the other Apostles
addressed themselves. These are the Graeco-Roman world
of the Roman Empire, and the Jewish religious background
of the many Jews scattered through the Empire, who were
usually the first to whom they addressed themselves.

All the writers of the New Testament had this double
background: even if St Luke was a Greek-Roman with no
Jewish blood, he, at any rate, acquired a working knowledge
of the Jewish thought of the time. All the writers of the New
Testament, with the possible exception of St Matthew (although it may well be that he translated his Gospel himself
into Greek before leaving Palestine, when an Aramaic Gospel
would be of little use), wrote in Greek, which was the "lingua
franca" of the Eastern part of the Empire. "The Roman
Government", wrote Professor Ramsay,[1] "far from being
opposed to Greek influence, acted in steady alliance with it.
It adopted the manners of Greece, and even recognised the
Greek language for general use in the Eastern Provinces . . .
Rome accepted the Greek language as her ally. Little attempt
was made to naturalise the Latin language in the East; and
even the Roman colonies in the province of Galatia soon

[1] W. M. Ramsay: *St Paul the Traveller and Roman Citizen* (5th ed.),
p. 131.

ceased to use Latin except on state occasions and in a few formal documents. A Graeco-Roman civilisation, using the Greek language, was the type which Rome aimed at establishing in the East."

The same thing, with regard to language, was true of the Jewish communities outside Palestine: beginning as far back as 200 B.C. the Jewish communities in Egypt were using Greek even as their liturgical language, and this is the origin of the Septuagint version of the Old Testament. Some later books of the Hebrew Scriptures were even composed in Greek (such as the Second of Maccabees in the second century B.C.). So it was that the united rule of Rome all over the known world of the time (the lands round the Mediterranean), together with the Greek tongue spoken all over the East, facilitated the travels of the Apostles and their labour of spreading the Gospel.

a. MESSIANISM IN ISRAEL AND ROME

It is easy for anyone who reads the Old Testament to see God's preparation for the coming of the Kingdom, by the choosing of the Jewish people as the recipients of his revelation, by the preservation of the worship of the True God in their midst, by the prophets and types of the Redeemer to come,[1] and finally by the very dispersion of the Chosen Race in the pagan world.

Less obvious, but surely equally true, is God's preparation of the Roman people for their destiny to be the vehicle of the Gospel, to bring them to the moment of perfection that held the whole world at peace when Christ was born,[2] and to give their very heart and centre to be the heart and centre of

---

[1] A prophet may be briefly defined as one who announces God's will to the people; a type is an historical person whose actions in some way foreshadow the Redeemer to come.

[2] As we read in the thrilling announcement in the Martyrology for December 25th: "Anno Imperii Octaviani Augusti quadragesimo secundo, toto Orbe in pace composito".

Christendom. The two cities of Jerusalem and Rome symbolize this double work of God's preparation. As Giovanni
Papini has put it:[1] "There were two Holy Cities . . . Jerusalem was the city of God; Rome, the city of Man. Jerusalem
willed to destroy the God-Man and was destined to destruction; Rome wished to destroy the Church of Christ, and was
saved from destruction because it was chosen to be the see of
the Head of the Church of Christ. Jerusalem gave the books
of the Promise, of the Covenant, and of the Revelation;
Rome offered the imperial network of her prefectures for
dioceses, her solemn language, the tradition of her law."

An elaborate account of the prophets and types of the
Redeemer, which are to be found in the Old Testament, is
not necessary here: the matter has been fully treated in Vol.
V of this series, *The Kingdom of Promise*, but as we are at the
moment studying the two Holy Cities, we cannot omit
a reference to the possibility of a parallel preparation in
Rome.

The Messianic prophecies of the Old Testament are of very
varying degrees of precision. It is rare that prophetic utter-
ances are exact with regard to time and place, or precise in
declaring the manner of the event. The descriptions of the
Messianic age are couched in symbolic language. But when we
listen to the *concentus* of the prophets, certain elements become very plain, even though each text taken singly may fail
to prove anything definite. A Child is expected who is to have
a divine origin (Is. 7. 14: "A virgin shall conceive and bear a
son, and his name shall be called 'God-with-us'"; Is. 9. 6:
"A child is born to us, and the government is upon his shoul-
der: and his name shall be called Wonderful Counsellor,
Mighty God, Father of the world to come, Prince of peace",
etc); further, he shall be the ruler of the earth, the anointed

---

[1] In *Gli operai della vigna*, 1929, the essay *Cristo Romano*. Translated by
Alice Curtayne (S. & W., 1930) as *Labourers in the Vineyard*, the essay
Caesar and Virgil.

one (Messias or Christ[1]), king of a kingdom "not of this world" (Jn. 18. 36) (II K. 7. 16, to David: "Thy throne shall be firm for ever"; Is. 16. 1: "Send forth, O Lord, the Lamb, the ruler of the earth", Mic. 5. 2: "Out of thee [Bethlehem] shall come the ruler in Israel" [2], etc.); thirdly, he will be rejected by the world (the whole of Is. 53); and lastly, his coming will bring the blessings of the Messianic age, when cruelty and discord will be abolished, and right will eventually triumph. These blessings are described in startling symbols taken from nature (e.g. Is. 11. 6: "The wolf shall dwell with the lamb, and the leopard shall lie down with the kid," etc.), and promises of peace (Is. 11. 9: "They shall not hurt, nor shall they kill in all my holy mountain"), and prophecies of the triumph of the Holy City of God (e.g. the last two chapters of Zacharias).

Now the whole medieval Christian tradition held that pagan Rome had parallel oracles, uttered by prophets unwittingly guided by God to speak of the Redeemer to come and the Messianic age. This tradition was probably inaugurated by Constantine the Great, the first Roman Emperor to embrace the Christian Faith, in his great "Oration to the Assembly of the Saints"[3] (Chapters XVIII–XXI). Constantine maintains unhesitatingly that the Sibylline Oracles announce the coming of Christ, and especially the Messianic age. The Sibylline writings have for the most part perished, but some fragments have been preserved which show striking likenesses to Isaias' description of the age of peace (e.g. the wolf and the lamb, the leopard and the kid).[4] Medieval art frequently put the Sibyls among the prophets (e.g. in the Cathedral of Florence, fourteenth century, culminating in

---

[1] Hebrew מָשִׁיחַ (Mashiah) and Greek χριστός mean "anointed".

[2] This was the prophecy that caused the Jewish clergy to give an immediate straight answer to Herod's question about where the Messias should be born (Mt. 2. 5).

[3] Given as an appendix to Eusebius' "Vita Constantini", published just after the Emperor's death in A.D. 335.

[4] T. F. Royds, *Virgil and Isaiah*, 1918, Appendix B.

B

Michelangelo's roof of the Sistine Chapel and Raphael's "Stanze" in the Vatican), and the same idea occurs in medieval liturgical texts, such as the Christmas sequence *Laetabundus* (lost in the Roman, but preserved in the Dominican rite):

> Isaias cecinit,
> Synagoga meminit,
> nunquam tamen desinit
>   esse caeca.
> Si non suis vatibus,
> credat vel gentilibus:
> Sybillinis versibus
>   haec praedicta.

More famous still is Virgil's "Messianic Eclogue" (the Fourth),[1] which was regarded by Constantine and later by St Augustine and the whole medieval tradition, including Dante, as a clear prediction of the coming of Christ. Constantine even held that Virgil himself knew it, but disguised his language in symbol for fear of persecution. Dante[2] makes the convert Christian poet Statius say to Virgil (*Purgatorio*, XXII, 73): "Per te poeta fui, per te cristiano." Virgil was generally regarded as a prophet who announced God's plan to the Roman world, and so continued to lead men to Christ. Modern scholarship is divided on the Messianic nature of the Fourth Eclogue, and modern opinion tends (not surprisingly) to go against it. But what is quite obvious is that the Eclogue contains the principal elements of Messianic utterance. There is the Child awaited, who is to have a divine origin (l. 7, the most celebrated quotation: "Jam nova progenies caelo demittitur alto"), there is his beneficent rule (l. 11: "decus hoc aevi, te consule, inibit"), yet there will still be sin in the world (corresponding to the rejection of the Messias) (l. 31: "Pauca tamen suberunt priscae vestigia fraudis"), but cruelty and discord will be banished, under symbols (as in Isaias) from nature (l. 24: "Occidet et serpens, et fallax herba

[1] For the whole study of this Eclogue, T. F. Royds' book is excellent.
[2] Dante wrote his *Divina Commedia* probably between 1309–1316.

veneni"), and victory will eventually come to truth and justice (l. 36: "iterum ad Troiam magnus mittetur Achilles" —in whom Constantine saw a figure of the victorious Christ). The prophetic words of the Eclogue are indeed little, if at all, more mysterious than the prophecies of the Old Testament, and we can permit ourselves to join the Christian tradition in looking upon Virgil as a prophet of Christ,[1] even if he was but an instrument in the hand of God, or was simply one who, with a poet's insight, understood that "every creature groaneth and travaileth in pain even till now" (Rom. 8. 22), and that the world was crying out for one who should save and bring the age of peace.[2]

b. THE POLITICAL SITUATION

The general outline of the growth of the Empire and its organization has been given in the introduction to a previous volume (Vol. IV: *The Church in the New Testament*), and some geographical notions were given in the last section. What is needed here is a glance at the events in history that led up to the fusion of the Greek and Roman civilisations in the Roman Empire of New Testament times, which was the background of the lives of the Apostles.[3]

It was about the year 264 B.C. that Rome first had begun to colonise beyond the confines of Italy. This was the beginning of the First Punic War, in which Rome and Carthage struggled for supremacy in the Mediterranean. Rome had nearly lost all when the redoubtable Hannibal brought utter destruction on the Roman army at Cannae in 216. The south of Italy was almost entirely occupied by the Carthaginians. The Romans were desperate except for Fabius, who earned for himself the title of "Cunctator" (or Dawdler), and Scipio, later called Africanus, who was planning his master-stroke at the Cartha-

[1] T. F. Royds, p. 69, and Papini's essay quoted above.
[2] Virgil was writing in the year 40 B.C. (*v. infra*, p. 19).
[3] The material will be found in any good Roman History, such as Liddell's *Student's Rome*, and Bury's *Student's Roman Empire*.

ginian bases in Spain. When he struck in 209, the tide soon
turned in favour of Rome. Hannibal evacuated Italy, and in
202 Scipio struck at Carthage itself, bringing the war to an
end.

In Rome's dark hour at Cannae, another power had dreams
of world-domination. This was Philip V of Macedon, who
was now the ruler of what had been the western part of
Alexander's great Empire. This Empire, after its founder's
death in 330, had eventually settled itself into three separate
Empires: the Macedonian, the Seleucid (Syria and Asia
Minor), and the Ptolemaic (Egypt). All three retained the
Greek language and customs introduced by Alexander.
Philip V of Macedon saw a chance in 215 of contributing to
the downfall of one rival who seemed dangerous, and made a
treaty with Hannibal against Rome.[1] When, however, Rome
recovered, Philip turned his attention to Asia Minor in the
East. But before long the Romans had invaded Greece, and
in 197 Philip was defeated at Cynoscephalae. The Romans
now dominated Greece. The Seleucids, now the friends of
Philip against Rome, entered Greece, but were driven out
and finally defeated in Asia Minor itself at Magnesia by
Scipio, the brother of Africanus and later called Asiaticus, in
190. This was called the Syrian War.

The complete subjugation of Asia Minor took a long time.
Shortly after Magnesia, the kingdom of Pergamus became a
vassal of the Romans, and in 133–130 was turned into the
"Province of Asia". The Jews in Palestine, under Judas
Maccabaeus, revolted against the Seleucids and concluded a
treaty with Rome in 161. The Seleucid Empire was tottering.
But in 120 a new power appeared in the East: the formidable
King Mithridates of Pontus. Rome's protection was invoked
against his ravages in Asia Minor. This was about the year
100 B.C., the year when Julius Caesar was born. Two years

[1] A very good and original study, from Philip's point of view, is F. W.
Walbank's *Philip V of Macedon* (1940).

later the long series of Civil Wars began, and Mithridates took advantage of this by trying to get the Greeks to throw off the Roman yoke. Many of the Greeks and Asians welcomed him as a liberator, and it was not until 86 that Athens was retaken by Rome. In 67 began the brilliant career of Pompey. The year 64 marks the complete conquest by Pompey of Asia Minor, Syria and Palestine (63). The Seleucid Empire was no more; Judea was instituted a vassal-kingdom of Rome under Antipater, father of King Herod the Great.

This completes the general outline of the Empire in the East as the Apostles knew it. (We have not attempted to describe Roman expansion in the West, that is, in Africa, Gaul and Spain, nor in the northern provinces along the Danube. They are not immediately relevant to the world of St Paul.)

In the year 61 Pompey returned and held a great triumph. From 58 to 50 Caesar was away in Gaul, and towards the end of this time plans were being laid in Rome for his downfall. It was in 49 that Caesar felt himself obliged to accept a state of civil war and "crossed the Rubicon" towards Rome with his army. Two bitter years followed, with the death of Pompey in 48. After this Caesar was in almost sole command until his assassination in 44.

Immediately a triumvirate led by Octavian took charge and defeated the conspirators at Philippi in 42. 31 marks the Battle of Actium and the beginning of Octavian's sole rulership of the Empire. In 27 he received the title of Imperator and Augustus. From this time dates the principal organization of the Empire mentioned above and the famous PAX ROMANA during which Christ was born at Bethlehem in the vassal-kingdom of Judea, where King Herod had been reigning since 40 B.C. Octavian Augustus reigned until his death in A.D. 14.

Augustus was succeeded by his stepson, Tiberius, who was Emperor during the Public Life and Passion of Our Lord, and until A.D. 37. The Emperors that followed during the

Apostolic Age were Caligula (37–41), Claudius (41–54), during whose reign most of St Paul's missionary labours took place, Nero (54–68), before whom St Paul was cited when he appealed to Caesar in 57, who started the First Persecution of the Christians in 64, and under whom St Paul was arrested the second time and put to death in 67. The year 68–69 was called the "year of the four Emperors" because during a stormy period after Nero, three others succeeded rapidly: Galba, Otho and Vitellius. Vespasian reigned 69–79, having been proclaimed Emperor while fighting the rebels in Judea. That war ended with the sack of Jerusalem in 70 under Titus, who, in turn, became Emperor (79–81). The remaining Emperors were Domitian (81–96), who brought about the Second Persecution of the Christians in 91–93 in which St John suffered his ordeal and exile, Nerva (96–98), who recalled many exiles including St John. At the turn of the century Trajan was ruling (98–117).

The organization of the Empire developed along the lines laid down by Augustus, with periods of notable expansion and internal prosperity during the reigns of Nero and Trajan.

Roman justice was administered in the provinces on the basis of local law. This was in accordance with the Roman principle of retaining local custom, language and religion. There is the obvious case of Gallio, proconsul of Achaia (Greece), residing at Corinth (Acts 18. 12–16), who refused to deal with the complaints against Paul, which were no "matter of injustice". The local squabble they had to settle for themselves. We see the same respect for local authority in the trial of St Paul at Jerusalem and Caesarea (Acts 21. 31 to 25. 12) and in the trial of Our Lord. The Roman authorities did, however, make two important modifications of local juridical rights: (1) no local tribunal was to have the *jus gladii* or right to inflict capital punishment (hence the cry of the Jews to Pilate in Jn. 18. 31: "Nobis non licet interficere quemquam"),[1] and (2) one who had the privilege of "Roman citizenship" had the right to appeal against the judgement of the local tribunal, to be judged by the Emperor himself (as Paul did in Acts 25. 11). Should a Roman citizen be condemned to death, he had the right to execution by beheading and not crucifixion (thus St Paul was beheaded and St Peter crucified). The question of Roman citizenship is intricate, as there were many various degrees, bestowed on whole towns (*jus latinum* and *jus italicum*) and (as was the case in the East in St Paul's time) spread by individual grant in return for political services. This citizenship appears to have been hereditary (cf. St Paul's "I was born so", Acts 22. 26).[2]

c. THE JEWS IN THE ROMAN EMPIRE

With the Greek-speaking unity brought by Alexander's conquests, there began the emigration of Jews from Palestine all over the Greek-speaking world from about 300 B.C. onwards, so that according to Strabo (quoted by Josephus, *Antiquities*, XIV, 7) by the time of Augustus "these Jews are already gotten into all cities, and it is hard to find a place in the habitable earth that hath not admitted this tribe of men, and is not possessed by it". These were known as the Jews of the Diaspora or Dispersion, as distinct from those in Palestine, and seemed generally to have lived as peaceful and prosperous members of society in most of the great cities. We meet them frequently with St Paul. They formed a community apart with their own religious observances. But it was not always entirely peaceful. On at least two occasions during our period there were decrees issued by the Emperors against the Jews. The first was during the reign of Tiberius, when the Emperor took measures against (compescuit) Egyptian and

[1] This matter is complicated, and the historical evidence is obscure. See, for instance, Lagrange's commentary on this and the next verse, or the note in WV.

[2] A complete study of this is Sherwin-White's *The Roman Citizenship*, 1939.

Jewish worship and ordered their vessels and vestments to be destroyed. At the same time the "mathematici" were driven out of Rome with them (probably these were in reality Eastern magicians). This is recorded by Suetonius (*Tiberius*, 36). The next time it is in the reign of Claudius, and Suetonius has a famous passage (*Claudius*, 25) which is by many believed to contain a garbled reference to Christians among the Jews in Rome: "Judaeos impulsore Chresto assidue tumultuantis Roma expulit". (Chrestus is an unknown figure, unless it is a confused allusion to Christians.) This expulsion of the Jews from Rome is confirmed by St Luke in the Acts (18. 2), when he recounts how St Paul met at Corinth (A.D. 50–52) two Jews, Aquila and Priscilla, "lately come from Italy . . . because that Claudius had commanded all Jews to depart from Rome." However, the banishment does not seem to have lasted for long, since it is evident that when St Paul wrote to the Romans there were many Jewish-Christians among his readers, and even his old friends Aquila and Priscilla have got back there (Rom. 16. 3), and this was little more than two years later.

With regard to the Jews of Palestine, their first relations with Rome took place in Maccabean times, when they made a treaty with Rome in 161 B.C. After the successful Maccabean revolt the Jewish state was more or less self-governing during about seventy years. Then in 63 B.C. it was overrun by Pompey, who took Jerusalem and entered the holy of holies "and saw all that which it was unlawful for any other men to see but only for the high priests. . . . Yet did Pompey touch nothing of all this, on account of his regard to religion" (Josephus, *Antiquities*, XIV, 4). The Romans then set up a vassal-kingdom in Judea, under the Idumean king, Antipater, who was the father of the Herod who slew the Innocents and who died in 4 B.C.,[1] and grandfather of the Herod who was

---

[1] Perhaps we should remind ourselves that our current reckoning of years A.D. is probably in error by four or six years. Christ was, of course, born before the death of Herod.

Tetrarch of Galilee at the time of Christ's Passion and of
Archelaus who was Ethnarch of Judea from 4 B.C. till A.D. 6
when he was deposed. This vassal kingdom was then turned
into an ordinary Roman (imperial) Province. For a short time
(A.D. 41–44) the vassal-kingship of Judea was restored by
Claudius in the person of another Herod (Agrippa), son of
Herod the Great (who slew the Innocents). (The Herod
Agrippa, known as II, who visited St Paul at Caesarea was the
son of the above Herod Agrippa (I) with the title of vassal-
king over northern Palestine.)

Julius Caesar is known to have been friendly towards the
Jews (cf. Suetonius, *Divus Julius*, 84). Josephus (*Ant.*, XIV, 10)
records his decrees in detail. During the cruel reign of Herod
the Great (40–4 B.C.) the Jewish intrigues caused much
trouble to Octavian. Josephus records his mercies to the
Jews, and indeed those of all the Emperors to those of his own
personal benefactor, Vespasian. Twice the country was torn
by internal strife, ending the first time with the abolition of
the kingship in 4 B.C., and the second time with the disastrous war in which Rome put down the revolt of the Jews in
A.D. 66, when thousands of Jews were slain and Jerusalem
and the Temple destroyed in A.D. 70. Josephus himself was a
witness of these last events, and of the misrule on the part of
Roman officials in Palestine that brought on the revolt, and
he wrote up the history of that war (*Wars*, especially Books
III–VII). More of Josephus later, in connexion with Hellenistic Jewish literature.

The destruction of Jerusalem marks the end of the Jewish
state in Palestine. Jews were excluded from the city, rebuilt
under the name of Aelia Capitolina, and they had no part in
the government of the Roman Province. The traditions
of the Rabbinic schools were allowed to continue at
Jamnia, near Jaffa. More of this when we study Rabbinic
learning.

d. RELIGION IN THE ROMAN EMPIRE[1]

In order to understand the impact of the Christian message on the Roman world, we must understand something not only of the expectancy and Messianic hopes as expressed by Virgil (section *a.* above), and of the political situation both of the Empire itself and the Jews within the Empire (sections *b.* and *c.* above), but also something of the organized systems of pagan religion existing in the Empire at the time of the preaching of the Apostles. Of the religious system of Israel we shall treat in the next section.

Four main systems can be distinguished in the religious thought of the Empire, and for the Roman these four elements in no way excluded each other, but provided due offices of piety were performed for public worship, the Roman felt free to follow whatever cult satisfied the needs of his own personal superstition or religious instinct.

The first and basic system was the traditional Roman cult of the classical deities. The principal gods of the Romans, such as Jupiter, Juno, Minerva, Venus, etc., were originally local gods, to whom were ascribed in the national system the various hidden forces of nature and of fortune. During the two centuries before Christ, when the Romans became acquainted with the various deities of the Greeks, these latter were adopted into the Roman system, the Greek gods being equated with the Roman and their offices more or less identified. Thus Zeus, the Lord of Heaven for the Greeks, was identified with Jupiter, who held a similar position for the Romans, and similarly Hera was equated with Juno, Athene with Minerva, Aphrodite with Venus, Ares with Mars, Hermes with Mercury, etc. The Greek cult of Apollo was taken over bodily by the Romans, as early, it would seem, as 212 B.C. when Roman games were instituted in his honour. Thus the national religion of Rome at the time of the Empire was already a synthesis of older Greek and Roman beliefs.

[1] A very good chapter (XXV) by G. Bardy in *Initiation Biblique*.

With the spread of Roman power in the East (see section *b* above) and with the Roman principle of toleration of local custom and law, came not merely toleration of local Eastern religion, but lively interest in it, curiosity about it and even sometimes adoption of it by local Roman officials. A case in point was Judaism, a tolerated Eastern religion: of the centurion in Lk. 7 it was said, "He loveth our nation, and he hath built us a synagogue" (Lk. 7. 5), and Cornelius, also a centurion and an Italian, was described as "a religious man and fearing God" (Acts 10. 2). This last phrase seems to have been a technical term for those pagans who were prepared to adhere to the monotheistic doctrine of Judaism without submitting to incorporation into the people of Israel by the rite of circumcision. A similar interest on the part of Romans in the provinces was shown in the various pagan religions and mystery cults of the East. The most important of these were the cult of Isis and Osiris in Egypt, of Attis and "the great Mother" in Asia Minor, and of Mithra in Persia and the surrounding lands. During the first century A.D. these cults had found their way into Rome itself, and providing that they did not interfere with the public worship of the national gods, no objection was normally raised. Yet one finds (as we have seen, recorded by Suetonius, *Tiberius*, 36) that the Emperor "Aegyptios Judaicosque ritus compescuit" and that "expulit et mathematicos". This seems to have happened when the foreign cults came to be regarded as a dangerous superstition, subversive of public safety. We have the same thing in Nero's persecution of Christians, who are referred to by Suetonius as "genus hominum superstitionis novae ac maleficae" (*Nero*, 16).

At the same time we find in the Empire in the Apostolic age an attempt, known to the historians of religion as "Syncretism", to synthesize the two elements we have studied, the national religion of Rome and various cults of the East. As the gods of the Greeks were identified with those of Rome, so an attempt was made to see in the far remoter Eastern deities manifestations under another name of the same powers represented by the gods of Rome. Thus Isis was identified with Ceres (the Greek Demeter, the goddess of the earth), Mithra with Apollo, etc.

The third religious influence that was present in Rome at this time was the general scepticism about the reality of the traditional gods of the national religion. This spirit is directly traceable to the Greek philosophers of the fourth century B.C. Socrates had been put to death in 399 B.C. principally because of his impious views about the traditional deities of Greece. Plato (*d.* 347 B.C.) had arrived at the idea of the Supreme Good which controlled the world, and Aristotle (*d.* 322 B.C.) had taught that there was a First Cause of all things. These doctrines led to a philosophical monotheism which was held by many cultured Romans in the early days of the Empire. For them the national religion was no more than "dope for the people". So St Paul could say in Athens in the middle of the first century A.D., after walking about and seeing their idols, that they were altogether too superstitious. And they, far from putting him to death, were anxious to give him a further hearing (Acts 17). He could say, amid the background of the many altars and among the teachers of philosophy, that the "Unknown God" whom they also worshipped was indeed the "God who made the world and all things therein, he being Lord of heaven and earth" (Acts 17. 24). There seems to have been little attempt to synthesize philosophical monotheism with the national religion, and indeed the "philosophi" were often regarded as dangerous, being subversive of national institutions. Domitian (*Suetonius*, 10) ordered their banishment.

The fourth element was the worship of the deified Emperors. The practice already existed in the Seleucid and Ptolemaic Empires, where the Emperors were sometimes even deified during their lifetime. It was, therefore, nothing new when Julius Caesar was placed, after his death, among the gods of Rome. Augustus erected the "aedem divi Iuli" (*Mon. Ancyr.*, XIX). The senate decreed that a temple should be built in his honour and dedicated to Clemency (Plutarch, *Caesar*, 67, for this was a special virtue of Caesar). In due course Augustus was deified,[1] and Caligula appears to have been the first to claim divine worship during his own lifetime. But by this time the worship of the deified Emperor had become part of the imperial political propaganda. It was an important element incorporated into the national religion. This cult of the Emperor was imposed upon all peoples of the Empire, whatever their local religion might be, with the solitary exception of the Jews. Gaius Caligula, however, insisted on the erection of his statue in the Temple at Jerusalem. Protests were made by the Jews of their "insuperable aversion to the reception of the statue", first, unsuccessfully, by Philo of Alexandria, and, finally, by the vassal-king Herod Agrippa II, when the matter was allowed to drop. (The complete story is in Josephus, *Ant.*, XVIII, 8.)

e. THE RABBINIC TRADITION IN ISRAEL

The Scriptures of the Old Testament are the basis of all the religious tradition of Israel. Every Jew had that background, whether he knew his Scripture in the original Hebrew, as it was read in the Jewish liturgy, or in the Aramaic paraphrases known as the Targumim which were read in the Aramaic-speaking areas such as Palestine, or in the Greek Septuagint version that was used in the Diaspora. Both the Targum and the Septuagint had their origin about the year 200 B.C. and the process of their compilation was a gradual one. The various Targumim were not complete until after the first century A.D. Targum (plural Targumim, a word meaning "interpretation", cf. the modern Arabic *turguman*, a

[1] Information comes to hand in the second number of *Ancient India*, 1946, of a Templum Augusti as far afield as south-east India in the first century.

dragoman or interpreter) was a Rabbinic production, and although certain Targumim were simple translations into Aramaic, others were elaborate paraphrases. They had their origin in the vernacular (Aramaic) homily after the reading of the Hebrew Scriptures. The two principal Targumim are the *Babylonian Targum* attributed to Onqelos (first century A.D., collecting older traditions, but not codified until after the third century at Babylon), and the *Jerusalem* (i.e. Palestinian) *Targum*, attributed to one Jonathan (usually called Pseudo-Jonathan, purporting to be first century A.D.). In one form or another the Old Testament was therefore the basis of all Jewish teaching. P. Prat has reckoned that St Paul in his Epistles quotes (with formula of quotation) from the Old Testament seventy-eight times, and that in 112 places his words are a clear allusion to an Old Testament text.[1]

St Paul had not only the background of his Roman citizenship and the Greek-speaking world of the Roman Province of Cilicia, but he also had an education in the best tradition of the Rabbis. He himself said: "I am a Jew, born at Tarsus in Cilicia, but brought up in this city (Jerusalem), at the feet of Gamaliel, taught according to the truth of the law of the fathers, zealous for the Law . . ." (Acts 22. 3) ". . . according to the most sure sect of our religion I lived a Pharisee" (Acts 26. 5).

The Pharisees were the traditionalists among the Jews, jealously guarding the traditions handed down among them from the fathers—a traditionalism which often degenerated into a burdensome legalism and hypocrisy as we know so well from the Gospels, but which at the same time had a truly religious foundation and provided a sound ethical and spiritual training. The names of Nicodemus and Gamaliel, and those we shall mention presently in the later tradition are great names indeed. The Pharisees traced their ancestry to the Maccabees, but their traditions of learning to a much earlier date. We can see what was the Rabbis' own tradition

[1] *The Theology of St Paul*, vol. I, 411 sq.

about the origins of their learning from the opening of the most well-known tractate of the Mishnah, called Aboth[1] (or in full, Pirqe Aboth, the Sayings of the Fathers): "Moses received the *Torah*[2] from Sinai, and he delivered it to Josue, and Josue to the elders, and the elders to the prophets, and the prophets delivered it to the *Men of the Great Synagogue*. They said three things: Be deliberate in judgement; and raise up many disciples; and make a fence round the *Torah*. Simon the Just was one of the last survivors of the Great Synagogue. He used to say: Upon three things the world is based: upon the *Torah*, upon the Temple service, and upon the practice of charity." This gives us a good idea of the ideals of the Pharisees, but the identity of the Men of the Great Synagogue remains a mystery. Simon the Just is most likely to be identified with the High Priest who was in office round the year 300 B.C.[3] However that may be, it is established that the body of Jewish laws known as the *Mishnah* was growing at the time of Christ and was not codified until about A.D. 200. Although, therefore, Rabbinic literature did not exist, written down as we have it now, until long after, much of the material existed in oral tradition at the time when St Paul was sitting at the feet of Rabbi Gamaliel and is to be traced much further back still.

Because this very teaching was the material of St Paul's Rabbinic education, it is important that we should have some notions of the extensive literature that came from it. The following outline is based on that in the *Rabbinic Anthology* of C. G. Montefiore and H. Loewe[4] (especially Excursus III for dates, etc.).

Rabbinic literature is primarily a legal and an exegetical

[1] To be found in any Jewish Prayer Book. Standard English edition (Singer), pp. 184 sq.
[2] i.e. teaching or guidance, used of the oral tradition of Israel, or in particular of the Pentateuch (the books Genesis–Deuteronomy).
[3] See *Rabbinic Anthology*, 1938, mentioned below.
[4] I would like here to pay tribute to these two Jewish scholars, who died in 1938 and 1940 respectively: the latter was my own master in Rabbinics.

literature. The legal books are the *Mishnah* and *Talmud*, and the exegetical books are the various *Midrashim*. The two literatures grew up parallel. They both have their basis in the Old Testament. Both are written partly in Rabbinic Hebrew (a development from Biblical Hebrew), partly in Aramaic (the language of Palestine for about three centuries on either side of the Christian era). Both make regular use of two methods of exposition: *Halakha* ("as we go along" we explain) and *Haggadhah* (we explain "by telling a story").

We shall now trace briefly the growth of the *Mishnah* and the *Talmud*. (The word Mishnah comes from the Hebrew Shanah "to repeat"—i.e. learning by oral method—Aramaic Tena, hence Tanna, "a teacher".) From 300–200 B.C. onwards we have the "Pre-Tannaitic" period, including the great names of Hillel and Shammai just before the Christian era. The "Tannaitic" period, when the teaching began to be written down, extends from A.D. 10 to A.D. 200. St Paul's time in the Rabbinic schools dates from the earlier part of this period, the period of the formation of the *Mishnah*. After the destruction of Jerusalem in A.D. 70 Rabbi Johanan ben-Zakkai founded the Academy at Jamnia (near Jaffa) where the work went on. Rabbi Gamaliel, St Paul's master, also belongs to this earlier period. One of the greatest names is that of Rabbi Aqiba, who died just before the fatal revolt of Bar-Kokhba in A.D. 135, after the failure of which Jews were banished altogether from Judea, and the Jamnia Academy came to an end. The scholars scattered into various outlying parts of Palestine, notably to Sepphoris in Galilee. Here, about the year 200, the codification of the Mishnah was completed by Rabbi Judah the Prince and the Tannaitic period concludes. After this there was a large migration of Rabbis to Babylon, and so we find two centres, one in Galilee and the other in Mesopotamia. The succeeding period after 200 is called the "Amoraic" or that of the Amoraim (i.e. the "speakers" or commentators of the Mishnah). The codified

Mishnah was worked upon, and this commentary is called the *Gemara*, which was written between A.D. 200 and 500, either in Palestine or in Mesopotamia. The original text of the *Mishnah* with the *Gemara* is the *Talmud*, either a work of forty-four volumes, the *Babylonian Talmud*, or a much shorter work which is called the *Jerusalem Talmud*. There is also a collection of commentaries from the Tannaitic period called the *Tosefta* (or additions).

Of course, the whole literature of the Talmud is very much later than apostolic times, but it deserves study not only for its own sake, but because it is the flower that came from the root that was already growing in the ground when St Paul was doing his Rabbinic studies at the feet of Gamaliel.

f. HELLENISTIC LITERATURE IN ISRAEL

The Rabbinic literature was confined to the Aramaic-speaking world of Palestine, and when, after A.D. 200, they moved further abroad, they remained a small and closed community. Much more numerous were the Jews of the Diaspora, scattered through the pagan world of the Empire. Yet it is interesting that Saul of Tarsus, being of a good religious family, was sent for his training to Jérusalem, the only centre at the time of Rabbinic studies. The Jews of the Diaspora adopted the lingua franca of the lands they lived in: Greek. They had their Scriptures and their liturgy in Greek. And when they wrote, they wrote in Greek.

The first obvious monument to Jewish Greek letters is the *Septuagint Version* of the Old Testament.[1] This seems to have

[1] It is a great pity that mistrust of legend prevents us from accepting the delightful story of the origin of the Septuagint, according to which seventy (or seventy-two) scholars were entertained at King Ptolemy's expense, and each shut up in a separate cell with a Hebrew Bible and writing materials. At the end of seventy (or seventy-two) days, by divine intervention (for such it must have been), each produced exactly the same translation into Greek, which was therefore called the version of the "Seventy" (Septuaginta), usually written LXX or 70 in roman figures. For material on the Greek versions, see a good account in Sir Frederick Kenyon's *Our Bible and the Ancient Manuscripts*, 4th ed., 1939, 1941, pp. 52 sq.

been made in Egypt about the year 200 B.C. So familiar had
this version become among the Jews of the Diaspora, that the
writers of the New Testament normally quote it for their
references to the Old Testament. Until the end of the second
century A.D. the great majority of Christians were Greek-
speaking and they adopted the LXX version of the Old
Testament and regarded it with as much veneration as an
original text (even sometimes attributing to it inspiration).
One of the results of this was that the Jews produced rival
versions in the second century A.D. There were three, by
Aquila (believed to be a disciple of Rabbi Aqiba, mentioned
above), *Theodotion* and *Symmachus*. These new versions never
had great popularity, though the Greek of Symmachus has
considerable merit and was used by St Jerome when he was
working on the Vulgate.

Then there are the various Books of the Old Testament
which were either written directly, or at least published, in
Greek only, and were incorporated into the LXX Bible, but
never accepted by the Rabbinic schools as canonical, not
appearing in the Hebrew Bible, and so are not accepted
by the Jews and are counted by the Protestants among the
"Apocrypha". They formed an integral part of the Catholic
Bible, since the whole early Church used the LXX version.

Of these books

Tobias
Judith   almost certainly were originally in Hebrew,
Baruch   but only the Greek has come down to us.
I Maccabees

Ecclesiasticus was certainly written in Hebrew, and
about half of the Hebrew text has come to light
since 1896, but the author's grandson, in a preface,
tells us that he translated the book into Greek before
publishing it.

Wisdom
II Maccabees were originally written in Greek.

Esther ⎫ existed in a long and a short recension, of which the
Daniel ⎬ longer is represented by the Greek, so that certain
⎭ parts of these books are not found in the Hebrew.

We can, of course, regard the New Testament itself as Hellenistic Jewish literature, though its popular style places it in a class apart. It is written in the Greek known as κοινή or "common" to all the Eastern part of the Empire at the time.

Two Jewish writers, almost contemporaries with the Apostles, and who wrote in Greek, stand out. The one is an historian and the other a philosopher.

The historian is *Flavius Josephus*.[1] He was born in A.D. 37–38 in Palestine where he joined the Pharisees in Jerusalem as a young man. When he was twenty-six he made a journey to Rome to plead a legal cause, and made many acquaintances there that were to prove useful to him later on. He was back in Palestine (living at Sepphoris in Galilee), when the revolt of A.D. 66 broke out. He took a prominent part in resisting the Romans, but was eventually taken prisoner. While a prisoner he got into the favour of Vespasian who had just been declared Emperor and was able to act as an intermediary between the Romans and the Jewish rebels, even while Jerusalem was being besieged. After the fall of Jerusalem in 70 he was invited by the Emperor to go to Rome in order to write up the history of the war. This he did, writing in Greek, under the title *The Wars of the Jews*, being an eye-witness' account in seven books of the events in Judea A.D. 66–70. He was made a Roman citizen and given every opportunity of writing (including a pension). He then set about his great work in twenty books, *The Antiquities of the Jews*, in which is related the history of Israel from Creation to the period of the war chronicled in his other work. The Christian reader is specially interested in the passage in XVIII, 3: "Now, there was about this time Jesus, a wise man, if it be lawful to call him a man, for he was a doer of wonderful

[1] His autobiography, and especially *Wars*, III, 8 and Pope, V, 410.

works, a teacher of such men as receive the truth with pleasure. He drew over to him both many of the Jews, and many of the Gentiles. He was the Christ. And when Pilate, at the suggestion of the principal men amongst us, had condemned him to the cross, those that loved him at the first did not forsake him; for he appeared to them alive at the third day; as the divine prophets had foretold these and ten thousand other wonderful things concerning him. And the tribe of Christians, so named from him, are not extinct at this day." The genuineness of this passage has been doubted and scholars (Catholics and non-Catholics alike) are divided. Some consider it to be a Christian interpolation. All the ancient MSS. include it, but then they are all of Christian origin. Origen (writing in A.D. 248) did not know of it, but Eusebius (writing in A.D. 311–325) quotes it in full. There is no direct evidence against it, but the fact remains that such a witness is very extraordinary coming from a Jewish writer.[1] Josephus added the name Flavius to his own, after becoming the protégé of the Emperor Flavius Vespasian. He died in Rome about A.D. 100.

The other outstanding Jewish Hellenistic writer is the philosopher *Philo*, a Jew of Alexandria.[2] Only one fact is known about his life: that he led the Jewish Embassy to Rome in A.D. 40 to protest about Caligula's statue (see end of sect. *d.* above). Eusebius tells us that while in Rome he is said to have met St Peter (II. 17. 1), but brings no evidence to prove it.

Philo's great importance lies in his philosophical writings. He was thoroughly conversant with both backgrounds, knowing intimately both his Jewish Old Testament and the current Greek philosophy of Plato. His contention was that since Truth is necessarily one, the revealed truth of the Bible and the philosophical truth arrived at by reason must necessarily be one and the same. He endeavoured to prove to the

---

[1] For discussion of this see Pope, V, 413 and (fully) F. J. Foakes Jackson, *Josephus and the Jews*, p. 89 and Appendix B. Also L. de Grandmaison, S.J., *Jesus Christ*, I, 9, for opinions of Catholic scholars.

[2] Pope, V, 414 sq., is very good on Philo.

Greek-speaking Jews that the philosophical system taught by the Greeks all round them was merely another aspect of the familiar revelation of the Bible, and to the Greeks that the Jewish revelation, so uninviting to the Greek mind, was no other than the truth about the Supreme Good and Beautiful, which they had arrived at by reason. Philo probably more than anyone else made the creed of Judaism known among the Greeks. Of particular importance is his synthesis of the Platonic notion of things coming into being as reflections of the ideas in God, with the Jewish notion of God creating things out of nothing. Philo taught that God brought things into being through a system of intermediate beings or Aeons (corresponding to Plato's self-subsisting Ideas) among which was the λόγος or "word" of God. This theory bridged the gulf between the Platonic idea of God as a purely spiritual supreme Being and the Hebrew idea of God as a Father full of loving care for his creatures, and it paved the way for the later Christian Neo-Platonists. Further, Philo's readers would be in a position to understand the beginning of St John's Gospel: "In the beginning was the λόγος, . . . and the λόγος *was God.*"

In addition to his purely philosophical works, Philo occupied himself much with exegesis of the Old Testament (LXX text). He began the "allegorical" method of interpretation, i.e. a study of biblical history and anecdote, not so much for the sake of the historical personage or his actions, but for the sake of the spiritual meaning symbolized by the person or event.

The allegorical method of exegesis was followed by many later generations of Christian interpreters, and actually Philo was widely read by the early Christians, especially in Alexandria itself.

Philo is presumed to have been born at about the beginning of the Christian era and to have died round A.D. 70. Since St Mark is believed to have come to Alexandria in about A.D. 50 to preach the Gospel, the first converts to Christianity would have been made while Philo was still teaching and writing there.

A REFERENCE TABLE OF A FEW
KEY-DATES IN THE APOSTOLIC AGE

Year A.D.	Roman Emperor	Roman Rule in Palestine	Apostles	Bishops of Rome
30—	Tiberius since 14	Pontius Pilate procurator since 26		
		36. Marcellus		
	37. Caligula	37. Marullus		
40—	41. Claudius	41. Vassal-king Herod Agrippa I		
		42. *Persecution*	42. James Gt. martyred	42. Peter
			Peter to Rome	
		44. Fadus procurator		
		46? Tib. Alexander	47. Paul begins his journeys	
		48. Cumanus	49. Council of Jerusalem	
50—	54. Nero	52. Felix	52. Paul meets Gallio	
		57. Festus	55–57. Paul in prison at Caesarea	
			58–60. Paul in prison in Rome	
60—		62. Albinus	62. James the Less martyred	
	64–67. *First Persecution*	64. Gessius Florus		
		66. Jews' Revolt		
			67. Peter and Paul martyred	67. Linus
	68–69. Four Emperors			
	69. Vespasian			
		70. Fall of Jerusalem		
70—	79. Titus			79. Cletus
80—	81. Domitian			
90—	91–93. *Second Persecution*		93. John's ordeal and exile	91. Clement
	96. Nerva		96. John's release	
	98. Trajan			
			100. John dies	
100				

PART II. SAINT PAUL

1. HIS LIFE

Note 1. A short outline of his life was given in Vol. IV of this series,
   The Church in the New Testament, pp. 121 sq. Parts of this chapter
   are taken verbatim from there.
Note 2. I have chosen to follow for the most part the dates given by
   Father Hugh Pope, O.P., in his *Aids*, V, 373 sq. The dates given by
   various authors vary by a few years, owing to the acceptance or
   rejection of different evidence, and to the fact that parts of years may
   or may not be counted as a year.
Note 3. There are only three key-dates in the chronology of St Paul's
   life that one can attempt to fix by contemporary history. These are:
      (i) St Paul's escape from Damascus when Aretas was king there
          (II Cor. 11. 32–33; Acts 9. 23–25).
      (ii) St Paul's stay in Corinth when Gallio was proconsul there
          (Acts 18. 12).
      (iii) The replacement of the procurator Felix by Festus, while St
          Paul was a prisoner at Caesarea (Acts 24. 27).
   Intermediate dates are fixed from these, since the scale of years
   within the life of St Paul are fairly clear. The historical evidence for
   fixing the key-dates will be examined in brief small-type paragraphs.[1]
Note 4. This chapter is intended as much for reference as for direct study.

Saul of Tarsus, afterwards to become Paul the Apostle of
the Gentiles, was remarkable from the beginning for his un-
tiring energy, his unswerving purposefulness and his inspir-
ing leadership. Beneath these qualities was a deep and ardent
love, a love of what is good and true, a love of his own people,
and a love of the service of God as he saw it. It was this very
passionate love that made him at first into a persecutor of
those whom he saw as enemies of his own Israel, "breathing
out threatenings and slaughter" (Acts 9.1).

His conversion was violent: the blinding light, the vision,
the voice of Christ, the trembling terror that followed and
the days of darkness. "And he received his sight, and rising
up he was baptized" (Acts 9. 18). He lost no time. "And
immediately he preached Jesus in the synagogues, that he is
the Son of God" (9. 20).

[1] For chronological arguments see Pope, V, 473 sq., Prat, I, 397 sq.,
WV Acts, Appendix II, to mention obvious places only.

Henceforth his burning love was consecrated: "I live, now not I; but Christ liveth in me" (Gal. 2. 20). His love of his own people is transformed: "I have great sadness, and continual sorrow in my heart: for I wished myself to be an anathema from Christ, for my brethren, who are my kinsmen according to the flesh" (Rom. 9. 2–3). His energy is canalised into ceaseless travel to preach Christ "in much patience, in tribulation, in necessities, in distresses, in stripes, in prisons, in seditions, in labours, in watchings, in fastings . . . by honour and dishonour, by evil report and good report . . . as dying, and behold we live; as chastised, and not killed; as sorrowful, yet always rejoicing; as needy, yet enriching many; as having nothing, and possessing all things" (II Cor. 6. 4–10). So his missionary labours continue for about seven years, founding new Christian communities and later writing to encourage them, visiting other communities or writing to them. Then making a pilgrim-visit to Jerusalem he was arrested in the Holy City.

For five years he was a "prisoner of Christ Jesus" (Philem. 1), first in Palestine, then in Rome. But his dauntless energy and trust in God did not desert him. Later he wrote: "At my first answer (i.e. trial) no man stood with me . . . but the Lord stood by me, and strengthened me, that by me the preaching may be accomplished, and that all the Gentiles may hear: and I was delivered out of the mouth of the lion" (II Tim. 4. 16–17).

So he was acquitted and started travelling again, only to be once more arrested. This time he knew it was the end: "I am even now ready to be sacrificed, and the time of my dissolution is at hand," he wrote in his last Epistle (II Tim. 4. 6). Then the end came with his glorious martyrdom, which tradition places on the same day as that of St Peter, June 29, A.D. 67.

Such is the story. Let us now examine it in detail. The life falls obviously into distinct periods, and we adopt here the same divisions as in the previous volume.

A. Before his conversion (to the year 33/34). Saul was born at Tarsus in Cilicia, "a citizen of no mean city" (Acts 21. 39), probably about the beginning of the Christian era, for at the martyrdom of Stephen (round the year 32) he was still a νεανίας (Acts 7. 57), so probably not much over thirty, and writing to Philemon from his Roman prison (A.D. 58–60) he calls himself "an old man" (Philem. 9), so perhaps about sixty. This means that his age corresponds roughly with the years A.D.

As a young man he attended the Rabbinic school at Jerusalem, having joined the Pharisees (Acts 26. 5), and studied "at the feet of Gamaliel" (Acts 22. 3). He voted (perhaps as a member of the Sanhedrin?) in favour of the persecution of the Christians (Acts 26. 10), and "consented" to the stoning of Stephen (Acts 6. 57–59). He then got the high priest's authority to put Christians into prison and even to death (Acts 22. 4–5, 26. 10–12). In the midst of these efforts, Saul was miraculously converted to Christ. There are three accounts of this in the Acts: by Luke the historian 9. 1–22, in speeches by Paul 22. 1–21 and 26. 2–23.

B. After his conversion (a period of three years: 34–37). Here we must sift our evidence from Acts and Gal., with one passage from II Cor.

Acts 9. 1–18. the account of his conversion
19. "with the disciples at Damascus for some days"
20. "immediately preached Jesus"

23–24. *"and when many days were passed,* the Jews consulted together to kill him ... and they watched the gates also"
25. "but the disciples conveyed him away by the wall, letting him down in a basket"

Gal. 1. 15–16. "he called me by his grace"

17. "neither went I to Jerusalem"
18. "but into Arabia, and again I returned to Damascus"

II Cor. 11. 32. "At Damascus, the governor of the nation, under Aretas the king, guarded the city"
33. "and through a window in a basket I was let down by the wall"

26. "and when he was come to Jerusalem"

27. "Barnabas brought him to the apostles"

28. "and he was with them in Jerusalem"

30. "they brought him down to Caesarea, and sent him away to Tarsus"

Gal. i. 18. "Then *after three years* I went to Jerusalem to see Peter,

and I tarried with him fifteen days"

21. "Afterwards I came into Syria and Cilicia"

The parallels are striking, yet it is not definitely established that the same visit to Jerusalem is intended, though that is most probable. What is plain, however, is that the "many days" of Acts represents a period of about three years, during which, after his conversion and short stay at Damascus, Paul went "into Arabia" before returning to Damascus, when the episode of the plot and his escape in a basket occurred.

Of his journey into Arabia we know nothing whatever. There is no other reference to it, and it is not clear what is meant by "Arabia". It may refer to any part of the territory that lay desert-wards or eastwards from Damascus and Palestine and was inhabited by Arab tribes. The suggestion has been made that during this period he may have visited Our Lady, but this is pure conjecture.

Of the years that follow his retirement to his home-town nothing is known either. The next thing that we hear is in Acts 11. 25, that Barnabas "went to Tarsus to seek Saul: whom when he had found he brought to Antioch". This is the second recorded act of friendship of Barnabas towards Paul, and he later accompanied Paul on his First Journey. As Barnabas was a Cyprian (Acts 4. 36), it is possible that he and Paul of Tarsus were already friends before.

The mention in II Cor. 11. 32 of King Aretas is a clue to the date 37 for this event. Aretas was King of the Nabataeans (Arabs who lived in the Syrian desert) who apparently got possession of Damascus and became a vassal-king for a time. He lived until about A.D. 40. We find Roman coins at Damascus of the reigns of Augustus and Tiberius, but none of the reign of Caligula or Claudius from which it has been inferred that it was not until the time of Caligula (37) that Aretas became vassal-king. Tiberius was apparently very hostile to the Arab tribes on the edge of the Empire.

C. His Missionary work (A.D. 46–55). Paul seems to have spent nine years since 37 in his home-town of Tarsus, when in 46 he was fetched thence to Antioch, where he and Barnabas "conversed there in the church a whole year, and they taught a great multitude" (Acts 11. 26). From here he set out on his missionary journeys, which can be dated as follows:

1st Journey (47–48) (Acts 13. 4 to 14. 27): Cyprus, Asia Minor, with a stay for "a long time" (14. 2) at Iconium. Probably about a year in all.

At the end of it "they abode no small time" at Antioch. Which brings us to

The Council of Jerusalem, probably in 49 (Acts 15. 2–30). This is probably[1] the visit referred to in Gal. 2. 1, "Then, after fourteen years, I went up again to Jerusalem with Barnabas, taking Titus also with me".[2] Then "after some days" at Antioch (Acts 15. 36) Paul proposes to set off on his

2nd Journey (49–52) (Acts 15. 39 to 18. 22), on which he re-visits his friends in Asia Minor (provinces of Galatia and Asia), sails from Troas to Macedonia, and so to Thessalonica, Athens and Corinth, where he stays one and a-half years (18. 11), and meets Gallio the Proconsul (18. 12). From Corinth, passing Ephesus, he returns to Antioch.

This meeting with Gallio has been an important key-date, especially since the discovery and publication in 1905 of the Delphic Inscription[3] which fixes the proconsulship of Gallio to the year 52–53. (Proconsuls held office for one year.)

3rd Journey (52–55) (Acts 18. 23 to 21. 17): St Paul sets off again after "some time" and again visits Galatia and Asia, this time spending two years at Ephesus (19. 10) ("till Pentecost", I Cor. 16. 8), after which he visits

[1] But see note on Gal., p. 155.
[2] Approximately fourteen years since his last visit in 37, counting parts of a year as a year.
Greek text in Pope, V, 418.

Corinth again (Acts 20. 2–3, I Cor. 16. 6), and returns by
sea (via Miletus, where he meets the clergy of Ephesus)
to Caesarea, reaching Jerusalem by Pentecost 55, just a
year after leaving Ephesus.

D. Period of imprisonment (55–60) (Acts 21. 33 to the end).
On the seventh day of his pilgrimage at Jerusalem Paul was
arrested. Within three days (indications of time are 22. 30,
23. 11–12, 23) he was removed to the prison at Caesarea,
under the governor Felix.[1] Thus he remained for two years
(55–57) without condemnation (24. 27), when the governor
was changed and Festus took over.

Another key-date. The new governor took over in 57. Eusebius tells us
that Festus came in the second year of Nero, who began his reign in
October 54, and so his first (complete) year began officially in September
55, his second year in September 56.

Paul almost immediately appeals to Caesar (25. 11), and is
duly shipped to Rome, travelling in winter (27. 9), and so
arriving early in 58. Here he remained "two whole years in
his own hired lodging" (28. 30), which brings the end of his
imprisonment to the year 60.

E. Period of liberty (60–65?). The rest of Paul's life is mostly
a matter of conjecture, with some guidance from tradition.
From his captivity he writes already to Philemon: "But withal
prepare me also a lodging. For I hope that through your
prayers I shall be given unto you" (Philem. 22). So he had
hope. In I Tim. and Titus he no longer writes as a prisoner,
but speaks of travel-plans (I Tim. 3. 14, Titus 3. 12). But
this liberty probably did not last long.

F. Second imprisonment and death (65?–67). There are no
certain dates here, but Nero's great persecution began in 64,
and the probability is that Paul was caught some time after
this, perhaps somewhere in the provinces (Nicopolis or
Troas[2] have been suggested). The probable date of his martyrdom, together with that of St Peter, is A.D. 67. The legends

[1] Felix was a freedman. See further note on him in Appendix C, p. 309.
[2] See note on II Tim. 4. 13, p. 222.

about their deaths are given in Vol. IV, *The Church in the New Testament*, pp. 211–12.

SUMMARY OF THE LIFE OF ST PAUL

A. Born at Tarsus in Cilicia
Studied at the Rabbinic school at Jerusalem
Led the persecution of Christians

B. Conversion 33 or 34
Went to Arabia
Returned to Damascus: Escaped 37
Visited Jerusalem (15 days)
Retired to Tarsus 37–46

C. Preaching at Antioch 46–47
1st Journey 47–48
Stayed at Antioch
Council of Jerusalem 49
2nd Journey 49–52
3rd Journey 52–55

D. Arrested 55
Imprisoned in Caesarea 55–57
Appealed to Caesar 57
Imprisoned in Rome 58–60

E. Acquitted 60
Period of liberty (travels) 60–65?

F. Second Imprisonment 65?–67
Martyrdom 67

(9)   ## 2. HIS LETTERS

St Paul's letters, like those of any man, reveal much of his thoughts and desires, and convey to us most vividly the teaching which the great Apostle was giving to the early Christians. At the same time, as in everyone's letters, many autobiographical details are given, which help us to follow yet more exactly the story of his life, and which bear out the history given by St Luke in the Acts in a manner which strikingly commends the historical accuracy of both.

The style of the letters is very familiar to all Christians, from reading, from hearing in the Liturgy and from frequent quotation in the literature and the conversation of the whole world. But already St Peter warned us ". . . as also our most dear brother Paul, according to the wisdom given him, hath written to you: as also in all his epistles, speaking in them of these things; in which are certain things hard to be understood, which the unlearned and the unstable wrest, as they do also the other scriptures, to their own destruction" (II Pet. 3. 15–16). Indeed St Paul is sometimes "hard to be understood", for at times his thought runs faster than his words, sometimes a parenthesis takes him away from the argument (like the famous one in Eph., where the sentence of 3. 1 is resumed in 3. 14 after an intervening parenthesis), and sometimes he makes up his own words or puts so special a meaning on them (e.g. "justification" in Rom.), that it is only after long familiarity that we can fully understand.

In many cases, of course, the original readers were those who had heard him preach, and the letters were reminders and encouragements to perseverance. But in God's plan the letters of St Paul are meant not only for Thessalonians or Corinthians, etc., but for us Christians ever since. We have not got the living voice of Paul to guide us to their full meaning, but we have the living voice of the Church's traditional interpretation and theological explanation. We also have the other books of the New Testament to help us, and we should bear in mind the fact even if some of the Gospels were already composed by the time the Epistles were written, it is most improbable that St Paul's readers were already familiar with them. It is likely that the synoptic Gospels were contemporary with most of the Epistles,[1] but unlikely that the new con-

[1] This is not the place for a discussion of the dates of the Gospels. Suffice it therefore to say that St Paul's Epistles date from 50–66, and Dr Bird's dates (in Vol. III of this series, *A Study of the Gospels*, pp. 3 sqq.) are these: Mt. (Aramaic) 40, (Greek) later, Mk. 42–49, Lk. 56–60 and Jn. 100.

verts had any written instruction apart from the Epistles of St Paul. We should also remember that St Paul's readers were all recent converts, with no traditional Christian support such as the most recent convert nowadays can get from the body of the faithful. Our study of the world in which these people lived will also help us better to understand the message that the Epistles brought to them.

The Chronology of the Epistles

We have seen (Intro., 1) that the order of the Epistles in the Bible is group-order and not a time-order. (The Westminster Version puts them in a time-order.) In the succeeding exegetical sections we shall study them in a time-order, and the annexed table places the Epistles in a chronological order which can be regarded as accepted except for the doubtful cases of *Gal.* and *Heb.*, where the internal evidence is by no means obvious and the scholars are divided. The evidence for the place of writing and the time in St Paul's life when they were written is very clear in all except *Gal.* and *Heb.* mentioned, and the Epistles of the period of liberty, *I Tim.* and *Titus*. The general period of these appears with a strong probability, but the place of writing is unknown.

An examination of the internal evidence in each of the Epistles, which enables us to determine its place and time of writing to within a year, will be left to the introductory matter of each Epistle. In general let it be said here that references are sought either to (1) the place of the writer's present abode (as in I Cor., II Cor., Epp. of the Captivity, II Tim. and possibly I Tim.), or to (2) his journeyings which can be checked by the Acts (as in I Thess.), or to (3) people, whose whereabouts at the period one knows, mentioned as being with the writer (as in II Thess. and Rom.).

The Epistles of St Paul are grouped chronologically as follows:
The "Great" Epistles (or the Missionary Epistles)
        written in the course of his 2nd and 3rd Missionary

Journeys 49–55. (He wrote none on his 1st Journey—
unless one holds the early date of Gal.: at the conclusion of the 1st Journey.)

I Thess., II Thess., I Cor., II Cor., Rom., Gal.

The Epistles of the Captivity
written from his Roman captivity 58–60.

Eph., Col., Philem., Phil.

The Pastorals and Hebrews
written after his acquittal in 60, during the period of
liberty, with the exception of II Tim. which was written from his last captivity just before his death. (The
insertion of Heb. into this period is conjectural.)

I Tim., Titus, Heb., II Tim.

St Paul's method

St Paul probably dictated most of his letters. In one case
the scribe adds a word of his own, in the Epistle to the
Romans: "I, Tertius, who wrote this epistle, salute you in the
Lord" (Rom. 16. 22). It seems likely that the concluding
paragraphs in all his letters were added in his own hand. He
expressly says so in four cases (II Thess. 3. 17, I Cor. 16. 21,
Gal. 6. 11 and Col. 4. 18). In the first of these (II Thess.),
which was only the second in the whole series, he adds a
remark to show that this piece of his own handwriting at the
end is a mark of genuineness: "The salutation of Paul with
my own hand: which is the sign in every epistle. So I write",
i.e. "this is my handwriting" (RAK). Usually some greeting
(obviously in his own writing) follows, such as "The grace of
our Lord Jesus Christ be with you all. Amen" (e.g. II Thess.
3. 18). Sometimes (as in I Cor. and Gal.) the P.S. is quite
long. In Romans, although there is no mention of his own
writing, the letter seems to come to an end with "Amen" in
16. 24, and the remaining four verses are probably a P.S. in his
own writing. In Col. the P.S. is a touching little reminder of
the fact that he is a prisoner: "The salutation of Paul with my
own hand. *Be mindful of my bands* (USA *chains*). Grace be

with you. Amen" (Col. 4. 18). These concluding salutations
in the author's own hand were common in the Greek world
of the time, as was the practice of dictating letters. Such a
mark of genuineness was called a ξύμβολον.[1] But we cannot
omit to notice the peculiar case of Gal. 6. 11: "Ἴδετε πηλίκοις
ὑμῖν γράμμασιν ἔγραψα τῇ ἐμῇ χειρί, WV: "See with what large
letters I am writing to you, with mine own hand!" The
Vulgate translated "qualibus litteris", which owing to the
fact that littera in the plural = epistola, has appeared in the
Rheims (and Authorised Version) as "what a letter". But the
reference is obviously to St Paul's large handwriting, probably more sprawling than that of the professional scribe
(perhaps Tertius again!). Dr Wand paraphrases: "Here is a
postscript in my own handwriting. (You can tell it is mine
by the big letters I make.)"; and Mgr Knox: "Here is some
bold lettering for you, written in my own hand," suggesting
that the additional verses were written especially large, to call
attention to them.

One epistle, the short one to Philemon, appears to have
been written entirely by Paul himself: (Philem. 17) "I, Paul,
have written it with my own hand."

St Paul's letters generally follow a fairly regular plan, as
we shall see when we pass on to the exegesis of them:

> Superscription in adapted Roman style
> Preamble connected with it
> The matter of the Epistle
> usually first dogmatic
> then moral
> Various personal greetings
> Concluding salutation
> ξύμβολον

In this context some allusion to the problem of the Epistle
to the Hebrews must be made. (For further detail see the
exegesis of the Epistle infra.) The above-mentioned plan is
not verified in the case of Heb.: there is no superscription (as
in all the other Epistles of St Paul or of the others). But there

---

[1] See Höpfl, O.S.B., *Introductionis Compendium*, vol. III on St Paul's
Epistles, for this and many other points of useful information.

C

is a ξύμβολον of the usual type, with personal salutations (with no mention of the author's own writing). The only possible indication of place is the obscure one of 13. 24. The style is more classical and different from the other Epistles: there is great abundance of quotation from the LXX. From the early centuries there have been doubts about its Pauline authorship (Paul's name does not appear at all). There are three main views about it: (i) (that of perhaps most non-Catholics) that it is not by Paul at all, and that there is no reason whatever to suppose it is; (ii) (that of most Catholics) that it is Paul's teaching, but not by direct dictation, the letter being "written up" by somebody else afterwards; and (iii) (that proposed by St Jerome[1]) that Paul, writing to Hebrews, wrote in eloquent Hebrew, and the letter was translated for subsequent general publication into equally eloquent Greek. Margaret Monro in *Enjoying the New Testament*, 1945, puts it well (p. 115): "For once he need not write so as to be understood by Gentiles as well as Jews! Hence he could fall back on what might be regarded as his 'natural' style, the style of a Jewish rabbi soaked in the ancient Scriptures and the lore of Israel."

A detail connected with St Paul's work, which can be found among the autobiographical hints, should not be missed. That is the question of St Paul's finances. In the earlier days of Thessalonians he mentions his working at his trade of tent-making "lest we should be chargeable to any of you", but later on (in II Cor. 11. 7–9), and while in prison (Phil. 4. 15–19) he acknowledges his debt to the Christian community of Philippi who provided for him.

Several of St Paul's letters are written as coming from Paul *and* a friend or friends, obviously with him at the time and joining in sending the letter. These are noted in the table on pp. 50-51.

---

[1] *De Viris Illustribus*, V; quoted in Pope, V, 261.

Lastly, we should notice St Paul's method of using a friend, who is travelling to the place in question, as a bearer of the letter. In some cases it is not proved from the text that the friend arrives with the letter: we have then added a query in the table.

The following table and the "Correspondence Map" on the back end-paper, which should be studied together with the table, were proposed and in substance prepared by two boys in the writer's Scripture class.

A CHRONOLOGICAL TABLE

Epistle	Period	Date	Companions	From	To
1. I THESS.	2nd Journey	51	Sylvanus & Timothy	Corinth	Thessalonica
2. II THESS.	2nd Journey	52	Sylvanus & Timothy	Corinth	Thessalonica
3. I COR.	3rd Journey	53/4	Sosthenes	Ephesus	Corinth
4. II COR.	3rd Journey	54	Timothy	Macedonia (Philippi?)	Corinth
5. ROM.	3rd Journey	54/5	—	Corinth	Rome
6. GAL.	3rd Journey[1]	54/5[1]	(all the brethren)	Corinth or Ephesus?[1]	Galatia[1] (which part?)
7. EPH.	1st Capt.	58/60	—	Rome	Ephesus
8. COL.	1st Capt.	58/60	Timothy	Rome	Colossae
9. PHILEM.	1st Capt.	58/60	Timothy	Rome	Colossae
10. PHIL.	1st Capt.	58/60	Timothy	Rome	Philippi
11. I TIM.	Liberty	60/5	—	on travels (Macedonia?)	Ephesus
12. TITUS	Liberty	60/5	—	on travels	Crete
13. HEB.	Liberty[1]	60/5[1]	—	Palestine or Italy[2]	Italy or Palestine[2]
14. II TIM.	2nd Capt.	66/7	—	Rome	Ephesus

[1] These are uncertain points.
[2] Depends on the interpretation of 13. 24: "the brethren of Italy salute you".

OF ST PAUL'S EPISTLES

Messenger	Group	Purpose	Length	Chaps.
—	Churches	Instruction	Medium	5
—	Churches	Encouragement and warning against Antichrist	Short	3
Stephanas? (16. 15–18)	Churches	Correction and instruction	Long	16
Titus and two brethren (8. 16, 18, 22–24)	Churches	Consolation and instruction	Long	13
Phebe? (16. 1)	Churches	Problems of the Christian	Longest	16
—	Churches	Problems, esp. of Jewish-Christians	Medium	6
Tychicus (6. 21)	Churches	Instruction esp. on unity	Medium	6
Tychicus and Onesimus (4. 7–9)	Churches	Instruction esp. on Life in Christ	Short	4
Onesimus (v. 12)	Personal	A personal matter	Shortest	1
Epaphroditus (2. 25)	Churches	Instruction	Short	4
—	Pastoral	Duties of a bishop	Medium	6
Zenas and Apollo? (3. 13)	Pastoral	Duties of a bishop	Short	3
—	(Special)	Christian Revelation fulfils that of OT	Long	13
—	Pastoral	Farewell advice	Short	4

PART III. EXEGESIS OF ST PAUL'S EPISTLES

NOTE ON THE EXEGETICAL SECTIONS THAT FOLLOW

It is obvious that not all the Epistles can be studied at full length in the course of a school year. Some method of selection must be used. We are going to use three types of exegesis: (1) a full exegesis, (2) a short exegesis only dealing with salient points, and (3) a sketch of the contents with notes on important texts. We shall select one of the "Great" Epistles for full exegesis, one of the Epistles of the Captivity and one of the Pastorals. For the others we shall have to confine ourselves to a short exegesis, or even only a sketch when the ground is being to some extent covered elsewhere.

We shall make a start with *Philemon*, because the matter is very straight-forward, the epistle is very short, the circumstances obvious, the style quite typical of St Paul, and the whole letter so delightful. After this intro-duction to St Paul's letter-style, we shall work through the Epistles in chronological order, as they come in the life of their author.

Before starting on each commentary we shall lead off with three short sections: (*A*) the time and place of writing, (*B*) the people to whom the Epistle was written, and (*C*) a summary of the argument of the Epistle.

It is taken for granted that students have the Rheims text at hand.

(10–11)   THE EPISTLE TO PHILEMON

A. Time and place. The first words show that St Paul was in prison. This letter was clearly written at the same time or in the same circumstances as the other Epistles of the Captivity. Timothy joins Paul in the address. At St Paul's end are found Epaphras, Mark, Aristarchus, Demas and Luke, all of whom appear again in Col.   Archippus at the other end appears again also in Col.   Tychicus is the messenger for Col. (Col. 4. 7–9) together with Onesimus, who is taking the letter to Philemon (v. 12), and he is messenger also to Ephesus (Eph. 6. 21). Timothy also joins in writing Phil.   Paul refers to his captivity in all four of the Epistles assigned to this period (Eph. 3. 1, 4. 1, 6. 20; Col. 4. 3, 18; Philem. 1, 9, 23; Phil. 1. 7). These things bring the four Epistles into a unity. Col. and Philem. obviously belong together, and it is likely that Tychi-cus was to take Eph. on the same journey: the sea-route from

Rome would be through Ephesus. That the imprisonment
was that of Rome (58–60) is rarely called in question. In the
first place it is evident that he sees a lot of people, and Luke
tells us (Acts 28. 30) that in Rome "he remained two whole
years in his own hired lodging: and he received all that came
in unto him", whereas at Caesarea he was kept in much closer
confinement, though the governor ordered (Acts 24. 23) that
his guard "should not prohibit any of his friends to minister
unto him". Further, in Philem. and Col. Luke is with him,
and the "WE-passages" in the Acts[1] show this to be true of
his journey to Rome and his sojourn there, but it is not
shown to be so of Paul's confinement in Caesarea. Then there
are the two places in Philippians which refer almost explicitly
to Rome: (Phil. 1. 13) "my bonds are made manifest ... in all
the court"—the word both in the Greek and the Latin is
"praetorium", which is left in English in USA and RAK
and rendered "the praetorian guard" in WV: it can be understood of the imperial court itself, but probably refers to the
imperial guard who would be charged with the custody of a
prisoner awaiting judgement by Caesar. The other reference
is to Christians in "Caesar's household" (Phil. 4. 22), probably slaves who were converts.These things all point with
reasonable certainty to Paul's Roman captivity as the period
of these Epistles, and this notion is confirmed by general
tradition, and also by the tradition that Mark (mentioned in
Col. and Philem.) lived in Rome.

B. To whom? Philemon was obviously a gentleman of
Colossae, since the same people are mentioned in Philem.
and Col., and since Onesimus, the slave of Philemon, is
described in Col. 4. 9 as "one of you". He was probably the
principal Christian at Colossae, and a man of means: "The
church that is in thy house" (Philem. 2). The houses of
those Christians who had sufficient accommodation were the
regular meeting places in the early times of the Church.

[1] Acts 16. 10–17; 20. 5–21; 27.1 to 28. 16.

"Thou owest me thy ownself also" (v. 19) probably indicates that he was a convert of St Paul, although the latter had never been to Colossae (Col. 2. 1: "for you and for them that are at Laodicea and whosoever have not seen my face in the flesh"). This letter was sent to him personally (the only one of its kind in the New Testament) by the hand of Onesimus, while Tychicus, travelling with Onesimus, took the common letter to the community at Colossae. It is the only one of St Paul's letters that was clearly written by himself (v. 19).

C. Argument. Onesimus, a slave of Philemon, had run away from his master, and probably robbed him as well (v. 18: "If he hath wronged thee in any thing, or is in thy debt . . ."). He had come to Rome—the big city would be a better hiding-place—and had met St Paul and become a Christian. Now St Paul is sending him back to his master with this letter, in which he asks that, now that both master and slave are Christians, Onesimus should be received back "now not as a servant, but instead of a servant a most dear brother" (v. 16). This is as far as St Paul will go discreetly to propose emancipation of the slave without proposing it in so many words. In fact, this was quite frequently done (especially a little later by Christian masters), though in early times rarely during the master's lifetime but more often through his will (see Appendix C on Slavery). The loss of a slave (quite apart from robbery) meant a serious loss in capital, and Onesimus was being sent back to make restitution in the only way he could: by his further service.

Address

(1-3)

> Paul (a prisoner) and Timothy (a brother, i.e. a Christian)
> to
> Philemon (a fellow-labourer),
> Appia (his wife?),

Archippus (probably the priest who conducted
services for them, cf. Col. 4. 17: "Take heed
to the ministry which thou hast received"),
and to the church which is in thy house,
grace to you and peace from God our Father, and from
the Lord Jesus Christ.

Note that this is an adaptation of the usual Roman letter
form, for which we have not got to go further afield than
Acts 23. 26–30:

Claudius Lysias
to
the most excellent governor Felix,
greeting.

Cicero's letters, for instance, are always headed, e.g. "Cicero
Attico S." i.e. Salutem. More formal is: "S.D." (Salutem
dicit) or "S.D.P." (Salutem dicit plurimam). The Roman
letter did not conclude with the author's name, as ours do,
but began with it. At the end one just added "Vale" (as in
Acts 23. 30), or something similar. St Paul has christianized
the style, wishing to the reader at the beginning not merely
"salutem" or health, but "gratia vobis et pax". At the end,
instead of a mere formal "farewell", he writes "Gratia
Domini nostri Jesu Christi cum spiritu vestro. Amen"—
phrases that have become so familiar in his letters, and of
which Philemon provides so typical an example.

A tradition preserved in the Martyrology for November 22
states that Philemon and Appia were killed during the reign
of Nero (therefore before 68, and so not many years after
this letter), when some pagans entered the church and the
rest of the congregation fled. Archippus is said to have died
in Asia on March 20.

Preamble

4. St Paul constantly prays for his friend: a normal Christian practice both then and now.

c2

5. His frequent phrase "in the Lord Jesus" or "in Christ" (cf. the modern "Yours sincerely in Christ"): we are brought together because we are all servants of Christ. All our actions are done "in Christ". The whole of Col. concentrates on this idea: "Christ, who is your life" (Col. 3. 4). Col. 1. 4 corresponds almost verbally with our present verse. The idea comes four further times even in this short epistle (vv. 6, 8, 20, 23).

"The saints": Paul's constant word for the Christians: τοὺς ἁγίους i.e. "the holy ones".

6. "That the κοινωνία of thy faith may be made evident" reading ἐναργής (from ἀργός shining), while the Greek text has ἐνεργής "effective". The word κοινωνία means "a having in common (κοινός)" and became a technical word of St Paul and the early Christians.[1] It is used for sharing the same teaching (e.g. Phil. 1. 5), for unity in the one Eucharist (hence our word "Communion") (e.g. the great eucharistic passage in I Cor. 10. 16), for the having-in-common by a contribution or benefaction (e.g. Rom. 15. 26), and for the unity or fellowship in the apostolate (e.g. Gal. 2. 9). The precise sense here is not certain, the most obvious being the fact that we share in the one Faith. The Rh "communication" is a literal translation that leaves the matter open. USA "sharing" also does so. WV translates the word consistently throughout as "fellowship". RAK interprets as "generosity".

Our faith is to show itself (become either evident or effective) by our good works. See notes on this teaching in Rom. and James.

7. Philemon was obviously a wealthy benefactor. "Refreshing the bowels" τὰ σπλάγχνα: in accordance with Greek usage St Paul uses this word metaphorically, first in that the bowels were supposed to be the seat of the emotions (cf. a "sinking feeling") for the "feelings" or emotions (II Cor.

[1] See special study of this word in Vol. IV, *The Church in the NT*, pp. 169 sqq.

6. 12, 7. 15), then in particular for the feeling of affection (and St Paul uses this phrase specially at this period: Philem. 12. 20 and Philippians 1. 8) and finally (here) for the "desires" or needs. So the meaning here is that Philemon's benefactions have "fulfilled the needs of the Christians". The modern versions all substitute the "heart" for the "bowels", using a commoner modern metaphor.

The Request

8-10. Although I *could* command you,
> yet I *ask* you
>> (as one old man to another, and I on the top
>> of it all a prisoner),
> I *ask* of you a favour for my son Onesimus.

Onesimus was the runaway slave, whom Paul had "begotten", i.e., as we should say, "received into the Church". Dr Wand paraphrases happily: "I want to enlist your sympathy on behalf of a convert I have made here in prison—a veritable son born to me while in chains. It is none other than Onesimus."

11. "Who hath been unprofitable"—to say the least, if he had robbed his master. There is a play on the slave's name, which means "useful", ὀνήσιμος, the verb from which is used, punning, in v. 20, q.v.

12. "Whom I have sent back to thee," the Greek then reads "him who is my very heart (σπλάγχνα)" (WV). Vulgate: "Tu illum, ut mea viscera, suscipe"—RAK happily: "Make him welcome, for my heart goes with him". The Greek word here refers to St Paul's affection for Onesimus.

16. "Servant" δοῦλος, the ordinary word for a slave.

"Both in the flesh (human forgiveness) and in the Lord (now that he is also a Christian)".

18. "Put that to my account": Paul undertakes to pay compensation for any loss Philemon may have sustained from Onesimus when he ran away. This he would do from

his own funds, which at this period he got from the community at Philippi (Phil. 4. 15–19), as we saw in the preceding chapter.

19. "I, Paul, have written it with my own hand"—the word "it" is not in the Greek or the Latin: it may refer to the whole epistle, or just to the signing of this undertaking. RAK paraphrases: "Here is a message in Paul's own hand", and Dr Wand freely: "This is a business matter, a formal I.O.U. I write it and sign it with my own hand. I, Paul, will pay the amount in full."

He adds: I need not remind you that you are already in my debt: "thou owest me thy ownself also", i.e. Philemon was one of Paul's converts—a debt that can hardly be repaid.

20. "May I enjoy thee" (Ego te fruar). The Greek has ὀναίμην (aor. opt. middle of ὀνίνημι). "Let me have this profit from thee" (WV), punning on the name Onesimus. USA covers both senses: "May I, too, make use of thee".

"Refresh my bowels", see above: either "correspond to my affection" or "fulfil my desires". USA: "Console my heart."

Conclusion

22. Having put his request that Philemon receive back Onesimus as a brother, and expressed his confidence that Philemon will do even more (Is this a hint at emancipation of the slave?), he asks Philemon to keep a spare room for him. He hopes to come and visit Colossae, and the fact that he makes this proposal suggests that he did not expect his imprisonment to last very much longer; yet he counts on the prayers of his friend.

23. Lastly he sends greetings: first those of Epaphras. He was the person who was the evangelist of Colossae (Col. 1. 7), who now was visiting Rome, and who was a Colossian himself (Col. 4. 12). So this was a greeting from an old friend. Epaphras is here described as a "fellow-prisoner in Christ Jesus". Note that the word is αἰχμάλωτος "a prisoner-of-

war", distinct from δέσμιος "a prisoner in chains" or a criminal convict, which Paul uses to describe himself in v. 1. (Bishop Lightfoot's observation.) So it conveys rather the idea of a prisoner of circumstances and not a legal prisoner, as Paul was. From this it is generally considered that "he is so much with me that he almost shares my captivity".

24. Then the greetings of Mark, the evangelist, now residing in Rome, of Aristarchus, who receives in Col. the title of "fellow-prisoner" as Epaphras does in this Epistle, of Demas, who apparently lived in Rome for he was still here at the time of St Paul's second captivity five or six years later when he abandoned the Apostle in his last struggle and went to Thessalonica "loving this world" (II Tim. 4. 9), and lastly of Luke, the evangelist and chronicler of St Paul's travels up to this moment, and his faithful companion since Caesarea. In Col. 4. 14 he is called "Luke, the most dear physician". He was the one who remained faithful to the very end: in II Tim. 4. 11 as Paul was awaiting death he wrote: "Only Luke is with me"—a moving witness to his constant friendship.

These people are all referred to as "fellow-labourers", as is Philemon himself in the address, i.e. labourers in spreading the Gospel. From this we conclude that although Epaphras first preached to the Colossians, Paul's convert Philemon took a leading part among the Christians there, especially during the absence of Epaphras in Rome.

25. The Christian final salutation: "The grace of our Lord Jesus Christ be with your spirit"; cf. the usual liturgical salutation, "Dominus vobiscum: et cum spiritu tuo".

Let us note that even in this little Epistle of only twenty-five verses the Holy Name of Jesus occurs no less than eight times (even when the matter is not theological): so much was St Paul's thought centred on Our Lord. It is said that the Holy Name occurs 219 times in the course of his Epistles.

Note.—The Epistles will now be studied in chronological order.

(On II Journey: I–II Thess.)

(12–13)   THE FIRST EPISTLE TO THE THESSALONIANS

A. Time and place. There is little doubt that the two Epistles to the community at Thessalonica in Macedonia were written from Corinth during St Paul's long stay there during the course of his II Journey. The first part of I Thess. recalls his travels at the time he first visited Thessalonica, and the events referred to fit in exactly with the account of this period in the Acts, as the following table shows.

First of all, let us go over the events of the II Journey until St Paul's arrival in Macedonia. Paul left Antioch in the company of Silas (Acts 15. 40), went through Syria and Cilicia and arrived at Lystra. Here he met Timothy (son of a Jewish mother and Gentile father), whom he took along with him on the remaining part of the journey (16. 1–3). So now there were three on the party: Paul, Silas and Timothy (cf. I Thess. 1. 1). They went through Phrygia and Galatia to Troas, where Paul had the vision of "a man of Macedonia, saying: Pass over into Macedonia and help us." Here a fourth member is added, the author of the Acts, for "sailing from Troas, we came . . ." (16. 11). They arrived at Samothracia, travelled to Neapolis and thence to Philippi, "the chief city of part of Macedonia" (16. 12). Here Luke leaves the party and apparently stays at Philippi, where he picks up with Paul again on his voyage to Troas on the III Journey about five years later. Here we could well put the passages from Acts and I Thess. in parallel columns.

Acts 16. 13–40. The Philippi episode, riot, Paul and Silas beaten and put into prison, released by an earthquake, gaoler converted, departure.	*I Thess.* 2. 2. "shamefully treated at Philippi"
17. 1. "through Amphipolis and Apollonia... to Thessalonica."	2. 1. "our entrance in unto you, that it was not in vain"

17. 2–3. "for three sabbath days he reasoned with them out of the scriptures . . . that the Christ was to suffer and to rise . . . and that this is Jesus Christ, whom I preach to you"

17. 4. "and some of them believed, and were associated to Paul and Silas: and of those that served God (proselytes) and of the Gentiles, and of noble women not a few"

17. 5–9. tumults in Thessalonica.

17. 10. Paul and Silas leave for Berea (also Timothy, 17. 14).

17. 14. Paul goes to Athens, but Silas and Timothy remain behind, at Berea.

18. 1. Paul leaves Athens and goes to Corinth.

18. 5. "And when Silas and Timothy were come from Macedonia, Paul was earnest in preaching. . . ."

18. 11. "and he stayed there a year and six months"

1. 5. "our gospel hath not been unto you in word only, but in power also"

1. 6. "and you became followers of us, and of the Lord"

1. 9. "you turned to God from idols"

1. 6. "in much tribulation"

2. 17. "we, being taken away from you for a time"

3. 1. "we thought it good to remain at Athens, alone"

3. 2. "we sent Timothy to confirm you and exhort you"

3. 6. "but *now* when Timothy came to us from you, and related to us . . ."

From the above it is plain that Paul wrote to the Thessalonians while he was at Corinth, after he had been rejoined by Timothy and Silas. The Acts do not tell us of Timothy's commission to go to Thessalonica, but it is obvious that he was sent there while he and Silas were at Berea (the two cities are only about fifty miles apart). Further, we know from Acts 17. 15 that Paul's parting instructions to Timothy and Silas when he went to Athens alone were "to come to him with all speed". The fact that they did not catch up until he had already got to Corinth supports the notion that Paul was anxious about the Thessalonians (where he had only spent three or four weeks) and changed his mind, instructing Timothy to visit Thessalonica instead of coming straight on to him, and to come on to him with Silas afterwards. So the two of them "come from Macedonia" and find Paul at Corinth. He had already started preaching there, but had not

yet met Gallio the proconsul. From Corinth he sailed back to
Palestine with only a brief stop at Ephesus (Acts 18. 18–22).
We reckoned (see above, Life of St Paul) that his II Journey was from A.D. 49–52, and that his long stay in Corinth
would begin early in 51. It seems that this letter was written
shortly after his arrival in Corinth (Timothy would not delay
more than necessary: Paul was evidently anxious, as the
letter shows), and so would be written at the beginning of
A.D. 51.

B. To whom? He is writing to the converts that he made
during his short stay. Acts 17. 4 suggests that there were few
only ("some of them believed") of those who heard Paul in
the synagogue, but states that there was a "great multitude"
of "those that served God and of the Gentiles": this represents the Vulgate "de colentibus gentilibusque", though the
Greek of Codices ℵ, B and most others omits the "and",
reading (WV) "and also of worshipping Greeks", the word
"worshipping" being σεβομένων, meaning those Gentiles
who attached themselves to Jewish worship without actually
becoming members of the Jewish people (cf. Intro. on
Religion in the Roman Empire and the case of Cornelius,
Acts 10. 2). Anyway there were, therefore, in the new Christian community a few Jews and a multitude of Gentile
Greeks, all or some of whom (according to the reading) were
already taking part in the worship of the true God. And St
Luke adds in his inimitable way: "and of leading ladies not a
few".

C. Argument. Paul was anxious about them, "I, forbearing
no longer, sent to know your faith: lest perhaps he that
tempteth should have tempted you, and our labour should
be made vain" (3. 5). But on getting their news from Timothy he was cheered (3. 6), and writes to tell them so, although
this was indeed only a confirmation of what he had heard in
between while in Greece and elsewhere, for they had become
"a pattern to all that believe in Macedonia and in Achaia

(Greece), for from you was spread abroad the word of the Lord, not only in Macedonia and in Achaia, but also in every place" (1. 7–8).

He goes on to recall his labours among them and his solicitude for them as a father for his children (c. 2). He then tells of his happiness about them and his prayer for them (c. 3).

The last two chapters (4–5) are devoted to their further instruction, first in general (4. 1–8), "For this is the will of God, your sanctification", secondly exhorting them to fraternal charity (4. 9–11), thirdly giving them words of warning about the "coming of the Lord" (4. 12 to 5. 11), a matter which he resumes in further detail in a sort of P.S. which is II Thess. Lastly he gives them various admonishments about the Christian conduct of life (5. 12–24).

The most important doctrinal teaching is that on the Second Coming or "$\pi\alpha\rhoου\sigma\acute{\iota}\alpha$"[1] of Christ, which will be studied, together with its elaboration in II Thess., in the exegesis.

Short Exegesis

Address

1. 1–2   Paul and Sylvanus and Timothy
                                  to
            the church of the Thessalonians in God . . .
                       grace be to you and peace.

The usual christianized Roman salutation. In view of the history in Acts there is no room for doubt that Sylvanus is the same person as Silas in the Acts. Paul mentions him three times (here and in II Thess., and as having preached with him and Timothy at Corinth in II Cor. 1. 19) and always under this name. Peter, similarly, says he wrote his

---

[1] This word (=presence), often written in Latin, "Parousia," is the word already used in Mt. 24, and by St Paul (e.g. 2. 19) for the Second Coming of Christ at the end of the world, and has become the theologians' technical term.

First Epistle "by Sylvanus" (see under I Pet.). The spelling
Syl- seems to be peculiar to the Rheims version. All modern
texts (with the printed Vulgate and the Greek) write Sil-,
which is more exactly the Roman form. It is obviously a case
like Saul-Paul of a Jew using a Roman name when travelling
outside Palestine, and again the name is assonant with the
original name, probably the Aramaic שאילא (Sh-ila),
which, curiously enough, is simply the Aramaic of the
Hebrew name שאול (Sha-ul) or Saul (the passive participle
in the two languages, meaning "asked-for").[1]

Preamble

1. 2–3. We give thanks to God always for you, making
remembrance of you in our prayers: as so often, Paul reminds
them that he supports them by his own prayer.

PART I: HISTORY

1. 4–10. He tells them of the good report he has had of the
Thessalonian community while he was in Greece. He reminds them how they "turned from idols" and are now
waiting for the "Son from heaven": his first reference to the
Second Coming of Christ.

2. 2–8. He recalls his conduct among them, trying to serve
God and not men.

2. 5. We never took "an occasion of covetousness": RAK
"an excuse for enriching ourselves".

2. 9. One of St Paul's few references to his trade: he worked
with his hands to earn his living, "lest we should be chargeable to any of you". He refers to this again in II Thess. 3. 8.
St Luke in Acts 18. 3 explains that Paul's trade was tent-
making and so he worked with Aquila and Priscilla in the
same trade while at Corinth. It was a Rabbinic custom that
every man should learn a trade, for among the Jews work
had a dignity unknown in the Roman world, which was run
on slave-labour (cf. Appendix C).

[1] See *Encyclopædia Biblica*, art. Silas.

2. 10–13. More about his stay with them.

2. 14–16. Just as the Church in Judea suffered from their countrymen, so do the Thessalonians—they had had to hurry Paul and his companions away (Acts 17. 10), and the chief trouble came from the Jews (17. 13), whom Paul now speaks of in bitter terms.

2. 17 to 3. 13. He speaks of his anxiety for them since he left them, and explains why he sent Timothy back to see that all was well.

3. 11. He hopes, with God's help, to return to them. In fact, he did not do so till about three years later, when he paid them two visits (at least a visit to Macedonia would probably include Thessalonica, especially when travelling from Greece). This was in 54, when he stayed till Pentecost at Ephesus (I Cor. 16. 8), and then moved to Macedonia, on to Greece, and back through Macedonia (Acts 20. 1–3, on the III Journey).

3. 13. He ends with a prayer that God may strengthen them, and so prepare them for "the coming of Our Lord"— the second reference to the Parousia.

PART II: INSTRUCTION

i. General principles (4. 1–8)

4. 1. "How you ought to walk": RAK "live". "That you may abound the more": USA "make even greater progress": RAK ingeniously "make more of it than ever".

4. 3. The great principle: "This is the will of God: your sanctification", and in particular the preservation of purity, for impurity is a thing that retards sanctification.

4. 6. "Circumvent his brother in business": Vulgate "in negotio", but the Greek has the article, so WV (and USA, which often follows WV): "overreach his brother in the matter" (i.e. of impurity, as the context shows). It does not, therefore, refer to "business-dealings".

ii. Fraternal Charity (4. 9–11)

4. 9. He will merely encourage them to "abound more".

4. 11. He encourages them to manual work, and they will not "need to depend on others" (RAK). This "would prevent any necessity of sponging on one another" (Wand).

iii. The Parousia (4. 12 to 5. 11 and II Thess. 1. 7–10, 2. 1–11)

We shall treat of St Paul's teaching in both Epistles together, since the second was obviously written both to calm those who were "troubled" (II. 1. 7), and to warn any of them who might be deceived by false teaching on the matter (II. 2. 2). He felt them to be in need of further instruction. He reminded them that he was merely going over what he had already taught them (II. 2. 5).

These passages are difficult, and a good plan is to study the following summary of the argument and so understand the teaching, and then to read it carefully in the various available versions, perhaps even marking off the stages in the exposition if one has a private copy.

St Paul deals in turn with various aspects of the question of the Parousia.

(1) *The living and the dead at the Parousia*

    (*a*) Be not sorrowful over the dead—Jesus, who died and rose again, will come back, bringing them with him (I. 4. 12–13).

    (*b*) The living at the time of the Parousia will join Christ after he has raised up those already dead (I. 4. 14–16)

                —so comfort one another with this.

(2) *The time of the Parousia*

    (*a*) The day is unknown, and will be a surprise—like "a thief in the night" (I. 5. 1–3).

(*b*) But it will not really be a surprise to you, who are "children of light" (I. 5. 3–10)

           —so comfort one another with this.

(3) *The manner of the Parousia*

(*a*) Christ with his angels will give you rest from your afflictions (II. 1. 7, 10).

(*b*) But in a flame of fire he will punish those who "obey not the Gospel" (II. 1. 8–9).

(4) *More about the time of the Parousia*

(*a*) Do not think the time is at hand—certain signs must come first: (i) the Apostasy must come first;
                  (ii) the Man of Sin, the Son of Perdition, must first be revealed (II. 2. 1–4).

(*b*) The "mystery of iniquity" is already at work—but there is a power which restrains the Wicked One: when that power is removed, he will be revealed—but then Christ at his Coming will destroy him (II. 2. 6–11).

Such is the line of St Paul's argument about the Parousia. Some particular points now require to be cleared up.

I. 4. 14.[1] "We who are alive." This is certainly the reading of the Greek and of the Latin. But it is patent from the following passages that St Paul did not think that the Parousia was so near that he and other living people would be still alive when it came. The notion that the Parousia was imminent occurs frequently in the early Church, and from II. 2. 2 we gather that even some of the Thessalonians thought so. Both St Paul in that passage, and St Peter (II. Pet. 3), are anxious that on the one hand the idea of the Parousia should not be forgotten, but that on the other hand it should not be expected at once. RAK paraphrases to explain: "Those of us

[1] Vv. 12–17 are vv. 13–18 in the Greek.

who are still left alive", adding the note that "he means by
'we' the living, at any given moment of history".

I. 5. 2. "As a thief in the night": a phrase used of the
Parousia also by St Peter (II Pet. 3. 10) and St John (Apoc.
3. 3, 16. 5) clearly echoing the words of Christ recorded in
Mt. 24. 43 sq. The phrase stands out as a striking Matthaean
parallel, but in all Paul's teaching on the Parousia so much of
the terminology finds its parallel in Christ's teaching in Mt.,
that it seems necessary to suppose that Paul was familiar with
the Gospel of St Matthew.[1] This is quite possible chronologically, for Mt. is almost certainly earlier than Thess. (It
could not be supposed that Paul's text is prior, since here we
have but fragments which are only adequately explained by
the connected discourse in Mt.) Of particular interest is the
study of certain words found in the NT only in the eschato-
logical[2] passages. For instance, the "trumpet" ($\sigma\acute{a}\lambda\pi\iota\gamma\xi$) comes
here (4. 15), in I Cor. 15. 52 (also eschatological), and in
Mt. 24. 31, and also in Apoc. The phrase "to meet him"
($\epsilon\grave{\iota}\varsigma\ \acute{a}\pi\acute{a}\nu\tau\eta\sigma\iota\nu$) involves a rare word, occurring only in 4. 16
here, and in Mt. 25. 6, the parable of the virgins, which is a
parable of the end of the world—apart from one instance of
everyday use in Acts 28. 15 (when disciples come from Rome
to meet Paul). The trumpet, the clouds, the angels, the false
security before the event, the thief in the night, and the picture of Christ coming in majesty: these things are all traceable to Christ's own teaching in Mt. The parallels in Mk. 13
and those scattered in Lk., especially 17. 22 sq., and also
12. 37 sq., appear again to be fragments corresponding only
in part to the connected teaching of Mt. There is one verbal
parallel between Thess. and Lk. (not in Mt.), in the phrase
"sudden destruction" in I. 5. 3 and Lk. 21. 34–36. It may

[1] This thesis is put forward in an original and very able article in
Biblica for 1938 (vol. 19, fasc. 1), with full treatment and many examples
in proof, by Dom Bernard Orchard, o.s.b., now Headmaster of St
Benedict's School, Ealing.
[2] This word means "descriptive of the last ($\acute{\epsilon}\upsilon\chi\alpha\tau\sigma\varsigma$) days, or end of the
world".

well be that this is a contribution of Paul which Luke later borrowed from his friend.

It is important to note that St Paul is bearing out Christ's teaching about the suddenness and unexpectedness of the Second Coming: Mt. 24. 36, "But of the day and hour no one knoweth, no, not the angels of heaven, but the Father alone" (cf. Mk. 13. 32).

I. 5. 5. "Children of the light" is a phrase that appears on the lips of Christ in Lk. 16. 8 and Jn. 12. 36. St Paul uses it again in Eph. 5. 8, and the idea comes in I Jn. 1.

II. 1. 7. "With the angels of his power": a somewhat puzzling phrase, unless (as Dom Bernard Orchard observes) taken with the phrases in St Matthew, "coming . . . with much power" (24. 30) and "shall come, and all the angels with him" (25. 31).

II. 1. 9. The doctrine of the eternal punishment of the damned, i.e. those who have refused the Gospel, given at the Last Judgment: cf. Mt. 25. 41, "Depart from me, you cursed, into everlasting fire".

II. 2. 3. "A revolt": all the modern versions have "the Apostasy", which is the Greek word, with the article.

"The man of sin, the son of perdition": usually referred to by John's word "the Antichrist" (I Jn. 2. 18, 22; 4. 3; II Jn. 7), though John himself gives the word a wider sense: "He who denieth that Jesus is the Christ . . . who denieth the Father and the Son". Later Paul speaks of "the man of sin" as "the wicked one" (II. 2. 8), more literally (WV) "the lawless one".

II. 2. 4. "Who opposeth", a participle, RAK "the rebel", which he uses again for "the wicked one". The identity of this person remains a mystery.

II. 2. 6–7. The power that restrains : "you know what withholdeth" (RAK "you know what I mean"). Cf. Mk. 13. 14: "He that readeth let him understand"; but here the reference is far from obvious to us. It was widely believed in the Early Church that the power that restrained Antichrist was the Roman Empire, and that when it fell, then the end would come.[1] But for us, the identity of the power that will unleash the son of perdition must still remain a mystery.

The teaching that the power of evil is already at work occurs also in I Jn. 4. 3: "Antichrist . . . he is now already in the world". His coming is according to the working of Satan (II. 2. 9).

Before leaving this section on the Parousia,[2] we must refer to the decrees of the Biblical Commission[3] on the Parousia in St Paul. (Full text in Pope, V, 215–6, or WV, Appendix IV.) The decrees were published in 1915 to safeguard Catholic teaching on the matter, and may be summarised as follows:

I. Can we maintain that the Apostles were giving their own human notions, whence error or deception might arise? NO.

II. Can we maintain that St Paul departs from the notion of mankind's ignorance of the time of the Parousia? NO.

III. Is it possible that "We who are alive" can refer to the Coming of Christ within Paul's lifetime? NO.

iv. The rest of the Epistle (5. 12–24)

Concerned with practical admonishments to spiritual perfection.

Conclusion

A final request for prayers, a greeting, an order that this Epistle be read out (an unusual thing: probably taken for granted in the later letters—except Col. 4. 16, where there is the order that it should be passed on to Laodicea), and the usual Christian salutation at the end.

[1] For instance, Hippolytus of Rome (c. A.D. 200) in his Commentary on Daniel, lib. IV, 21, "Who is it that withholdeth until now, if not the fourth beast?", i.e. Rome (cf. IV, 5 and 8).

[2] The teaching on the Parousia is admirably expounded in Pope, V, 208 sq., also in Prat, I, 71 sq.

[3] See p. 194, n. 3.

THE SECOND EPISTLE TO THE THESSALONIANS

This Epistle is so obviously an addition to the First, that there is no doubt that it was written shortly after it, perhaps after some reports about difficulties of some of the brethren about the Parousia had reached Paul during his stay at Corinth. It is written in the name of the same party as the previous letter.

The main doctrine in 1. 7–10 and 2. 1–11 has already been studied together with that of the First Epistle.

Other points of special interest are these:

2. 5. His reminder that this teaching on the Parousia is what he taught them when he was with them.

2. 14. His insistence that they hold fast to the "traditions which you have learned, whether by word or by our epistle". These two passages help us to understand the importance of tradition in the earliest times of the Church, and the use of the apostolic writings to implement and confirm it.

3. 1. His request again for their support of his work in prayer.

3. 7–12. His earnest recommendation of manual work, recalling the example he gave them himself, as he explained already in I. 2. 9. He reminds them of a saying of his: "If any man will not work, neither let him eat" (II. 3. 10).

3. 17. The famous example of his own handwritten salutation and signature as a proof of genuineness (see Part II, Sect. 2, St Paul, his letters).

(On the III Journey: I–II Cor., Rom., and ? Gal.)

(14–20) THE FIRST EPISTLE TO THE CORINTHIANS

Note. This Epistle is selected from among the "Great" Epistles for more elaborate treatment for several reasons. It is relatively easy; it is typical of an Epistle that is in reality a spiritual treatise; it contains much teaching that has a practical importance for all time; it includes so many famous texts; and lastly, it is second only to Romans in the extent to which it is used in the Liturgy. It has been taken rather than Romans, for this is a difficult Epistle, and much of the argumentation, e.g. about the Old Law, if studied in full detail, would require very full explanation.

A. Time and place. Paul on his II Journey spent one and a half years at Corinth, and from here (as we have seen) he wrote to the Thessalonians. From Corinth he sailed almost straight to Palestine, stopping only at Ephesus for a short while (Acts 18. 19–20). But he promised to return (18. 21). The convert Jewish couple, Aquila and Priscilla, with whom he had been staying at Corinth, came with him as far as Ephesus. He went on to Palestine, and after "some time there" he set off on his III Journey (18. 23) through Galatia and Phrygia, seeing his friends of the two previous journeys.

Meanwhile an interesting person had arrived at Ephesus, and obviously made a great impression. This was the Alexandrine Jew, Apollo (or more correctly Apollos,[1] as the other English versions have it), who had been baptized by John the Baptist, and was "one mighty in the scriptures" and "an eloquent man" (18. 24). "Knowing only the baptism of John" his Christian instruction was of course defective, and St Luke tells so discreetly how Aquila and Priscilla took him gently aside and "expounded to him the way of the Lord more diligently" (18. 26). Apollo then departed from Ephesus and went to Corinth with a letter of recommendation from the Christian community at Ephesus to that at Corinth (18. 27).

It was after Apollo had come and gone that Paul arrived at Ephesus for his promised visit (19. 1). The autobiographical details in I Cor. make it quite clear that the Epistle was written from there. He stayed there two years (Acts 19. 10), "at Ephesus until Pentecost" (I Cor. 16. 8), which, reckoning from the date of the meeting with Gallio in 52, would be the Pentecost of 54. The letter was therefore written some time

[1] The name in Greek is Ἀπολλώς, distinct from that of the god Apollo, which is Ἀπόλλων.

late in 53 or early in 54, at any rate at a time when one refers to the following Whitsun as simply "Pentecost". He was once more (not surprisingly) lodging with Aquila and Priscilla (I Cor. 16. 19), in their new home, and sends the greetings of the churches of Asia (ibid.), referring also to the visits he made in Galatia on his way to Ephesus (I Cor. 16. 1).

Not without interest is to compare Paul's travel-plans as recorded in Acts and in I Cor.:

Acts 19. 21	*I Cor.* 16. 5–6
Paul purposed in the spirit, when he had passed through Macedonia and Achaia (Greece), to go to Jerusalem, saying: After I have been there I must see Rome also.	Now I will come to you (at Corinth) when I shall have passed through Macedonia. And with you perhaps I shall abide, or even spend the winter: that you may bring me on my way whithersoever I shall go.

We know that after his visit to Corinth he did go to Jerusalem in time for the Pentecost following his departure from Ephesus, i.e. 55 (Acts 20. 16), and that he was arrested a week later. He did indeed "see Rome also", but as prisoner and not till early in 58.

While he was at Ephesus, before the riot of the silversmiths at the very end of his stay (the occasion of the riot was most probably the annual festival of Diana of the Ephesians, the "Artemisia", which took place in May[1]) he sent Timothy into Macedonia (Acts 19. 22), and obviously thought that Timothy might quite likely appear at Corinth at the same time, so he wrote to the Corinthians (I Cor. 16. 10), "Now if Timothy come, see that he be with you without fear . . ."

So the letter was probably written after the departure of Timothy.

B. To whom? St Paul had left Corinth only two years ago when he wrote this letter. He had founded the Christian community there and fostered its early growth for eighteen months. The original nucleus was the faithful couple Aquila

[1] Morton, *In the Steps of St Paul*, p. 333. The whole section on Ephesus, pp. 321 sqq., is very valuable.

and Priscilla, who, being Jews, had been expelled from Rome by Claudius, and whom Paul found on his arrival (since they were Jews and also of the same trade), and he stayed with them and worked with them. (Were they already Christians, converts of St Peter in Rome—who knows?) There was, as in all the great trading cities, a large Jewish community in Corinth, and Paul began his work, as usual, by preaching in the synagogue on the Sabbath days. But gradually they began to resist his efforts, "gainsaying and blaspheming" (Acts 18. 6), and Paul left them, saying, "From henceforth I will go unto the Gentiles" (ibid.), and after that he spoke at the house of one Titus Justus, who was one of those pagans who were attracted to the Jewish worship of the True God without attaching themselves to the Jewish community officially. (They were called σεβόμενοι or φοβούμενοι τὸν θεόν, cf. Acts 18. 7, here, and 10. 2 and 13. 43, and Hist. Intro. *d.*, p. 25.) However, the ruler of the synagogue, Crispus, was converted (Acts 18. 8), and Paul himself baptized him (I Cor. 1. 14). He was succeeded by a certain Sosthenes, who was publicly beaten after Paul's arraignment before the pro-consul (Acts 18. 17), and it is presumably the same Sosthenes who himself became a Christian and left the city with Paul and apparently stayed at Ephesus, for this name is associated with Paul's when he writes I Cor. from Ephesus.

Pagan Corinth was at the time famous for its wickedness. It was a new Roman city with the most heterogeneous population brought there by trade (cf. Geographical Intro.). "With no aristocracy, but that of wealth, and no tradition but that of making money, Corinth had become a by-word for every vice in the short space of a century. The pleasures of Corinth and the expense of living there were notorious throughout the ancient world. The word 'Corinthianize' was coined to describe an evil life.[1] ... It is necessary to realise

---

[1] See Liddell and Scott s.v. κορινθιάζομαι used already by Aristophanes.

the immorality of Corinth if we are to understand the meaning of St Paul's letters to the Corinthians."[1]

The struggle with the Jews came to a head when a new proconsul was appointed to Corinth. The Jews hoped to induce him to condemn Paul for introducing worship contrary to the law (which recognised and tolerated Judaism). But the proconsul refused and the crowd sided with him and beat up the principal Jew, "and Gallio cared for none of these things" (Acts 18. 12–17). This man Gallio is a person of unusual interest. He was the brother of Seneca the philosopher and tutor of Nero. His amiable and upright disposition is commemorated by Seneca (*Nat. Quaest.*, IVa, praef.) and in the famous lines of the convert Christian Statius (*c.* A.D. 61–96), when he says that Spain (the land where Gallio was born) "dulcem generasse Gallionem" (*Silvae*, II, vii, 32). Until the discovery of the Delphic Inscription (cf. supra, p. 41, in the dating of St Paul's life) the only corroboration of his proconsulship recorded in Acts was a remark of Pliny (*Hist. Nat.*, 31, 33) about his going for a cruise for his health "post consulatum". Seneca also reports his ill-health while in Greece (Ep. Morales, 18, 1 otherwise 104, 1). (Other references to Gallio are in Tacitus, *Annales*, 6, 3 and 15, 73; and in Dio Cassius' history, 60, 35 and 62, 25.)

The new city of Corinth, the administrative capital of Greece and residence of the proconsul (the title, correctly given by St Luke, of the governor of a senatorial province, cf. supra in Geogr. Intro., p. 6), had a population drawn from all ranks and races of the Roman world. The Christian community must have been equally heterogeneous, and this is not only reflected in the advice given in the Epistle, but also probably explains the strife and contentions among the Christians themselves. Yet by the end of the century the Corinthian Christians had become famous for their piety, as is shown by the Epistle to the Corinthians of St Clement, the third suc-

[1] Morton, p. 296. Very good on Corinth, pp. 289 sqq.

cessor of St Peter: "Who that hath sojourned among you hath not experienced the firmness of your faith and its fruitfulness in all good works; admired the temper and moderation of your piety in Christ; proclaimed the magnificent spirit of your hospitality; and thought you happy in your perfect and certain knowledge of the Gospel?"[1] Such was the fruit of St Paul's labours by his visits and epistles.

C. Argument. St Paul, while at Ephesus doing a work there similar to his previous work at Corinth, obviously kept himself very much *au courant* with what was going on at the earlier foundation at Corinth. He even mentions his informers in I Cor. 1. 11. The Corinthians had written to him for guidance on certain matters (I Cor. 7. 1), and he had written to them before: "I wrote to you in an epistle, not to keep company with fornicators" (I Cor. 5. 9). This earlier epistle has been lost. (A discussion of the lost Epistles to the Corinthians will be found in the Introduction to II Cor.)

The argument of the present Epistles falls clearly into four sections, which include two typically Pauline digressions.

I. Certain things must be corrected
      i. Party-spirit (c. 1–4).
      ii. Immorality (c. 5).
      iii. Litigation before pagans (c. 6).

II. Answers to Questions
      i. On Marriage (c. 7).
      ii. On pagan food (c. 8–10).
      (*Digression* on his own freedom and his own apostolate, with a warning from the OT, 9.1 to 10. 13.)

III. Corrections about the Liturgy
      i. Women's headdress (c. 11. 2–16).
      ii. The Eucharist   (c. 11. 17–34).

[1] Ep. of Clement, c. 1 (Dr Brownlow's translation in his excellent little book, *The Early History of the Church of God*, C.T.S., 1901, p. 170).

iii. Spiritual gifts   (c. 12–14.)
      (*Digression* on Charity, the greatest of all,
      c. 13.)
IV. The Doctrine of the Resurrection (c. 15).
      (c. 16 is entirely taken up with practical matters
      and salutations.)

Exegesis
Address
  1. 1–3. Paul (called to be an apostle) . . . and Sosthenes
                  to
         the church at Corinth
         (to them that are sanctified
         called to be saints)
         together with
    all those who call on the name of Jesus
        grace to you and peace

St Paul, as usual, has varied the Roman form of beginning
a letter. Note here a favourite phrase: "called to be an
apostle . . . called to be saints". Sosthenes is almost certainly
the "president of the synagogue" from Corinth (Acts 18. 17
WV, USA). His presence with Paul at Ephesus would be of
the greatest interest to Corinthian readers. The Martyrology
commemorates him as a martyr at Corinth on November
28th, adding that his being beaten before the proconsul
"consecrated the beginning of his faith". Timothy had gone
to Macedonia (Acts 19. 22).

Preamble
  1. 4. Again (as in I Th.) Paul begins by thanking God for the
grace that has been given to his readers, adding a prayer that
Christ will stand by them (confirm them) and keep them without crime.

  1. 7. "On the day of our Lord Jesus Christ", a frequent
phrase for the last day. Our translations insert "of the
coming" as an explanation.

1. 9. "You are called"—again the idea of their vocation, as in the address—"unto the κοινωνία of his Son": here the word clearly has its simplest meaning of "fellowship".

I. CERTAIN THINGS MUST BE CORRECTED

i. Party-spirit

1. 10. "That there be no schisms among you", i.e. divisions (RAK), or dissensions (USA). "Schism" has acquired a technical meaning in theology: the refusal to accept the authority of the Church, though without disagreeing about doctrine. Thus the schismatic churches of the East have retained the name "Orthodox", since (at any rate at the time of the Photian Schism in 863 or its renewal in the Great Schism of 1054 and 1472) the belief of those who fell away was not heretical but orthodox (i.e. "right-thinking").

1. 11. Someone had reported trouble at Corinth.

1. 12. The division was on the matter of baptism. Various parties claimed to be superior to others, according as to who had baptized them.

> "I am of Paul
> I am of Apollo
> I am of Cephas (Peter)
> I am of Christ—i.e. I don't belong to any of these parties."

1. 13. "Is Christ divided?" They are all wrong. Whoever baptized them, they belong to Christ; they were baptized in his name, and not in Paul's or anyone else's. It is the grace of Christ that is conferred through the sacraments, and who the minister is, is of no consequence.

1. 14. "I give God thanks that I baptized none of you" but Crispus, the ruler of the synagogue at Corinth who became a Christian at the time when Paul gave up preaching in the synagogue (Acts 18. 8), Caius, with whom Paul later stayed

at Corinth (Rom. 16. 23), and the household of Stephanas, a family spoken of in I Cor. 16. 15 as "the firstfruits of Achaia". All these were obviously converts of the beginning of Paul's work at Corinth.

So we know who were those "of Paul", and we know that Apollo had gone to Corinth before Paul arrived at Ephesus on the III Journey. What of those "of Cephas"? Had Peter visited Corinth on his way to Rome *c.* 42? Were Peter's converts at Corinth emigrants from Rome, like Aquila and Priscilla? Eusebius, however, reports (II 25) Dionysius, Bishop of Corinth about A.D. 180 (and famed for his devotion to the see of Rome), referring to "the flourishing seed that had been planted by Peter and Paul at Rome and at Corinth . . . both of these having planted us at Corinth, likewise instructed us".

Some translators (the Greek is a genitive) render "I am *for* Paul, etc" (WV, RAK) as a party-cry, and then "I am for Cephas" may be a cry of the Judaizers (cf. infra on Gal. pp. 161 sq.), though there is no sign in this Epistle of that difficulty. Some authors take "I am of Christ" to be an exclamtion of the Apostle and not the cry of a fourth party.

1. 18. What is the *remedy* for this party-spirit? An understanding of the doctrine of the Cross. This is true wisdom. It is not the wisdom of the world, the σοφία λόγου or scientific wisdom so much sought after in the Greek world of the time. Party-spirit was so strong among the philosophical schools of the time: party-spirit and boasting about men and leaders come from the wisdom of this world.

1. 19–21. By the Cross the wisdom of this world is made foolish. "What has happened to the sage and the scribe? What has become of the worldly critic? Has not God stultified worldly wisdom?" (Dr Wand).

1. 22. The Jews require signs (God gave them a "sign" sixty-eight times in the OT, and in the NT Christ rebukes them, e.g. Mt. 12. 39, "An evil and adulterous generation

D

seeketh a sign", cf. Mt. 16. 4 and Jn. 6. 30), and the Greeks run after wisdom.

1. 23. "But we preach Christ crucified, unto the Jews indeed a stumbling-block, and unto the Gentiles foolishness." (Cf. the same idea in Gal. 3. 1.) Foolishness is the antithesis of wisdom.

1. 24. He is all the time contrasting the wisdom of this world with that of Christ. What appears to the world foolishness, the Cross, is mightier than the world's own wisdom: the Life of Christ was by worldly standards a failure, the Crucifixion was a shameful death in the Roman world (Cicero, *In Verrem*, 5, 64, "crudelissimum teterrimumque supplicium") abolished in A.D. 313 by Constantine out of respect for Our Lord. Yet this apparent foolishness is the strength of Christ.

1. 27. "The foolish things of the world hath God chosen, that he may confound the wise."

1. 29. "That no flesh should glory in his sight." For of ourselves we are nothing: as creatures we owe our very life to God, to Christ, and to his Cross we owe our δικαιοσύνη (St Paul's famous word, "Justification", life of grace, admitting us to eternal life—to be discussed later in Rom. pp. 140 sqq. which is specially concerned with this teaching), our "sancti- fication", our "redemption". Cf. Jn. 15. 5, "Without me you can do nothing".

1. 31. "Qui gloriatur, in Domino glorietur." The phrase is a précis of Jer. 9. 23–24 and is used again in II Cor. 10. 17.

2. 1. Paul has tried to put this into practice himself: "I came to you (about three years ago) . . . not in loftiness of speech or of wisdom . . . not in the persuasive words of human wisdom, but in the showing of the Spirit and power."

2. 5. "That your faith might not stand on the wisdom of men, but on the power of God." The reason or motive for our belief is not the doctrines of men, but God's authority in

Revelation: "Auctoritas Dei revelantis" in the words of the Vatican Council (Denz., 1789, 1811; cf. St Thomas II–II, 1, 1). Similarly, the Catechism, n. 9: "Faith is a supernatural gift of God, which enables us to believe without doubting whatever God has revealed."

2. 7. "But we speak the wisdom of God, mysterious, hidden" (USA), God's plan of redemption that is a μυστήριον, "his secret" (RAK), but that has now been made known.

2. 8. "None of the rulers of this world could read his secret" (RAK), or "they would never have crucified the Lord of glory".

2. 9. The famous verse from Isaias 64. 4, with adaptation: the Hebrew is best read (with Dr Kissane), "From of old no ear has heard, no eye has seen a God like thee, who works for them that hope in thee". The last verb in Hebrew means "to wait for, long for", and St Paul deliberately changes it to "love".

2. 11. "Who else can know a man's thoughts, except the man's own spirit that is within him? So no one else can know God's thoughts, but the Spirit of God" (RAK). To understand spiritual things one must be spiritual: that is what is necessary for us. To the "carnal man" God's wisdom remains an unintelligible mystery.

2. 16. "But we have the mind of Christ." And it has become a commonplace of spiritual advice to try and look on life and people and things in the way that Christ looks at them: "we share the standpoint of Christ" (Dr Wand): this is to be a real Christian, to have a Christian outlook. And here St Paul gives the first hint of his teaching on the "Mystical Body" of Christ, which he develops later in 6. 15, 10. 17 and especially 12. 12 sqq.

3. 1. Yet it is clear that the Corinthians are not yet spiritually-minded: they are still earthbound and worldly-minded if they have these rivalries and contentions among them.

3. 4–5. Dr Wand paraphrases: "After all, who is Paul, and who is Apollos? Just ministers by whose means you were brought to conversion." St Paul then develops the idea in two metaphors, that of a garden and that of a building.

3. 6–9. The metaphor of the garden: "I have planted, Apollo watered, but God gave the increase." He denies any rivalry between them. We know from Acts 18. 24 that Apollo was considered "an eloquent man", while Paul has been protesting his lack of wisdom of this world, yet they are one, they are but God's helpers, "ministers of Christ and the dispensers of the mysteries of God" (4. 1).

3. 10–15. The metaphor of the building. The argument is this (cf. especially RAK and Dr Wand): "You are God's house. I laid the foundation, which is Christ. Other people, including yourselves, build upon it. The quality of workmanship will be shown up in the fire of Judgement-Day. The man whose work lasts will be rewarded, and the man whose work collapses will only escape through the flames." The implication is, of course, that the work of the ministers of Christ will last, while that of the quarrellers will not.

3. 16–17. An idea is developed from the metaphor of the building: the Christian community is not merely a building, it is the dwelling-place of God. "If anyone destroys the temple of God, him will God destroy" (USA).[1]

3. 18–21. The contrast of worldly wisdom and the wisdom of God is summed up.

3. 22–41. The only aim of the ministers of Christ is to lead men to Christ, everything they do, their life, their death, it is all for that purpose. This and the following passages are a good meditation on the vocation, ideals and work of the Christian priesthood and its apostolate. The original words for the "minister" (so also AV, RV, WV, but USA, RAK, Wand

[1] One might recommend here Fr Bede Jarrett's book for boys, *Living Temples*.

"servant") and "dispenser" (the others have "steward", but Wand "trustee") are ὑπηρέτης (more properly an "attendant") and οἰκονόμος (a manager of a household).

4. 2. The first thing required of a "dispenser" is that he should be faithful: "a trustee should be trustworthy".

4. 3–5. Judgement on those who have preached to them belongs to the Lord; the Corinthians are not to make rash judgements.

4. 6–7. WV note: "In what Paul has said since 3. 5 the Corinthians might think that he had only Apollos and himself in view, whereas his real anxiety was about those teachers who made their two names a cloak for faction. He would have them take to heart such passages from Holy Writ as those quoted in 1. 19, 31 and 3. 19–20 (about the vanity of worldly wisdom), and so not transgress by arrogance or the like 'what is written'."

4. 8. A rather difficult verse. He is about to speak of the hardships of the apostolic life (and we should remember that the priest's life can be expected to be a hard one, a life of selfless devotion to the salvation of souls). This verse is probably an ironic description of the self-satisfaction of the Corinthians (far from the realisation that all they may have they have received): (Dr Wand's paraphrase) "You think you already have all you need, that you are already millionaires, that you are kings in your own right apart from us. Well, I wish you were in full possession of your kingdom, and then perhaps we could reign along with you."

4. 9–13. The contrast with the difficult life of the apostles.

4. 9. "The last": WV note: "The apostles are like men thrown to the beasts, to make the grand finale in the games. It is a very different ideal that the Corinthians and their teachers have set before themselves!"

4. 12. St Paul refers to his working for his living, tent-making with Aquila and Priscilla both when he was among

them at Corinth (Acts 18. 3) and now, as he is writing, at
Ephesus (I Cor. 16. 19).

4. 13. "Refuse" and "offscouring": two words used of the
heathen practice at Athens of sacrificing "some cheap life,
in the hope of averting ill fortune" (cf. notes in WV, RAK).
It is a continuation of the idea in 4. 9.

4. 14–16. He is reprimanding them, but lovingly as a father
does to his children. He is, after all, their spiritual father
("by the gospel I have begotten you"), and the idea of Catholics calling their priests "Father" is already indicated here.

4. 15. The words "As I also am of Christ" are added in the
current texts of the Vulgate and the translations therefrom.
They are not in the Greek or in the older texts of the Vulgate,
but are taken from 11. 1 where the preceding sentence in this
verse occurs again, so that it easily happened that the continuation from 11. 1 came to be inserted here.

4 17. Timothy's departure from Ephesus, recorded in
Acts 19. 22.

4. 18–19. USA: "Now some are puffed up, as if I were not
coming to you. But I shall come to you shortly, if the Lord is
willing."

4. 19–20. "Power" (cf. in 2. 4, "not in the persuasive words
of human wisdom, but in showing of the Spirit and power")
may refer to miraculous powers, but more likely to the
"effectiveness" (Wand) of the word of God, contrasted with
the mere rhetoric of worldly wisdom.

4. 21. When he does come, he hopes that these matters will
have been put straight, and that he will have to come to them
not "with a big stick" but in "love and gentleness" (Wand).

ii. Immorality

5. 1. "It is actually reported that there is immorality among
you, and such immorality as is not found even among the
Gentiles, that a man should have his father's wife" (USA).

Ὅλως originally = altogether, and colloquially "actually". Πορνεία can refer to any illicit union. Incest is the term for such unions between members of the same family (either by consanguinity, i.e. blood relationship by descent or common descent, or by affinity, i.e. relation by marriage). The case in point, of a man and his stepmother, is one of affinity. According to the OT this sin was punishable with death (Lev. 20. 11) and in the pagan world was regarded with special horror (Cicero, *Pro Cluentio*, 5, 6: "O scelus incredibile, et praeter hanc unam in omni vita inauditum!").

5. 2. "And you, it seems, have been contumacious over it, instead of deploring it, and expelling the man who has been guilty of such a deed from your company" (RAK). In 5. 9 he reminds them that he has already written to them "not to keep company with fornicators"; the report of incest in the community therefore makes him more than ever indignant.

5. 3–5. They have here Paul's judgement: they are to act according to it in their own assembly, and are to excommunicate the man. This probably is the meaning of "to deliver such a one to Satan". St Paul does this himself once (I Tim. 1. 20): ". . . Hymenaeus and Alexander, whom I have delivered up to Satan". (Such excommunication was known also among the Jews, e.g. Jn. 9. 22, "If any man should confess him to be the Christ, he should be put out of the synagogue".) An excommunication is not only a punishment, and a protection of the faithful, it is also to be a remedy for the malefactor. Here "for the destruction of the flesh" (i.e. of lusts of the flesh), in I Tim. "that they may learn not to blaspheme". If the man referred to in II Cor. 2. 6–8 is the same man (which is not certain), the passage shows how the road to forgiveness is to remain open: "For such a one this punishment meted out by many is sufficient. On the contrary, then, you should rather forgive and comfort him, lest perchance he be overwhelmed by too much sorrow. Therefore, I exhort you to assure him of your love for him" (USA).

5. 6. "A little leaven corrupteth the whole lump": the evil influence of one person can have an effect on the whole community. St Paul uses the metaphor again in Gal. 5. 9: in both cases of an evil influence. Our Lord compares the working of leaven or yeast in the dough to both a good influence (Mt. 13. 33, Lk. 13. 21) and a bad (Mt. 16. 6 sqq., Mk. 8. 15, Lk. 12. 1).

5. 7. When commercial yeast is not used, a little dough is left over and allowed to ferment. This then provides the leaven for the next baking. At the Passover, or feast of un- leavened bread, the Jews were commanded to remove all leaven from their houses and for a week to eat their bread unleavened (Exodus 12. 15 sqq.). This was to remind them every year of God's mercy in bringing them out of Egypt. After the Passover octave they were to make a new start. St Paul uses this figure to tell the Corinthians that they are to remove all the corruption of their former lives and make a new start with new dough or paste. Meanwhile, they are to be "unleavened" until the new dough is made. It has been argued from this mention of the Paschal celebration that this Epistle was written round the time of the Passover (before Pentecost 54).

The mention of the unleavened bread of the Passover brings St Paul to speak of the deep reason of the necessity of a new start. "For Christ *our* pasch is sacrificed." The Last Supper, united with the Sacrifice of the Cross, was the last Paschal Meal of the Old Law,[1] the consummation of the Old Testament and the inauguration of the New. There was no lamb killed for that Paschal Meal: Christ himself was the Lamb: "This is my blood of the New Testament" (Mt. 26. 28, cf. Mk. 14. 24, Lk. 22. 20, I Cor. 11. 25).

5. 8. Christ himself is the Paschal Lamb of the Christians, and so the Christians are to celebrate (ἑορτάζω from ἑορτή a feast-day) their Passover not with the old corrupt leaven of

---

[1] Last Supper was the Paschal Meal: Mt. 26. 17; Mk. 14. 12; Lk. 22. 7–8.

their former lives, but with the new unadulterated unleavened bread of sincerity and truth.

It is these verses (7–8) that are used at the Epistle on
Easter Sunday, the Christian Paschal Feast.

5. 9. The reference to the previous (lost) letter to Corinth.

5. 10–11. "I did not mean (in that letter) that you could
avoid all contact with immoral people, or that you could never
meet people who are lustful, rapacious or idolatrous. To do
that you would have to leave this world altogether. But this
letter is to bid you not to associate with any of our own brethren who has been convicted as immoral, lustful, idolatrous,
abusive, drunken, or as a robber" (Wand). We should recall
the immoral state of Corinthian society at the time (cf.
Intro.) and the close connexion between the idolatrous cult
especially of Aphrodite and the exaltation of harlotry
as an act of religion. This explains the frequent juxta-
position, and even combination, of the ideas of "fornication"
and "idolatry" in St Paul and already in the OT.

5. 12–13. St Paul claims definite "jurisdiction" (RAK)
over the community he has founded, but says that neither he
nor they should judge outsiders.

iii. The matter of litigation before pagans

6. 1–3. To bring Christian quarrels before a pagan judge
brings discredit upon the Christian name. "Don't you realise
that Christians will judge the whole world?" (Wand).

6. 4. The difficulty of this verse is (a) that the verb may be
present indicative or imperative ($\kappa\alpha\theta\iota\zeta\epsilon\tau\epsilon$), and (b) that some
MSS have a query at the end and others a full stop. It can
thus be translated in various ways:

When you have to make judgements on everyday things

do you set up contemptible people to judge them? (Why then do you choose pagans?)	set up simple folk to judge them. (As a lesson in humility)	you might as well set up any insignificant people to judge them. (But of course you do not do this, so why have pagans?)

6. 5. They are to find an arbitrator among their own number.

6. 6–8. It is better to suffer wrong from one of the brethren in silence, than to sue him in the pagan court of law.

It is worth observing here that the Law of the Church (Codex Juris Canonici, canon 120) accords to clergy the "privilegium fori", which means that a cleric is to be judged in an ecclesiastical and not a civil court. This privilege goes back to Roman times, but is not recognised in most modern countries; the Codex therefore orders that the Bishop is to be consulted, if possible, before a cleric is cited in a civil court.

6. 9–10. It were much better if they were to avoid misdeeds altogether. The wicked shall not inherit the kingdom of God.

6. 11. "Such some of you were, but now you are washed, sanctified, justified (cf. 1. 29) in the name of our Lord Jesus Christ."

A summary on immorality (*taking up the second point*)

6. 12. "All things are lawful to me." The phrase comes twice in this verse and again in 10. 22 and 23. RAK note: ". . . looks as if it were a catchword, perhaps a quotation from St Paul's own lips, by which the Gentiles reminded themselves of their freedom from the ceremonial obligations of the Jewish law. There seems to have been reason to fear that some of the Corinthians were in danger of holding themselves dispensed from its moral obligations as well." The application of the phrase to the matter of eating food that had been offered to idols (10. 23) bears this out. "But St Paul's chief anxiety in this place is to distinguish sharply these indifferent matters from that of purity, to which some misled Corinthians appear to have been applying this maxim" (WV note). Dr Wand sees it as an imaginary dialogue: "There are some who claim that as Christians they have a right to do anything. Perhaps, but not everything is fitting. 'To us', they say, 'everything is lawful.' Perhaps, but as far as I am concerned, I will not let myself fall under the power of any bad habit."

6. 13. " 'Food is for the belly, and the belly for food'; still, God will end the functions of both the one and the other" (WV). Another quoted maxim, a slogan of materialism, with Paul's quick retort. Our bodies do not belong merely to ourselves, they are not there just for our own pleasure; they belong to God.

6. 14. And how much more is this so, when we realise that at the Resurrection our bodies will rise again, even as Christ's own Body rose. This is further worked out in c. 15: Christ is "the first-fruits of them that sleep" (15. 20).

6. 15. "Know you not that your bodies are members of Christ?" An explicit enunciation of St Paul's teaching on the "Mystical Body", which is developed in 12. 12 sqq. (cf. 2. 16).

6. 15–20. Sins of the flesh are sins against a man's own body. And "you are not your own" (v. 19): herein lies the whole force of the specifically Christian argument for purity. Our bodies are sacred, "the temple of the Holy Spirit" and destined for eternal life. RAK paraphrases beautifully: "Glorify God by making your bodies the shrines of his presence".

II. ANSWERS TO QUESTIONS
i. On Marriage and Celibacy

These are matters which were raised by the Corinthians by letter. He answers them sometimes expressly saying that he speaks by revelation: about marriage being indissoluble (7. 10 "Not I, but the Lord commandeth") and about the excellence of Christian widowhood (7. 40 "I think that I also have the spirit of God"); other times he expressly says that it is his private opinion (7. 6 "I speak", 7. 7 "I would that . . .", 7. 8 "I say", 7. 12 "I speak, not the Lord", 7. 17 "So in all the churches I teach", 7. 25 "Concerning virgins I have no commandment of the Lord, but I give counsel").

7. 1–9. His first principle: "It is good for a man not to touch a woman", i.e. virginity is a good thing ($\kappa\alpha\lambda\acute{o}\nu$), not a

bad thing as the pagans sometimes held. But the married state is also a good thing: "every one hath his proper gift from God; one after this manner, and another after that" (v. 7). Yet he places marriage after virginity, adding "I would that all men were as myself". But, he says (vv. 2 and 9), it is better to marry than to "burn", i.e. be consumed with passion. He urges chastity in marriage but says he is "imposing no rule" (v. 6 RAK). To the unmarried he recommends remaining unmarried (his own opinion), widows he advises to remain widows, if they can (he returns to this in v. 38). What is the reason for the excellence of virginity? The married man "hath not the power of his own body, but the wife" and vice-versa (v. 4). The unmarried man is freer for the service of God. This is, of course, the reason for the celibacy of the clergy in the West.

7. 10–11. The doctrine of the indissolubility of marriage he gives as God's command, not his own. Cf. Christ's own words in Mt. 19. 6 (Mk. 10. 9) about marriage, "What God hath joined together, let no man put asunder". When the Pharisees objected that Moses allowed divorce (Deut. 24. 1), he said "From the beginning it was not so". He allowed for the possibility that a man should "put away his wife" in the case of fornication, but that does not leave him free to marry again. St Paul similarly allows for separation (though urging reconciliation), but forbids remarriage.

7. 12–16. "To the rest, I speak, not the Lord." Who are "the rest"? Those not united in Christian marriage. "The mixed-marriage tie is weaker," writes P. Prat,[1] "Paul does not even call it a marriage, reserving this name for the sacrament which unites two Christians." Be it said at once that a legitimate marriage between two unbaptized persons is of course recognised by the Church as a legitimate contract, but naturally is not the Christian Sacrament, although (as Leo XIII said in the Encyclical *Arcanum* in 1880) it is "of

[1] Prat, I, 113.

its nature something sacred". A marriage contracted by a Catholic with an unbaptized non-Christian is invalid (the impediment "disparitatis cultus") unless a dispensation has been obtained from the Holy See (CJC, canon 1070-1). Such is a "mixed marriage", and although (if the dispensation is obtained) the marriage is a true marriage contract, yet (in the opinion of most theologians) the Sacrament is not received, since Baptism is the first requirement for the valid reception of the Sacraments. This is also the reason why the "mixed marriage" of a Catholic with a baptized non-Catholic (such as a Protestant) is not only a legitimate contract but also a true Sacrament, although it is strictly forbidden unless a dispensation is obtained (from the impediment "mixtae religionis") not for its validity, but to render it licit (CJC, canon 1060-4).

Now in St Paul's time it might have happened that a person was converted to Christianity and their husband or wife was not. In such a case, if the pagan party "consent to dwell" with the other, all is well. If not, he indicates a possible line of conduct, which has come to be known as the "Pauline Privilege" which still exists in Canon Law today (canon 1120-7). This means that if one of two (unbaptized) pagan married people becomes a Christian, and the other refuses thereupon to live peaceably together and to respect the Christian religion, after formal requests to do so have been made and refused, the convert is entitled to leave the pagan and to contract a new Christian marriage. (Naturally, cases that fit these circumstances nowadays are very rare, but in the pagan world of the time it would have been important.) The reason why this is allowed is that the interest of the Faith comes first, before that of the pagan marriage, if this is going to ruin the Christian life of the convert.

7. 17-24. An interlude on contentment with our vocation: "as God hath called every one, so let him walk: so in all the

churches I teach". It matters not if one is a Jew or a Gentile, or a slave or free man: the slave becomes Christ's freedman, the free man becomes Christ's slave.

7. 25–28. He returns to the question of virginity or marriage. He applies to this what he has just said. If a man is married or unmarried, let him remain so and be content, though "for the present necessity" (ἀνάγκη the Greek idea of compelling fate) (RAK "such times of stress") virginity is good (RAK "the best condition for a man to be in").

7. 29–31. He reminds them that whatever is their walk of life, they must be detached from this world, "for this world and all its concerns are merely transitory" (Wand). St Paul's references to the Parousia or Second Coming of Christ in this Epistle are few. His teaching on the matter is especially to be found in I and II Thess. (cf. notes on I Thess. 4. 12 sqq.).

7. 32–40. A final recommendation of the state of virginity, but, as before, only recommended and not imposed. Yet virginity has always been highly esteemed in the Christian tradition. (i) He gives more explicitly his reasons for asserting the advantage of virginity: "He that is without a wife, is solicitous for the things that belong to the Lord, how he may please God. But he that is with a wife, is solicitous for the things of the world, how he may please his wife: and he is divided" (vv. 32–35). (ii) He advises parents or guardians about their daughters: "He that giveth his virgin in marriage, doth well; and he that giveth her not, doth better" (vv. 36–38). (iii) Finally, although he fully allows a second marriage to a widow, he says that "more blessed is she" if she remain a widow—this, he says, is his own advice, but "I think that I also have the spirit of God" (vv. 39–40).

ii. The awkward matter of idol-offerings

The problem about εἰδωλόθυτα is of no immediate consequence in the modern world, but it was a very real problem in a pagan city of the time, when the whole fabric of society was shot through with pagan cult and ritual. The animals offered at a sacrifice were not wholly consumed on the altar: a large part of the meat was given to the family who offered the sacrifice. This meat was called an εἰδωλόθυτον (θύω I sacrifice). Some of it was often given to relatives or friends, sometimes some of it was sold cheaply to the butchers. Furthermore, public holidays and civic occasions were usually celebrated with a sacrifice followed by a public banquet, at which, of course, the εἰδωλόθυτα were given to the guests.[1]

These practices raised a triple problem for the converts from pagan society. (i) Could they buy meat at the butcher's, if there was a possibility that it had formed part of a pagan sacrifice? (8. 1, 10. 25). (ii) Could they take part in a civic banquet, when εἰδωλόθυτα were eaten? (8.10). (iii) What were they to do when invited to a meal with a pagan friend and such meat is on the table? (10. 27). These were the problems about which the Corinthians had written to Paul.

8. 1–6. St Paul first lays down two quite clear principles. (RAK's translation is masterly here, for the literal translations are not easy to follow.) First of all, "we all know, to be sure, what is the truth about it" (γνῶσις or inner knowledge, "inside information") (v. 1): "we can be sure of this, that a false god has no existence in the order of things; there is one God, and there can be no other" (v. 4). So far, so good. The matter is plain "in foro interno", in our own minds.

But, "knowledge only breeds self-conceit, it is charity that binds the building together" (v. 1), and this comes from our love of God. For the love, therefore, of our brethren we must respect their conscience, and, however clear it may be to us that the sacrifice to valueless idols can only itself be valueless, yet "in foro externo", as regards our exterior practice, it may in certain circumstances be wise to abstain.

8. 7–12. What are these circumstances? Although we know

[1] Cf. Prat I, 115.

that in itself the thing does not really matter, there are some converts from paganism who (by force of old habits), when they eat these things, feel in their conscience that they are actually worshipping an idol. In such cases it is better for them to abstain. And for fear of offending such a person it may often be wiser for others to abstain also. What would such a person think, if he saw one of the faithful sitting at a civic banquet in the temple-precincts (v. 10)? "We gain nothing by eating, lose nothing by abstaining" (v. 8 RAK).

8. 13. If, therefore, to eat meat should shock anyone, "I personally would avoid eating meat per omnia saecula saeculorum!": εἰς τὸν αἰῶνα is the Greek liturgical phrase. It is obviously introduced in a gay manner, hence the happiness of Dr Wand's gay paraphrase: "So if the eating of such meat is a source of offence to my brother, rather than offend him I will become a downright vegetarian for as long as I live." St Paul is simply telling them what his own attitude in such circumstances would be. He would not let his own "liberty become a stumbling-block to the weak" (v. 9).

The importance of this teaching lies in its treatment of the matter of "giving scandal". The verb "scandalizo" is used in Greek, Latin and English in v. 13, and the word σκάνδαλον (properly a snare, hence a "stumbling-block") is frequently used in the NT. It simply means a device by which someone is made to fall. In the moral sense it is an action which causes another to fall from his principles or fall into sin. An action perfectly harmless in itself, may in certain circumstances cause scandal (such as eating idol-meats). Therefore, Christian teaching always insists that the circumstances of an act must always be taken into account when the act is to be judged as good or evil. When St Paul returns to this theme in c. 10, we find him using again the maxim: All things may be lawful, but not all are expedient (10. 22–23).

Finally, we should note how fully Paul has entered into the mind of the pagan so as to understand his difficulties—"I

became all things to all men, that I might save all" (9. 22)—
and yet how remote are these scruples of the pagan convert
from the problems of the Jewish convert, which must have
been so easily understandable to Paul the Pharisee himself.

A Digression on his own Apostolate

This discussion arises directly out of the principles given
above, namely that certain things may be perfectly lawful,
but that it may be inadvisable or inexpedient to do them here
and now; that as Christians we may have certain liberties,
but in some circumstances it may not be expedient to make
use of them. Similarly, an Apostle has certain privileges, but
it may be inadvisable to use them at the moment. He now
claims these privileges, but says that in fact he does not use
them for fear "lest we should give any hindrance to the Gospel of Christ" (9. 12): he would not "give scandal" even
though he is within his rights.

9. 1–2. "Have I not certain liberties? For am I not, after all,
an Apostle? How am I to prove this? Have I not seen Jesus
our Lord? And if I may not be looked upon as an Apostle by
anyone else, I have certainly been an Apostle to you Corinthians."

9. 3. "My defence to those who criticise me is as follows"
(Wand).

9. 4. What are the privileges of an Apostle? (i) To receive
sustenance from the faithful.

9. 5. (ii) To accept the service of Christian women, as the
other Apostles have done, even the "Brethren of the Lord"
(James the Less, Simon and Jude, cf. Mt. 13. 55, Mk. 6. 3)
and Cephas.[1] The Greek has ἀδελφὴν γυναῖκα "a sister-
woman", and the word "woman" in Greek (as in French) can
equally well mean "wife", wherefore many (chiefly Protestant) commentators, following AV, translate "take a wife
from among the sisters, i.e. Christian women". And indeed

[1] Note that St Paul always (except in Gal. 1. 18) uses this Greek form of
Peter's Aramaic name (I Cor. 1. 12, 3. 22, 9. 5, 15. 5, Gal. 2. 14).

St Peter certainly was married (Mt. 8. 14, Mk. 1. 30, Lk. 4. 38). Catholic tradition has, however, consistently interpreted the passage as meaning simply "a Christian woman", and this is indeed the more obvious sense with the two words standing in the order they do stand in. Further, the right to take a Christian wife could hardly be regarded as a special privilege of the Apostles, although it could be maintained that Paul is expressly permitting it here, though not doing so himself (in view of his argument of not using rights and his statements of his own celibacy in 7. 7 and 8). Lk. 8. 3 (Joanna, the wife of Chusa, and Susanna) and Mk. 15. 40–41 (Mary Magdalen, Mary the mother of James, and Salome) are passages that mention the women who looked after Our Lord and the Apostles. Joanna and Susanna "used to provide for them out of their means" (USA). So the generally accepted meaning of this passage of St Paul refers to "priests' housekeepers" of apostolic times.

9.6. (iii) "Or is it I and Barnabas alone who have not the right to forbear from work?" (WV following the Greek text: the Vulgate has "*hoc* operandi" in place of "*non* operandi", in which case "hoc" refers to the foregoing.) In the Greek text the third privilege is that of not plying a trade for their living. The following verses suggest this in any case.

Note that Paul includes Barnabas among the Apostles, as the Liturgy does also (June 11, though of lesser rank than the feasts of the twelve).

9. 7. Some analogies. A soldier: he is paid. A vine-tender: he gets a share of the grapes. A shepherd: he gets a share of the milk. (v. 10) A ploughman or thresher: he gets a share of the grain.

9. 8–9. Even the text of Deuteronomy 25. 4 about not muzzling the ox that treads out the grain (i.e. threshing not with a flail but by the animal's hoofs stamping out the grain) can be applied to this: even the ox who works is to get his share. (Or does God's word in the Bible refer to oxen only?)

9. 11. "Here are we (apostles), who have sown in you a spiritual harvest; is it much to ask that we should reap from you a temporal harvest in return?" (RAK) Here we have obvious evidence of the fifth precept of the Church: "to contribute to the support of our pastors." Church collections, Mass-stipends and Stole-fees are offerings made by the faithful for the sustenance of the clergy, in return for the spiritual goods provided in the administration of the Sacraments, Christian instruction and the performance of the Church's official prayer. Modern Law (CJC, canon 142) forbids the clergy to engage in ordinary trade or business.

9. 12. Yet Paul has not made use of these privileges. He has worked with his own hands for his living (I Thess. 2. 9, II Thess. 3. 8, I Cor. 4. 12, Acts 20. 34).

9. 14. "The Lord ordained that they who preach the gospel, should live by the gospel." Did St Paul already know the passage in Mt. 10. 10, "The workman is worthy of his meat"? It may well be so, or it may be that Christ's dictum had been handed down in tradition. In I Tim. 5. 18 he quotes (in a similar context) as Scripture the dictum, "The labourer is worthy of his hire (or reward)". The quotation is (verbatim in Greek) from Lk. 10. 7, which by the time he wrote I Tim. he would certainly have known textually (after A.D. 60).

9. 15. "I have not written all this so as to get things out of you: I would rather die!" The same plea in I Thess. 2. 5.

9. 16–18. The only reward he looks for is to be able to fulfil his desire, nay more than desire, his necessity to preach the Gospel.

9. 19–22. In order to preach to all kinds of people, he has made himself "all things to all men". We see him entering into the minds of Jews and pagans alike, to bring them to Christ.

9. 24–27. But preaching the Gospel requires more than this. He has shown that it is a hard life in itself, but it requires

discipline and training, abstention from the good things of this world. He compares it to the ἄσκησις (whence we get the word "ascetic") or training of an athlete. "I chastise my body, and bring it into subjection: lest perhaps when I have preached to others, I myself should become a castaway" (v. 27). The Corinthians, and we also, are to understand the necessity of mortification and self-denial which have been so earnestly recommended by spiritual writers from the beginning. We are to profit by St Paul's own example. In a very practical way he teaches them by his own example: he has found this the only way, and they will find it so too. The priest and preacher especially cannot but take these words to heart. We see here St Paul "in constant anxiety about his own salvation" (Mgr Knox in notes on Septuagesima Sunday): the Corinthians are to be anxious too and to take practical steps by disciplining themselves.

A further digression arising out of this: against self-confidence

This self-discipline is necessary. We must not think that we shall be saved simply because we are baptized. The danger of falling into idolatry, immorality (we have been speaking of these things) and murmuring remains with us. The thing happened before, in the Old Testament: they had the protection of God and the promise of the Redeemer, yet they fell.

10. 1–5. "They were all in a sense baptized in the water of the cloud and of the sea" (Wand), baptized εἰς τὸν Μωσῆν "into" Moses (not "in"), which can only mean "into fellowship with Moses" (RAK) or "unto the following of Moses" (WV) or something similar. Moses was a type or foreshadowing of Christ, and Paul says (12. 13) "we were all baptized into (εἰς) one body". The cloud: the cloud that guided the people on their march through the desert. The sea: the Red Sea, through which the people walked dry-footed at the

Exodus. The spiritual food and drink: the manna and the miraculous water from the rock, both types of Christ.

10. 6. "These things happened as warnings to us that we should not give way to evil passions as they did" (Wand).

10. 7–11. We are warned "not to turn idolatrous, . . . not to commit fornication, . . . not to try the patience of Christ, . . . nor to complain. The record was written as a warning to us, in whom history has reached its fulfilment" (RAK).

10. 12–13. The conclusion: "Wherefore he that thinketh himself to stand, let him take heed lest he fall." V. 13 is difficult: "May no temptation take hold of you (the Greek has 'no temptation has taken') but such as man is equal to. God is faithful and will not permit you to be tempted beyond your strength, but with the temptation will also give you a way out that you may be able to bear it" (USA).

The matter of idol-offerings concluded

10. 14. "Keep far away, then, from idolatry" (RAK).

10. 15–17. Why? We cannot take part in two kinds of worship, the worship of Christ and the worship of idols. When it is a question of taking part in a sacrificial meal, we have our own. At our sacred banquet the chalice is the sharing in the Blood of Christ, the bread is the sharing in the Body of Christ. It is that which binds us together, which makes us One Body, because we all partake of the One Bread. St Paul takes the Eucharist Doctrine entirely for granted, merely bringing it in as part of an argument. But in so doing in vv. 16–17 he has one of his sublimest passages. In v. 16 for "sharing" he has his wonderful word κοινωνία, having in common, which is so often (and rightly) translated simply "communion". In v. 17 we find, stated so briefly, the wonderful teaching that the Eucharist is the great Sacrament of unity. We become one Mystical Body through receiving the One Bread. These are verses to have by heart.

10. 18–22. Those who partake of sacrificial food, partake in

some way of the sacrifice (in the Jewish sacrifices, for instance). Now, idols are nothing, but "the things which the heathens sacrifice, they sacrifice to devils, and not to God . . . and you cannot be partakers of the table of the Lord, and of the table of devils" (vv. 20–21). To do this would be to provoke God's displeasure, and who is strong enough to resist that?

10. 23–29. The points raised at the beginning of this section are answered in a practical application of principles. (i) What you buy at the shambles,[1] eat and ask no questions. (ii) At civic banquets, and (iii) private invitations, eat and ask no questions, but, if someone says the meat is an εἰδωλόθυτον, then, for the sake of appearances, abstain.

10. 30–33. "Si ego cum gratia participo", if I "say grace over it" (RAK), I can in no way be blamed. The main thing is to do everything for the glory of God, and to take care to give no offence, either to Jews, or to pagans, or even to fellow-Christians.

III. CORRECTIONS ABOUT THE LITURGY

i. Women's Headdress in Church

11. 1–16. Among the pagans it was customary to pray bareheaded[2] while among the Jews it was, and is, *de rigeur* for both men and women to have the head covered at times of prayer. Among Christians, however, a distinction is to be made. Man is to pray bareheaded, woman is to be veiled. It is remarkable that this practice is so consistently observed throughout Christendom. The matter is believed by many[3] to have arisen through the fact that Christianity had greatly raised the dignity of womanhood in the pagan (as well as the

---

[1] "Shambles" is an old English word (in Rh and AV) for a market-stall where meat was sold. Cf. the old street in York. Later it came to be used of a slaughter-house, and so of a scene of chaos.

[2] Sales, Commentary in loc.

[3] For instance notes to WV and USA, and Prat, I. 120.

Jewish) world of the time, and that perhaps some of the women at Corinth had pushed their equality with men beyond due limits.

St Paul is very definite about it and gives various reasons. (i) A sort of theological argument: man looks only to Christ as his head, he is the "image and glory of God"; whereas the woman looks to her husband as her head, she is the "glory of man"; that is, man has no other master than Christ, while his wife owns her husband as her immediate lord (vv. 3, 7). (ii) An argument from universal custom among civilised people: there is no shame in a man being bald (St Paul apparently was himself) or wearing his hair short—it was the usual thing among the Greeks and Romans as it is now, for their haircuts were similar to ours—but for a woman it is disgraceful and ugly: she rightly takes care of her hair, for it is her glory. So it is no shame for a man to be bareheaded, but it is for a woman (vv. 5, 6). (iii) An argument from nature: woman's hair grows longer, showing that it is natural for her to be covered (vv. 14–15). In general, when we pray it is for God, not for man, so that women should cover that which is for the glory of man. And if all this is unconvincing (which perhaps it is), there is a last argument (v. 16): if anyone objects, tell him we have no other custom anywhere in the Church of God.

Although St Paul seems to emphasize the subjection of woman, and the veil as a sign of this, yet he also speaks (v. 11) of the equality of the sexes and their dependence on each other.

The matter seems to us unimportant, but we have had to delay because the argument is obscure. One verse is most obscure, v. 10: "She ought to have authority (ἐξουσίαν power to command or control) over her head, because of the angels". This "power" perhaps = "a sign of another's power over her, i.e. a veil" (though the interpretation seems a little far-fetched). Or it possibly = "power to choose a coiffure".

(The former is the more usual.) Who are the "angels"? Either the invisible angels who attend the liturgy, or possibly the ministers in the church (cf. the angels of the Churches, Apoc. 2–3).

ii. The Eucharistic celebration

In the early centuries the Christians met together, especially on Saturday night (e.g. Acts 20. 7: the midnight mentioned was that which begins Sunday) and had a common meal. This began after the Sabbath evening-service of the Jewish Christians, and was intended especially to help the poorer brethren. Some time after midnight the bread and wine were consecrated, with prayers and reading and instruction before and after. Thus the Mass came to its present form, and this is also the explanation of the usual early hour of Mass. All this is the obvious background of this part of I Cor. This common banquet held at night, which in the early hours of Sunday turned into Mass at which everyone received Holy Communion, was called the Agape or Love-feast (ἀγάπη love). As we see at Corinth, it was open to abuse, and it began to fall into disuse and was formally abolished in the fourth century.[1]

11. 17–18. There are schisms (cf. c. 1) when you come together to the ἐκκλησία (not literally a church, of course, but a place of assembly).

11. 19. "Heresies" or different opinions among you.

11. 20–22. The Agape at Corinth was no longer a Love-feast. Each one προλαμβάνει ἐν τῷ φαγεῖν, which means either "has his meal beforehand" or "eats it before anybody else". And the poor go hungry. (The second meaning is supported by v. 33, when it appears that late-comers get nothing.) They were becoming selfish. Some did themselves so well that they got drunk. P. Prat says the Agape had become "a vulgar

---

[1] See for instance (for the Agape in general) Cabrol, *Liturgical Prayer*, pp. 54 sq., Schuster, *Sacramentary*, I, 30, Prat, I, 120, 122.

picnic, as little religious as were heathen revels". This is far from "the Lord's supper". Fr Lattey in WV suggests that St Paul is trying to abolish the supper party before the Eucharist altogether ("Have you not houses to eat and drink in?").

11. 23–26. St Paul's great eucharistic passage.

11. 23. "I have received of the Lord", i.e. by direct revelation from God. It is important to see how Paul's revealed knowledge corresponds so closely with the Gospels composed as human histories. Tradition has it that St Luke got his information largely from St Paul, and it is indeed striking how St Luke's account of the institution of the Eucharist corresponds for the most part verbally with the account here (Lk. 22. 19–20). St Luke's Gospel was probably written within six years of this Epistle.[1]

For St Paul's revealed knowledge, compare I Cor. 15. 3, "For I delivered unto you first of all, which I also received: how that Christ died for our sins . . . etc."; and Gal. 1. 11–12, "For I give you to understand, brethren, that the gospel which was preached by me is not according to man. For neither did I receive it of man, nor did I learn it; but by the revelation of Jesus Christ."[2] It must remain a matter for speculation exactly when, where and how Paul received his revelation from God. In the life of Paul there are many divine interventions, even divine guidance as to where he should go (e.g. Acts 16. 6, "they were forbidden by the Holy Ghost . . ."); but without doubt what to Paul himself stood out more than any other after the vision at his conversion is the ecstasy described in II Cor. 12. 2–4, "rapt even to the third heaven . . . heard secret words which it is not granted to men to utter" (see note on this passage), which took place "above fourteen years" before he wrote II Cor. (A.D. 54), so

[1] Lk. written before A.D. 60 (the date of Acts).
[2] Fr Lattey (in WV) and P. Prat (I, 30–1) hold that the "Gospel" in Gal. refers only to his teaching on the relation of Jews and Gentiles.

before the year 40, i.e. during the period of his retreat to Tarsus, before his active apostolate had begun. It is impossible to say how much of what Paul taught he received in this way by infused knowledge, but he certainly seems to claim this for some of his doctrine. (Cf. Prat, I, 29–30.)

11. 24. "This is my body . . ." Lk. 22. 19 adds *"given* for you". Paul omits the participle, according to the earliest Greek manuscripts, so that WV translates "This is my body, on your behalf", although the Vulgate has "quod pro vobis tradetur" (Lk. "datur") and some manuscripts of the Greek have the participle "broken".

"This do for the commemoration of me" is verbatim as in Lk. (it is neither in Mt. nor Mk.), and has found its way into the Canon of the Mass. This is one of the few texts whose exact meaning has been authoritatively declared by the Church:[1] "If anyone say that by the words 'This do for the commemoration of me' Christ did not constitute his Apostles priests, or did not ordain that they and other priests should offer his Body and Blood, anathema sit" (Council of Trent, session xxii, canon 2—Denz., 949).

11. 25. *"After* he had supped," as in Lk. verbatim. Mt. and Mk. have "while they were eating" (Mt. 26. 26, Mk. 14. 22 identical words in Greek). But note that Mt. and Mk. describe the consecration of the bread as being *during* the meal, while Lk. and Paul place the consecration of the wine *after* the meal. From this one concludes that the bread was the unleavened bread of the Paschal Meal, consecrated at the very end, and the wine came after the meal. At the Agape, the consecration of the bread and wine took place at the end of the common meal.

11. 26. "You shall shew the death of the Lord" describes the unity of the sacrifice of the Cross (his death) and of the Mass (the Last Supper): cf. Catechism, n. 278, "Mass is one

---

[1] Pius XII in the Encyclical *Divino Afflante Spiritu* (1943) reminds us that such texts are few (para. 49, C.T.S. ed.).

and the same Sacrifice with that of the Cross" (cf. Trent, Denz., 940, "Una eademque est Hostia"). "Until he come", i.e. to the end of the world.

11. 27-29. St Paul's affirmation of the real presence: "discerning the body of the Lord". "Whosoever shall eat this bread *or* drink of the chalice of the Lord unworthily, shall be guilty . . ." shows that the Body and Blood of Christ are received entire under *either* species, a matter that was laid down as a doctrine at the Council of Constance in 1415 (Denz., 626), since it was being impugned by the heretic John Hus, the Bohemian.[1] This is one of the few places where the AV has falsified the text (corrected in RV) with no support from the early manuscripts, by reading "eat . . . *and* drink" to signify the need for communion under both kinds.

This text also lays down the need for worthy preparation, which is interpreted by the Church to mean freedom from mortal sin, as the Council of Trent explains (Denz., 880).

11. 30-31. "Infirm . . . weak . . . asleep": usually interpreted of the chastisements of illnesses and death consequent upon their unbelief or bad preparation for the Eucharist. ("Therefore" is translated by USA and RAK "That is why".)

11. 32. But he reminds them that God's chastisement in this world saves us from everlasting punishment by correcting us in time.

11. 33-34. At the communal meal they are to be polite and kind ("wait for one another") and not to make it an occasion for gorging themselves.

There were obviously other questions connected with these, which they had written to St Paul: these he will explain by word of mouth when he comes. (Other references to his

[1] The practice of elevating the Host after the consecration at Mass, which only began in the Latin rites in the twelfth century and only became general in the fourteenth, probably had its origin in the desire to combat a similar false notion, namely, that transubstantiation did not occur until both consecrations were complete. Cf. A. A. King, *Notes on the Catholic Liturgies*, p. 44.

future visit are in 4. 19, 21 and 16. 5–7.) This text is sometimes adduced as evidence for the existence of apostolic
teaching in tradition, but having no place in the Scriptures.

iii. Spiritual Gifts

12. 1. What were these "spiritual gifts" ($\pi\nu\epsilon\upsilon\mu\alpha\tau\iota\kappa\acute{\alpha}$)?
They were special supernatural powers, such as the working
of miracles, given by God to many of the first Christians for
the purpose of helping to establish the Faith. The Church
at the beginning needed this divine intervention in order to
achieve the task, impossible by purely human means, of
establishing herself throughout the world. These gifts, often
called "charismata" from $\chi\acute{\alpha}\rho\iota\varsigma$ a favour (cf. 12. 9), had as
their function to confirm the word of God as it was preached.
Later on God withdrew these special favours, once the Faith
was fairly established in the known world.

These extraordinary manifestations happened also at the
Christian assemblies, and here St Paul is trying to regulate
them.

12. 2. He asks them to remember how, when they were
pagans, they used to go and consult oracles, and how various
strange manifestations sometimes followed.

12. 3. Now, it is obvious that if anyone says "Jesus is
anathema (or cursed)" this cannot come from the Spirit of
God. On the other hand, "no man can say 'the Lord Jesus',
but by the Holy Ghost." Probably the phrase has to be taken
as subject and predicate: "Jesus is Lord" (WV, USA, RAK),
in contrast to the preceding blasphemy. Everything depends
on the attitude to Jesus.

12. 4–7. If then something so simple and yet so fundamental as a simple confession of Christ's Divinity can only come
from the Holy Spirit, how much more do the various extraordinary gifts also come directly from him.

We should remember that it was less than two years before
writing this, and in the very city where he was writing, here

at Ephesus, that St Paul had had the remarkable experience of finding a little group of Christians who said (as St Luke so delightfully puts it, Acts 19. 3), "We have not so much as heard whether there be a Holy Ghost". Paul had laid his hands on them and the Holy Spirit had come upon them, and "they spoke with tongues and prophesied". This seems to have been a familiar manifestation of the presence of the Holy Spirit since Pentecost (cf. Cornelius, Acts 10. 46).

12. 8–10. A list of the charismata or "manifestations of the Spirit", as found at Corinth. (A similar list is in vv. 28–30 and in Rom. 12. 6–8.)

(1) Words of Wisdom (σοφία sapientia).

(2) Words of Knowledge (γνῶσις scientia).

> (The distinction between these is not clear. St Paul's own use of "wisdom" in cc. 1–2 suggests a penetration of the highest truths, while "knowledge" in c. 8 suggests practical conscience.[1])

(3) Faith (of the kind that "could remove mountains", cf. 13. 2.[2])

(4) Healing.

(5) Miracles.

(6) Prophecy (i.e. not merely foretelling the future, but probably including any inspired utterance, cf. 14. 1–3).

(7) Discerning of spirits (i.e. good or evil spirits, cf. the control enjoined in 14. 29, "let the rest judge").

(8) The gift of tongues (further explained in c. 14).

(9) The interpretation of tongues (cf. 14. 27–28).

12. 11–13. These gifts are all from the One Spirit, and the possessors of them should no more be jealous of one another

---

[1] St Thomas, studying the gifts of the Holy Ghost in I–II, 68. 4, says that "wisdom" is of speculative judgements, while "knowledge" is of practical judgements, with the slight alteration in II–II, 8. 6 and 9. 3 that both are speculative, while "knowledge" leads to practical action. In any case his teaching seems to follow closely St Paul's own usage.

[2] A striking Matthaean parallel in Mt. 17. 20 and 21. 21 (which has a further parallel in Mk. 11. 23). The parallel is not verbal, but the striking figure is the same. Cf. on Thess., p. 68).

than are the various members of the body, for indeed we have all been "baptized into one Body . . . the Body of Christ" (vv. 13 and 27).

12. 14–26. The members of the human body are all necessary for their particular function, and none can do without the others. Some are nobler than others, according to the closeness with which they serve the reason and will: for instance, the reasoned control of the hands is more exact than that of the feet (as is shown, say, in the relative fineness of construction of the manual and pedal keyboards of an organ). The less noble members (remoter from reasoned control) we surround with "more abundant honour" (v. 23), i.e. with clothing, and the noblest are left uncovered (the face and hands). It is interesting here to have (quite by the way) St Paul's philosophy of clothes, entirely consonant with Christian tradition on the matter.

Further, the unity of the body is shown in the fact of sympathetic suffering of one member when another is in pain— we all know how a toothache incapacitates us (v. 26).

12. 27. "Now you are the Body of Christ, and members of member." This is an exact translation of the Vulgate, which clearly read the Greek as μέλη ἐκ μέλους, though the present Greek text has μέρους (one letter different), i.e. you are "members each of you", or "severally" (WV), cf. the phrase κατὰ μέρος "in turn" (τὸ μέρος = part or share). The Greek reading is much easier.

12. 28–30. God has called each one of them to possess a certain gift: each one should be content with that. Cf. 7. 17–24 on contentment with one's vocation. There follows a list, which corresponds fairly closely with that in vv. 8–10. It may be that the apostolate is here identified with the gift of wisdom of v. 8, and the doctorate with that of knowledge. The primacy of the apostolate should be noted.

12. 31. "You should try to cultivate the more useful gifts" —this thread is picked up again in 14. 1—"but I can

show you an even better way than that, the way of love"
(Wand).

Digression: the great Hymn of Charity (c. 13)

Better than any of these extraordinary charismata is Charity, that Love of God which overflows into love of mankind.
"Thou shalt love the Lord thy God . . . this is the greatest
and the first commandment. And the second is like to this
. . . " (Mt. 22. 37–39, cf. Mk. 12. 30–31). The Greek word is
ἀγάπη which came to have this specifically Christian theological meaning, and Catholic tradition, following the Vulgate
rendering "Charitas",[1] translates it "Charity" (Rh, WV,
USA, RAK, also AV), but the Protestant versions generally
(including RV) translate it "Love".

It would be presumptuous to do anything other than to
urge careful reading of this chapter: commentary is all but
superfluous and distracting. The beauty and dignity of the
Rheims-Challoner version is incomparable[2] and this chapter
is without doubt one of the highest flights of St Paul's writing. One or two observations may, however, be made.

13. 2. "Remove mountains": the Gospel parallel has been
noted above, p. 107, note 2.

13. 12. "In a glass": St Paul was thinking of a metal mirror
which easily got dim, and not of the modern glass mirror,
where the image is bright and clear.

"As I am known": I shall see God as clearly as he sees me
now, i.e. perfectly.

13. 13. "There remain faith, hope, and charity", i.e. they
are permanent things in this life, unlike the transient charismata, which are concerned with the passing moment. Faith
and hope, of course, being concerned with the unknown, will

[1] More accurate latinity spells it "Caritas". It is connected with the
Sanskrit "karu" and not the Greek χάρις (vide Lewis and Short s.v.).
[2] As is well known, AV owes much to the original Rheims of 1582.
Challoner's alterations of Rh are few in this chapter. He alters it in favour
of AV with "kind" for "benign" (v. 4), and "child" for "little one" (v. 11).

be replaced by vision in the next life, though Charity or the Love of God will remain for ever.

To return to the matter of spiritual gifts

14. 1–6. St Paul first commends Charity as the most important thing, and then most of the chapter is devoted to the comparison of "prophecy" with the "gift of tongues" (or "Glossolalia").

When the nature of these two gifts is understood the whole chapter becomes quite plain. "Prophecy" means some form of inspired preaching, since it edifies and instructs the hearers (vv. 3, 4, 6); "Tongues", however, seems to refer to a mysterious kind of ecstatic speech in a language strange to the speaker, but sometimes intelligible to a hearer, as at Pentecost, and therefore patient of interpretation or translation, either by himself afterwards or by a hearer who knows the language, or one who has the "gift of interpretation" (vv. 5, 13, 27, 28). To speak with "Tongues", being a divine gift, of course edifies the speaker (vv. 2, 4, 14), but it is no use to anyone else without an interpreter (vv. 6, 9, 11, 16, 19).

Prophecy is therefore much more valuable than the Gift of Tongues (vv. 1, 5, 12).

14. 7–8. An analogy from musical instruments, the flute, harp and trumpet. The musician must play in such a way that the tune is intelligible or recognisable.

14. 9. Similarly your speech should be intelligible or recognisable.

14. 10. "No doubt all these different languages exist somewhere in the world, and each of them has its significance" (RAK).

14. 11–17. But if nobody can understand, although it may be excellent prayer for the man himself (v. 17), it is not much use to the others, and they cannot be expected to add their "Amen" to it (vv. 11, 16).

14. 18–19. The Vulgate reading can be understood from

the Greek: "Thank God, I can rather (μᾶλλον) speak the languages of all of you (genitive)", i.e. Greek. But the more obvious reading of the Greek is: "Thank God, I can speak with tongues more (μᾶλλον) than any of you (genitive of comparison)"; but, he goes on to say, he would much rather preach to them.

14. 20–25. "Tongues" are usually regarded as a phenomenon that will benefit foreigners and infidel strangers (v. 22), but is there not a danger that it will be mistaken for sheer lunacy (v. 23)? (At Pentecost, the Apostles were thought to be drunk, Acts 2. 13.) Surely, intelligible preaching would be more profitable to an infidel visitor (vv. 24–25).

14. 26–35. St Paul gives the Corinthians rules for the managing of their liturgical assemblies when these manifestations take place. Various brethren would contribute to the prayers with a psalm or some instruction, or a hymn (cf. v. 15), or some revelation or even some ecstatic utterance in a "tongue" or an interpretation (v. 26). But things must be done in an orderly way: he has always taught this to all the groups he has started (v. 33), and women should not be allowed to address the assembly (vv. 34–35).

14. 36. Dr Wand paraphrases: "If you don't like this ruling, I must remind you that the word of God did not originate with you, nor are you the only ones who have received it."

14. 37–38. The proof of a genuine possessor of spiritual gifts will be his obedience, his recognition that what I have written is God's will.

14. 39–40. Summary: cultivate "Prophecy", but do not forbid "Tongues", and let everything be done in an orderly manner.

IV. THE DOCTRINE OF THE RESURRECTION

15. 1–4. The principal points of St Paul's preaching of Christ's work of redemption. He had "received" this doctrine, i.e. by revelation (cf. 11. 23 and Gal. 1. 11–12 with note above

E

on 11. 23). The principal facts on which our faith rests are that

     (i) Christ died for our sins.
    (ii) He was buried (i.e. he was really dead).
   (iii) He rose again on the third day.

15. 5–7. The fact of the Resurrection is established by various witnesses, most of whom are still alive and could be questioned on the matter. First of all, there is Cephas (Peter), whom some of you probably know (cf. Lk. 24. 34 on Easter Sunday, to the disciples returned from Emmaus, "The Lord is risen indeed, and hath appeared to Simon"); then there are the Apostles to whom he appeared behind closed doors, at the lakeside and in Galilee (Lk. 24. 36, Jn. 20. 19, 26, 21. 1, Mk. 16. 14, Mt. 28. 16); then there are other witnesses, whose sight of him after the Resurrection is not elsewhere recorded: the "more than 500 brethren at once", and James.

15. 8–11. Lastly, there is Paul's own witness: "He was seen also by me, as by one born out of due time". Paul ranks his vision at his conversion with those other visions of the Risen Christ, even though it happened much later. He therefore ranks himself among the Apostles, though he is "the least of the Apostles" and unworthy of the name because he had been a persecutor. Then the wonderful phrase of his humility: "By the grace of God I am what I am" (v. 10), and although admittedly he has laboured and travelled more than any of the other Apostles, "yet not I, but the grace of God with me": cf. Gal. 2. 20 (probably written a year or so later), "I live, now not I; but Christ liveth in me".

15. 12–19. The Resurrection of Christ is central to Christian doctrine: "If Christ be not risen again, then is our preaching vain, and your faith is also vain" (v. 14). Why? Because we are redeemed. Redeemed what for? For eternal life, and life-after-death means resurrection: our looking-forward to eternal life would make no sense without resurrection. "If

with this life only in view we have had hope in Christ, we are of all men the most to be pitied" (v. 19 USA).

15. 20. "But as it is, Christ has risen from the dead, the first-fruits of them that sleep" (USA).

15. 21–23. The idea of Christ as the Second Adam is more fully worked out in Romans 5. 12–21, which was written less than a year after this. "It is in virtue of their solidarity with Christ, the Head, whose members they are, that the bodies of the just are to rise again" (WV note).

15. 24–28. Mgr Knox's translation of these difficult verses is most helpful. The idea is that Christ, the Son of Man, is our King, and he will continue to fight for us and with us against all other "principality, power and virtue". At the "end" (RAK "full completion") of history, he will present to the Father "his kingdom, his chosen followers, as his trophy of victory" (Sales), and then he himself, according to his human nature, will be "subject", in the everlasting kingdom of his Father. Apoc. 11. 15 (in Handel's "Hallelujah Chorus"): "The kingdom of this world is become the Kingdom of Our Lord and of his Christ, and he shall reign for ever and ever."

15. 29. "Baptized for the dead": a very puzzling phrase. It is usually supposed to refer to the unorthodox practice of being baptized, as it were by proxy, on behalf of those who had died unbaptized; but if this is so, it is odd that St Paul in no way reproves them for such a practice. More likely, perhaps, is the suggestion that they used some ceremony as an intercession on their behalf (cf. WV). Others think it means death-bed baptism, as a proof of the dying man's belief in the Resurrection (cf. Sales). On the other hand it is possible that it refers somehow to the "daily death" (v. 31) suffered by the Christian, who is "baptized into the death of Christ" (Rom. 6. 3) and so shares his suffering. Lastly, it is quite probable that the sense is ironic: "What are those wretched

people going to do who get baptized only to die and just remain dead? What is the good of it if there is no resurrection? Baptism is not worth while (if that is what they think)!"

15. 30–34. Furthermore, what is the use of danger and death, if death is merely a dead-end? The Resurrection makes sense of suffering and death. If the dead do not rise again, it would be much more reasonable to act upon the maxim of the materialists (quoted from Isaias 22. 13): "Let us eat and drink, for to-morrow we die". No, "do not be led into such errors; bad company, they say,[1] can corrupt noble minds" (vv. 32–33 RAK). The reference to fighting with beasts at Ephesus cannot refer to the silversmiths' riot, for Paul left Ephesus straight after that (Acts 20. 1), but it probably refers to a similar occasion, one of the many "dangers of every hour".

15. 35–47. People want to know what the Resurrection will be like. These verses (which become much clearer in Mgr Knox's version) are nevertheless obscure. But the general line of the argument is fairly plain. We cannot really imagine the risen body, any more than when we sow seed we could from seeing this imagine the plant that will grow. So when our body is buried, we cannot from this imagine the body that will rise. And anyway God's creation is so diversified and every part of it is in itself a wonder. The variety is found in the humblest creatures and in the noblest, even "star differeth from star in glory". So will the variety be in the Resurrection, and so also will the risen body have a glory inconceivable when we consider the mortal body that is buried like a seed in the ground. And how will this be? Because the first Adam was indeed "a living soul", but Christ, the Second Adam, is the very source of life. The first Adam was a man of this earth, while the Second Adam is a Man from Heaven.

[1] This proverb is from the *Thais*, a lost comedy by Menander of Athens (342–291 B.C.).

15. 48–50. Now we, who belonged to the earthly first Adam, must now belong to the heavenly Second Adam, and, although we are mortals, in the Resurrection we shall share his immortal life.

15. 51–53. "Behold I tell you a mystery": all the dead will rise again "in a moment, in the twinkling of an eye, at the last trumpet".[1] But there is a textual difficulty in v. 51. (The main problem is where the "not" comes in.) The Greek uncial MSS represent three readings:

(i) All shall *not* sleep, but   all shall be changed (B and most later MSS).
(ii) All shall   sleep, but *not* all shall be changed (אּ, A, C).
(iii) All shall   rise, but *not* all shall be changed (D and Vulg.)[2].

The explanation of these is this:

(i) Some will *not* be dead at the last day, but they will be changed (i.e. glorified).
(ii) All will die (and rise), but some will *not* be changed (i.e. the wicked will rise, but not glorified).
(iii) All will rise, but the wicked will *not* be glorified.

The interesting thing is that (i) has the support of most of the early manuscripts, is the usually accepted Greek text, and is followed in most translations from the Greek (such as AV, RV and WV). It is also supported by the phrase, "He shall come to judge the *living* and the dead", and perhaps by I Thess. 4. 16.   The elect who are still alive will not experience death, but will pass straight into a heavenly existence. The reading (ii), however, has the support of the oldest of the uncial manuscripts, and has the same meaning as (iii), which is read by one uncial and is represented in the Vulgate and

[1] The trumpet (as in I Thess. 4. 15) is again a striking parallel with Mt. 24. 31.
[2] These letters are the designations of the great uncial manuscripts: אּ (Codex Sinaiticus, fourth century) is in London (BM); A (Codex Alexandrinus, fifth century) is there also; B (Codex Vaticanus, fourth century) is in Rome; C (Codex Ephraemi Rescriptus) is in Paris; and D (Codex Bezae, fifth to sixth century) is in Cambridge.

the translations therefrom (such as Rh, USA and RAK). According to this, everyone will die (one cannot of course rise from the dead unless one has died), and the second clause distinguishes the fate of the just and of the wicked. Because of this textual difficulty it is impossible to decide whether those who are alive at the last day will suffer death or not.[1]

These and next verses form the text of some of the most famous numbers in Handel's *Messiah* (v.g. No. 48, "The trumpet shall sound").

15. 54–55. When the mortal puts on immortality at the Resurrection, it will be true what Scripture says: "Death is swallowed up in victory. O death, where is thy victory? O death, where is thy sting?" The first quotation is generally traced to Is. 25. 8 where we read, "He (God) hath swallowed up death for ever" (or possibly, as in AV ". . . in victory") in the Hebrew, but the LXX has "Death has swallowed up, conquering", and it might be possible that St Paul took the verb as a passive (Pual): "Death has been swallowed up". The second quotation appears to be from Osee 13. 14, where the LXX reads "Where is thy right, O death? Where is thy goad (or sting), O Hades?" The Hebrew word אֱהִי for "where" is a very exceptional variant of the ordinary word אֵי; or else it might conceivably be a verb: "I will be", whence we have the Vulgate rendering "*Ero* mors tua, o mors, morsus tuus *ero*, inferne", which appears in the Liturgy (1st Antiphon at Lauds) in the Tenebrae of Holy Saturday.

15. 56. "It is sin that gives death its sting, just as it is the law that gives sin its power" (RAK), i.e. knowledge of sin comes from knowledge of a law.

15. 57–58. Conclusion of the teaching of the whole Epistle: thank God for the victory, but be persevering.

[1] The whole problem is discussed in Appendix I to WV (by Fr Lattey).

A FEW PRACTICAL AFFAIRS MENTIONED

16. 1–2. The collection for the poor among the Christian community at Jerusalem: the details we have from the same request made a little later on the same journey in Rom. 15. 26.

16. 3–9. His travel-plans which he actually carried out (cf. Intro. to I Cor.), writing II Cor. from Macedonia, and leaving straight for Palestine with the money he had collected in Macedonia and Greece (Rom. 15. 26).

16. 10–11. His recommendation of Timothy, whom he had probably already sent into Macedonia (Acts 19. 22).

16. 12. His recommendation of Apollo. Apollo seems to have returned to Ephesus while Paul was there, and he apparently was unwilling to go to Corinth again—perhaps owing to the factions there using his name? (I Cor. 1, etc.) Paul promises that he will come back.

16. 15–18. Stephanas and his friends are specially recommended. They were certainly Corinthians (1. 16), but were apparently with Paul at Ephesus at the time of writing, for he rejoices in their presence. Had they brought the letter with the questions in it? Were they taking back the present letter?

16. 19–20. Greetings from Aquila and Priscilla, well known to the Corinthian Christians, and from the others of Ephesus and Asia.

16. 21–24. Paul's ξύμβολον (see Introductory chapter on St Paul's letters pp. 46-7), or P.S. in his own handwriting. It includes the Aramaic phrase אתא מרן (Maran atha), "Our Lord has come" (which is the form given in the Peshitta, or Syriac, i.e. later Aramaic, version). The precise inflection of Aramaic as spoken in St Paul's time is uncertain, and it may be a participle: "Our Lord is coming". If it is a past tense it refers to Our Lord's life on earth; if it is a participle it refers to his Second Coming. Fr Lattey, however (in WV), divides the words otherwise, מרנא תא (Marana tha), which makes the verb an imperative: "Come, Lord", similar to the Greek

invocation in Apoc. 22. 20. The words may be the beginning
of an Aramaic prayer of the earliest Palestinian tradition,
which had become current in other communities. The same
may be said of אבא (Abba), which may possibly be the
beginning of the Our Father in Aramaic. It is certainly true
of the word "Amen", which has remained current everywhere.

Note. The foregoing study of I Cor. need not be considered of dis-
proportionate length: in a school-course like the present it is important
that the students should have experience of one full-scale commentary of
the kind. But one consequence is that we must be content with a very
brief treatment of II Cor. In view of the fact that II Cor. presents one of
the greatest literary problems of the New Testament, the intricacies of
which could only be studied adequately at very great length, I have
thought it wisest only to outline the problem as a guide to maturer study,
and to give briefly the argument of the Epistle with a very few notes on
outstanding texts.

(21–22)   THE SECOND EPISTLE TO THE CORINTHIANS

A. Time and place. As we saw, it is quite clear that I Cor.
was written from Ephesus, some time before Pentecost of
A.D. 54 (cf. I Cor. 16. 8). After the silversmiths' riot about
that time, Paul left Ephesus, and "set forward to go into
Macedonia" (Acts 20. 1). In II Cor. 2. 12 he mentions
passing through Troas (the port in Asia Minor from which
one would sail across the Aegean to Macedonia), where he
had hoped to meet Titus[1] returning from Corinth with news
for him. Titus, however, had not arrived (2. 13), so Paul goes

[1] This is the first time we read of Titus in the NT, although the event
of Gal. 2. 1, when Paul takes him to Jerusalem, is much earlier, probably
A.D. 49. He was therefore already a friend of Paul. It is possible that he is
the same person as the Corinthian Titus Justus (a "worshipper of God",
i.e. a pagan attached to Jewish worship) in whose house Paul preached
after abandoning the synagogue (Acts 18. 7), who afterwards became a
Christian, and might well be a suitable emissary to Corinth (though his
name in some MSS of Acts is spelt Titius, and in others he is simply
called "Justus"). Further notes on him will be given in our study of the
Epistle addressed to him. The only references to him are in II Cor., Gal.
2. 1, 3, II Tim. 4. 10 and Titus 1. 4.

on to Macedonia. This is as far as Paul's account of his travels in II Cor. goes. In Acts 20. 2 we read that "when he had gone over those parts ... he came into Greece", presumably to Corinth on the visit he promised in I Cor. 16. 5–6: "I shall come to you, when I shall have passed through Macedonia ... and with you perhaps I shall abide, or even spend the winter". This would be the winter of 54–55, though Luke in Acts 20. 3 tells us that he only spent three months there. (This visit is also referred to in II Cor. 12. 14, 20 and 13. 1.) Anyway by Pentecost of 55 he had reached Jerusalem, where he was arrested.

From this it is fairly obvious that II Cor. was written from Macedonia (perhaps at Philippi, the principal city and one where he had friends already), after Pentecost and a stay at Troas and before the winter of A.D. 54, probably less than a year after I Cor.

B. To whom? To the Church of Corinth, who were clearly still in a state of unrest. He had sent Titus to get a report of what was going on there, and the good report that he received from Titus when they met in Macedonia (II Cor. 7. 5–7) consoled him greatly. (An account of the Corinthian community is given in the Introduction to I Cor.)

C. Argument. In contrast to I Cor., where the argument is straightforward and consecutive, the structure of II Cor. is very difficult to analyse, and not only are the arguments interspersed with digressions more notably than in any other Epistle, but the mood of the writer seems to change very sharply between what we have put down as the first and the third parts. Further, it is difficult to identify exactly the visits and the letters to Corinth, to which references are made in II Cor. The general lines can, however, be seen clearly enough:

Address (1. 1–2).
    Paul and Timothy to the Corinthians (and to all the Christians of Greece).

Preamble (1. 3–7).
"Blessed be God, who comforteth us in all tribulation."

I. Paul's ministry (c. 1–7).
  i. History of his relations with Corinth (1. 8–2. 13).
  ii. Exposition of his own motives (2.14–7.3).

> "Not that we are sufficient to think anything of
> ourselves, as of ourselves; but our sufficiency is
> from God who also hath made us fit ministers
> of the new testament" (3. 5–6).

But this section includes several digressions:

> (*Digression* on the "spirit and the letter", 3.
> 6–18).

"We preach not ourselves but Christ" (4.5).

> (*Digression* on the "treasure in earthen ves-
> sels": we suffer tribulation and persecu-
> tion, but we know that he who raised up
> Jesus will raise us up also, and we look for-
> ward to our home "not made with hands,
> eternal in heaven", 4. 7–5. 8.)

"The love of Christ impels us" (5. 14 USA).

"For Christ we are ambassadors" (5. 20).

6. 4–10 is an account of his trials.

> "We are frank with you, O Corinthians; our heart
> is wide open to you. In us there is no lack of
> room for you, but in your heart there is no
> room for us. Now, as having a recompense in
> like kind—I speak as to my children—be you
> also open wide to us" (6. 11–13 USA[1]).

> (*Digression* on keeping away from idolatry, cf.
> I Cor. 8–10; 6. 14–7. 1.)

"Make room for us. We have wronged no one"
(7. 2 USA).

---

[1] A particularly good translation of these beautiful verses.

iii. His present consolation about the good report brought to him from Corinth by Titus (7. 4–16). (*The central point of the Epistle.*)

II. The practical matter of the collection for the poor at Jerusalem (c. 8–9).
  i. The request for alms (8. 1–15).
  ii. The steps he has taken to arrange it (8. 16– 9. 5).
  iii. On the excellence of almsgiving (9. 6–15).

III. Paul's "Apologia pro vita sua"[1] (10. 1–12. 13).
  i. His claim to authority (10. 1–11. 6).
      "For his epistles indeed, say they, are weighty and strong, but his bodily presence is weak, and his speech contemptible" (10. 10).
      "But we will not glory beyond our measure" (10. 13).
      "Even though I be rude in speech, yet I am not so in knowledge; but in every way we have made ourselves clear to you" (11. 6 USA).
  ii. His preaching the gospel free of charge (cf. I Cor. 9) does not disqualify him (11. 7–15).
      (He adds a warning about "false apostles", 11. 13.)
  iii. He has every claim to boasting (if it will help his claim to authority)—but, "he that glorieth, let him glory in the Lord" (10. 17).
      (*a*) His sufferings as an apostle are a witness (11. 16–33).
            (*Digression* on pride in Hebrew race, 11. 22.)
      (*b*) The revelations made to him (12. 1–6).
      (*c*) The "thorn in the flesh" (12. 7–10).
      (*d*) His apostolate is not inferior to that of any other preachers (12. 11–13).
            "Even if I am nothing, I am not at all

[1] Fr Robert Eaton's title in his Intro. to the C.T.S. edition.

inferior to your super-apostles.[1] I
have displayed all the signs of apostle-
ship among you by all that I have
endured, and by the performance of
miracles, wonders and works of
power" (12. 11–12 Wand).

IV. His coming visit to Corinth (12. 14–13. 10).
   i. He will not be a burden to them (12. 14–18).
   ii. He hopes he will find nothing to distress him (12. 19–
      13.10).
Conclusion (13.11–12).
ξύμβολον (13. 13).

The Literary Problem. There are four principal difficulties
in this Epistle, which we shall study in order. It should be
borne in mind that the events referred to must all have taken
place in the matter of the few months between the Pentecost
of 54 (Paul's departure from Ephesus) and the ensuing winter
(his arrival in Corinth).

(i) The first question is to establish the number of letters
which he wrote to Corinth. It is fairly generally held that he
wrote *four*. The *first* is that referred to in I Cor. 5. 9, "I wrote
to you in an Epistle not to keep company with fornicators
(i.e. heathen)", now he is going further and is telling them
not to keep company with such a one in their own midst:
this is in his *second* letter, which is our I Cor. Then there are
references in II Cor. 2. 3, 4, 9 and 7. 8 to a previous letter,
which was written "with many tears" and made them sorrowful, and which is usually referred to as the "stern"
Epistle. It is, in the opinion of most writers, not to be identified with I Cor., which does not seem as stern as all that.
The "stern" Epistle would be the *third*. The *fourth* is our
II Cor. It would seem that the first and third Epistles have
been lost.

[1] This is a very clever translation of the colloquial Greek τῶν ὑπερλίαν
ἀποστόλων.

(ii) The next problem is to decide how many times Paul visited Corinth. The first visit is that on which he founded the Christian community there on the II Journey (Acts 18), referred to often in the Epistles. The only other visit we know of is that promised in I and II Cor. for the following winter. Yet II Cor. 12. 14 and 13. 1 refer to his coming visit as the "third". There are various solutions: (1) He paid them an otherwise unrecorded visit, a sorrowful visit (cf. II Cor. 2. 1) probably some time after the "stern" letter. (2) 12. 14 especially may point to a mere intention of coming, and may mean that the second time he did not in fact come (cf. 1. 15, "I had a mind to come to you before"), but that now this third time he really will. (3) The approaching visit is the second, and a third may be necessary later. (4) "Come to you" may refer to a letter, as when we write, "I come to you again with a request. . . ."

(iii) What was the crisis at Corinth that called forth the "weighty and strong" letter that is II Cor.? There seems to have been a strong anti-Paul party there, perhaps a relic of the factions described in I Cor. 1. It has been supposed that they were Judaizers,[1] attaching themselves still to the name of Peter as against Paul. Timothy had been sent to Corinth before (Acts 19. 22, I Cor. 16. 10), and had returned, for he is with Paul when he writes II Cor. (1. 1), and now Titus has been sent as a further emissary, and the trouble seems to have been laid, for he brings back a good report to Paul whom he meets in Macedonia (II Cor. 7. 5–7). Titus and his companions are sent back to Corinth with the present letter (II Cor. 8. 16–24), which Paul still feels needs to contain some vindication of his own position.

(iv) This brings us to the biggest problem. The letter contains two apologias. In the first (c. 1–7) he explains his

---

[1] Judaizers were those Jewish-Christians who held that converts to Christianity must become Jews first. See Acts 15 (the Council of Jerusalem) and the whole matter discussed by St Paul in Rom.

motives with great tenderness, concluding with the announcement of his joy at their mended ways (7. 4–16). After the
matter of the alms comes another apologia (c. 10–12), this
time written with passion and clearly intended for very
antagonised readers. What is the relation of these two vin-
dications, whose tone is so different? The visit of Titus seems
(when we get to c. 7) to have settled the matter. Why does
Paul break out again and put his case with renewed vigour?

There are two principal solutions: (1) (the more popular
among Catholic writers) Corinth always had a mixed community, and the Jewish party (as was clear even when Paul
was there) was the more difficult, and easily resentful of the
ex-pagan elements. Most of the community had been "made
sorrowful unto penance" by Paul's "stern" Epistle (7. 9), but
certain elements continued in their feeling against Paul, i.e.
those quoted in 10. 10 ("his speech contemptible", etc.). The
second apologia would be written for them, and if they were
Jewish elements there is special force in the phrases in 11. 22
("They are Hebrews: so am I", etc.). The drawback to this
theory is that the supposition of the divided audience and the
address of the two apologias to the obedient and disobedient
sections respectively is quite gratuitous.

The other solution is this: (2) The second apologia is none
other than the supposedly lost "stern" Epistle, or third letter,
which has got tacked on to the end of the fourth letter, which
is our II Cor. 1–9. The verses 9. 6–15 could quite well be a
concluding paragraph to an Epistle. (12. 14 to the end may
belong to either: if it belongs to the "stern" Epistle, it would
seem that Titus was the bearer of that one also, according to
12. 18.) We should observe that the Epistles as they stand in
the Bible are not in chronological order in any case, so that in
itself there would be nothing surprising in finding the
earlier "stern" Epistle II Cor. 10–13 standing after the later
II Cor. 1–9. The drawback to this fascinating theory is that
such a division of the text is no more than a hypothesis, as

there is no trace of proof or manuscript evidence in support of it: one would have to suppose that the two Epistles were joined together at a very early date. If II Cor. 10–13 is the "stern" Epistle, written to the whole community, we can certainly understand how he made them "sorrowful unto penance" as he writes afterwards (7. 9), and we remember how he wondered how they would accept his earlier corrections in I Cor., when he wrote, "Shall I come to you with a rod; or in charity and meekness?" (I Cor. 4. 21). There is not much doubt how he "came to them" in his "stern" Epistle.[1]

The above is no more than an outline of the problems of II Cor. The commentaries and introductions will provide fuller discussion.[2]

Some passages that should be noted.[3]

I. The First Apologia

1. 8. "Tribulation in Asia": probably the silversmiths' riot (Acts 19. 23–40).

1. 15–16. The proposed second visit to Corinth which never came off. It is worth tabulating St Paul's plans and his actual travels between the Pentecost of 54 and that of 55.

proposed travels I Cor. 16. 3–6	*proposed travels* Acts 19. 21	*proposed travels* II Cor. 1. 15–16	*actual travels* Acts and II Cor.
Ephesus	Ephesus	Ephesus	Ephesus
		Corinth (cancelled, II Cor. 2. 1)	Troas (II Cor. 2. 12)
Macedonia	Macedonia	Macedonia	Macedonia (Acts 20. 1; II Cor. 2. 13)
Corinth	Corinth	Corinth	Corinth (Acts 20. 3)
straight to		straight to	via Troas, Miletus, etc. (Acts 20. 5–15)
Palestine (Acts 20. 3)	Palestine Rome, Spain (Rom. 15. 24)	Palestine (Acts 20. 3)	Palestine (Acts 21. 2)

[1] If II Cor. 10–13 really is the *third* Epistle, this passage might bear out the interpretation of 12. 14 and 13. 1 "the *third* time I am coming to you" as meaning a letter.

[2] For instance Fr H. Pope's *Aids* and WV on II Cor.

[3] These notes are confined to important passages not hitherto noticed, which might cause some bewilderment to the rapid reader.

1. 17–20. His travel plans may hesitate between Yes and No, but not so the message that he and Timothy and Silvanus have been preaching.

1. 22. "Sealed us": probably a reference to the Sacrament of Confirmation (RAK note). The Byzantine Rite uses the word σφραγίς "seal".

2. 5–8. The pardon of a sinner. Probably the incestuous man of I Cor. 5. 1–5.

3. 6–18. "The letter killeth", i.e. the observance of the Jewish Law is now valueless in itself since the coming of Christ. The Old Law, when it was graven on the tables of stone at Sinai, had its glory, reflected in the shining countenance of Moses, who had to cover his face with a veil (Exodus 34); but now "how much more the faces of Christ's ministers shine with the reflection of his glory!" (RAK note). For Christ's "spirit quickeneth".

4. 7. We carry the treasure of Christ's ministry in frail "earthen vessels", i.e. Christ's ministers are also subject to human frailty, weakness and troubles.

5. 16. "Christ according to the flesh" is a difficult phrase: it refers either (i) to his mere human appearance, or (ii) to his human Hebrew descent, or (iii) to Paul's human knowledge of him before conversion. Anyway, all those things "are passed away".

5. 17–18. Christ's reconciliation to God of the human race, who through sin had become his "enemies" (Rom. 5. 10).

6. 15. "Belial": a Hebrew word meaning "worthlessness", used here of the falseness of idolatry.

II. The Almsgiving

8. 1. He had collected for the poor in Jerusalem in Galatia (I Cor. 16. 1), in Macedonia (here, 9. 2 and Rom. 15. 26), and now in Greece (I Cor. 16. 1, here, and Rom. 15. 26), and proposed to take the offerings himself to Jerusalem (I Cor. 16. 3, Rom. 15. 25 and 28).

8. 6. Titus was to do the collecting on his visit to Corinth.

8. 18–19. "With him (Titus) the brother whose praise in the Gospel is throughout all the churches", who was also the "companion of our travels for this grace", i.e. the collection. One thinks of Paul's various companions on the III Journey, and in Acts 20. 4 there is a list of the party who started on the final stage of the journey to Jerusalem with Paul, to which must be added Luke himself, who was writing "We". Obviously it is a well-known person that is meant, and Luke is a probability.[1] (This was St Jerome's opinion.) It was Fr Hugh Pope[2] who suggested that the word "brother" here and in 12. 18 (where the Greek has the article, which could easily mean "his" brother) should be taken of a natural brother to Titus, and if this were Luke, it would explain Luke's complete silence about Titus in Acts (like John's silence about himself and his mother[3]) and open up many interesting possibilities.

8. 22. The third member of the delegation. Again it is a matter of guesswork, but Silvanus is quite likely, especially in view of his absence (on the delegation?) from Macedonia when Paul writes the address of II Cor. with Timothy only (1. 1).

9. 4. "The Macedonians": in the list of the party taking the alms to Jerusalem in Acts 20. 4, Aristarchus and Secundus of Thessalonica are, of course, Macedonians.

III. The Second Apologia

10. 7. (In the midst of a fierce passage) lit.: "Look at the things before the face". Translations are various: USA "Look at what is before you", RAK "Wait and see what happens when we meet", Dr Wand "Don't ignore this obvious fact".

[1] The Epistle on the feast of St Luke includes this passage.
[2] *Aids*, V, p. 241 (on Titus).
[3] i.e. if we equate Jn. 19. 25, "His (Jesus') mother's sister" with Mt. 27. 56, "the mother of the sons of Zebedee."

10. 13. "A measure to reach even unto you": USA "limits which include you also", i.e. the Corinthians are within "the province which God has assigned to us" (RAK).

11. 32. One of the guiding passages in dating St Paul's life, see p. 40.

12. 2–4. "The third heaven . . . paradise". St Thomas held (I 12. 11 ad 2, and II–II 175. 3) that St Paul had momentarily the Beatific Vision (i.e. the immediate vision of the Essence of God, which is the privilege of the blessed in heaven), and that this was granted to Moses as instructor of the Jews (Exodus 33. 11) and to Paul as instructor of the Gentiles. In this St Thomas is following St Augustine, though several other Fathers (Ambrose, Cyril, Gregory and Leo) and many modern theologians hold that he only received some special revelation. The "third heaven" probably refers to a supernatural heaven above the natural heavens of the atmosphere and the stellar space.

12. 7. "A sting of my flesh, an angel of Satan": "sting" σκόλοψ, i.e. some pointed object, a thorn. The meaning is much disputed, but the most likely is some physical ailment, though persecution and temptation have also been suggested.

IV. His coming visit

12. 16. "Being crafty, I caught you by guile": ironically expressing the thoughts of his readers.

13. 9. "We rejoice when we are weak" (WV). This is either to be taken together with 13. 4: we share the weakness of Christ in his crucifixion; or else that we rejoice when we need not show our strength when the Corinthians are strong in faith themselves.

Note. All the foregoing material is designed to provide for about twenty-two classes, an average length for a Michaelmas Term.

(23–26)   THE EPISTLE TO THE ROMANS

A. Time and place. There is no doubt that this Epistle was written from Corinth during Paul's three months' stay there during the winter of A.D. 54/55 (Acts 20. 3) on his III Journey. This was the visit so many times referred to in I–II Cor. as about to take place after he had gone through Macedonia (see note on II Cor. 1. 15–16, p. 125).

How do we know this?

(*a*) 15. 25–26. He has made the collection for the poor in Jerusalem already in Macedonia, and now also in Greece (cf. I Cor. 16 and II Cor. 8) and is about to set off with the alms to Jerusalem. This shows that his journey had at least reached Greece.

(*b*) 16. 1. "I commend to you Phebe . . . who is . . . at Cenchrae" (the port of Corinth to the east).

(*c*) 16. 23. "Caius my host"; and we know Caius of Corinth, a friend of Paul and baptized by him (I Cor. 1. 14).

(*d*) 16. 23. "Erastus, the treasurer of the city"; cf. II Tim. 4. 20, "Erastus remained at Corinth".

(*e*) 16. 21. Greetings are sent from Timothy and Sosipater, and Timothy and "Sopater" (most probably the same man) are in the party which leaves Corinth to go to Jerusalem with Paul in Acts 20. 4. After leaving Corinth they did not stop anywhere for any length of time.

So it remains fairly clear that the Epistle was written from Corinth just before Paul and his companions left for Palestine.

B. *To whom?* "To all that are at Rome, the beloved of God, called to be saints (i.e. Christians)". But one of the reasons why this Epistle is difficult is that it is addressed to a community that contains many different elements. Sometimes St Paul speaks to them all, sometimes to a particular section of the community, sometimes to their friends who are not yet Christians. Several times he says explicitly whom he is addressing, as in the cases of the references added to the following list; other times the argument makes it fairly clear to which section he is speaking. The result of this is that we can distinguish the intended hearers of each section as follows:

1. 1 to all Christians in Rome (1. 7 "to all").
1. 18 to their heathen friends (context).
2. 17 to Jewish-Christians (2. 17 "but if thou art called a Jew").
5. 1 to all (e.g. 6. 3 "all we who are baptized").
7. 1 to Jewish-Christians (7. 1 "I speak to them that know the Law").
8. 9 to all (8. 9 "You are not in the flesh", and context).
9. 1 to their Jewish friends (9. 3–4 "my brethren who are Israelites").
11. 13 to Gentile-Christians (11. 13 "I say to you, Gentiles").
12. 1 to all the community (context).

It is important to bear this in mind while studying the Epistle, though, of course, the whole letter is meant for them all, since each section will thereby be helped to understand the difficulties of the others. The address is "to all".

This mixture, therefore, of Jewish and Gentile converts, some of them still retaining great pride in their origin, together with their respective Jewish and heathen friends, is St Paul's audience.

But what else do we know of the Christian community in Rome?[1]

Their "Faith is spoken of in the whole world" (Rom. 1. 8), and Paul is only writing to "strengthen" them (1. 11) (a contrast to what he had to write to Corinth!). He wants to come and preach to them (1. 15), though he understands that they are "another man's foundation" (15. 20)—whose? Peter's? (See last paragraph of this section.) Yet very many of them seem to be known to Paul, for he sends greetings to no less than twenty-eight people in c. 16 (more than in any other Epistle). Some of these at least are probably his converts, such as Epenetus, "the first-fruits of Asia" (16. 5).

We know also that there were many Jews in Rome: in A.D. 6, according to Josephus (*Wars*, II, 6, 1) there were 8,000 Jews in Rome who supported the impeachment of Archelaus; and later (A.D. 58–60) we find Jews coming to visit Paul and dispute with him in his prison-billet in Rome (Acts 28. 17–29.). But meanwhile the Jews had been driven out of Rome by Claudius, about A.D. 50, and Paul had met two of

[1] See excellent notes in Pope, V, 83–94.

the refugees at Corinth shortly afterwards, Aquila and Priscilla (Acts 18. 2)[1]. Yet this ban on Jews living in Rome does not seem to have lasted long, for, by the time Paul is writing this Epistle, that good Jewish-Christian couple are once more installed in their old home, for he sends them greetings to Rome, together with a very touching witness to their goodness and hospitality, which we know he himself enjoyed both at Corinth on his first visit (Acts 18. 3) and at Ephesus (I Cor. 16. 19, Rom. 16. 3–4).

Lastly, we should notice the important tradition, mentioned by Eusebius (II 14) and St Jerome (*De Viris Illustribus*, 1), that St Peter first settled in Rome in the second year of the Emperor Claudius, i.e. about A.D. 42. This fits in well with Peter's sudden disappearance from the story of Acts, when after being imprisoned by Herod and escaping miraculously, he "went into another place" (Acts 12. 17). The writer evidently wishes to conceal from the casual reader the fact (if indeed it be so) that the Prince of the Apostles had taken up his residence in Rome, as early as that. And St Paul's reference to "another man's foundation" (Rom. 15. 20) is also remarkably guarded, but, of course (like that in Acts), instantly intelligible to any Christian living in Rome under the pontificate of Peter (who, according to tradition, was martyred there about A.D. 67). These guarded references are very interesting, and clearly *intend* to conceal something important, and when we take them together with the tradition, it is legitimate to suppose that the important fact is Peter's residence in Rome. In this way we can also understand the silence on this matter of Paul's letters from Rome, of Acts (written in Rome) and of Peter himself when he disguises the name of the City under the title of "Babylon" (I Peter 5. 13).

C. Argument. The Epistle to the Romans is certainly one

[1] For Claudius' decree, cf. Hist. Intro., Jews in the Roman Empire, p. 22.

of the most famous of St Paul's Epistles. Dr Challoner's note, printed at the head of the Epistle in the Rheims NT, says that it is placed first among the Epistles "on account of the sublimity of the matter contained in it, of the pre-eminence of the place to which it was sent, and in veneration of the Church".[1] Without a doubt it is one of the most important from the point of view of theological teaching, particularly the doctrine of Justification, for which the key-passage is 3. 21–26. A constantly recurring theme is that of the relation within Christianity of the Jewish-Christian and the convert from heathenism, or Gentile-Christian.

The general argument of the Epistle is clear enough and continuous. Autobiographical material is restricted to the Introduction and Conclusion to the Epistle.

I. The Gospel brings "salvation to every one that believeth, to the Jew first, and to the Greek" (1. 16) (c. 1–4).

    i. But the *pagans* have in the past perverted the idea of God (1. 18 sq.).

    ii. And the *Jews* have been too proud, and have looked for salvation from their Jewish descent (2. 17 sq.).

II. The Christian is "justified" (δικαιοῦται), i.e. enters a state of grace, through Faith in Christ (5. 1) (c. 5–8).

    i. This releases *everyone* from the slavery of sin (c. 5–6).

    ii. And in particular releases *Jews* from the bondage of the Law of Moses, which was there till Christ, for prevention of sin (c. 7–8).

III. The Jewish Question: "The *Gentiles*, who followed not after justice, have attained to the justice of the

---

[1] The non-chronological order of the Epistles in the Bible is probably simply a length-order (longest first, shortest last) in each group, missionary and pastoral Epistles, with Heb. standing alone.

Faith" (9. 30), "but *Israel*, by following after the
Law of Justice, is not come to this justice" (9. 31),
for "they have not submitted themselves to the
justice of God" (10. 3) (c. 9–11).

IV. Practical Problems of the Christian life (c. 12–15. 13).

     i. Peace among yourselves (12. 3 sq.).

    ii. Obedience to the civil power (13. 1 sq.).

   iii. Kindness to each other (13. 8 sq.).

   iv. Matters of "clean and unclean" food (especially with reference to Jews: cf. idol-offerings in I Cor. 14. 1. sq.).

    v. Patience (15. 1 sq.).

Conclusion: personal matters (15. 14–33).
salutations (c. 16).

Short Exegesis

Address

1. 1–7. We have seen how Paul, for instance in I Cor.,
inserts a phrase such as "called to be an apostle" after his
own name in the address. This time he inserts the same
phrase, but with it a whole parenthesis vv. 1–6, only bringing
the second (dative case) part of the address "to all that are at
Rome" in v. 7. Such digressions become more frequent in St
Paul's style now.

1. 4. Christ was "predestinated the Son of God" ὁρισθέντος
(from ὁρίζω to "limit", whence our word "horizon"), so
WV RAK "marked out" as the Son of God by the fact of
his resurrection. The Rh of this verse follows the exact order
of words in the Greek.

1. 6. "The called (κλητοί) of Jesus Christ", the Christian
vocation, applied by Paul also to his vocation of an Apostle
in v. 1.

Preamble

1. 8. As usual in his Epistles to the Churches (except II

Cor. and Gal., where the tone at the beginning is more severe) he leads off with a praise of their faith and a thanksgiving to God for it.

1. 9. Again as often (I Thess., Eph., Philipp., Col.) he tells them how he prays for them (cf. also Philem. 4): an important Christian habit.

1. 11–12. "I long to see you". Apparently he had not been to Rome, and we know that such a visit was part of his plan while he was at Ephesus (Acts 19. 21): cf. note on II Cor. 1. 15–16.

1. 13. He says he had often proposed to come, but we do not know when this would have been. But he has not come so far, because he has made a point of preaching in places where "Christ has not already been named", lest he should "build upon another man's foundation" (15. 20) and we have seen that this probably refers to Peter's foundation in Rome. Now, however, his work in "these countries" (Asia Minor, Macedonia and Greece) is done, and he is making further plans, which he outlines in 15. 24–28, saying that after he has taken the alms to Jerusalem he hopes to make a journey to Spain and to visit Rome on the way. But of course all these plans came to nothing, since he was arrested a week after his arrival in Jerusalem and came to Rome only as a prisoner about four years later.

1. 14. "I am a debtor", i.e. "I have a duty" (RAK), I *owe* something to the Gentiles, and what I owe to them is to preach to them.

I. SALVATION THROUGH THE GOSPEL

1. 16. The main theme of the whole Epistle: "The Gospel is the power of God unto *everyone* (inculcating the universality of Redemption) that *believeth* (since it is through Faith that we can benefit by the Redemption), to the *Jew* first (since the Jews received the revelation) and to the *Greek* (i.e. the Gentile world, to whom Redemption is open equally).

1. 17. For it is the Gospel that reveals to us God's δικαιοσύνη. This is St Paul's famous word. Originally it simply means "the character of the δίκαιος"[1] or just man; but St Paul has given it a specifically Christian theological meaning, viz. the process by which God brings us from a state of sin into a state of grace. This is called by the theologians "Justification" (e.g. St Thomas I–II 113. 1), and Fr Spencer translates it so in the text. The Vulgate has "justitia", whence Rh and USA "justice"; WV (thinking of the original meaning of the word) insists on "justness", while AV and RV have "righteousness". RAK (wishing to bring out the theological meaning) paraphrases "way of justifying us". The corresponding verb is translated by almost everyone "justify". The word is a key to the teaching of the Epistle (see especially notes on 3. 20 and 21).

"From faith unto faith" is a literal translation of the Greek. It is a Hebraism (according to Lagrange) meaning "with ever-increasing faith", cf. Ps. 83. 8 (Heb. 84. 7), "They will go from strength to strength" (AV). The Hebrew of Habacuc 2. 4 reads "the just man lives by his faithfulness" and St Paul is following the LXX.

i. What is the sin of the Gentiles   *to pagans*

1. 18. God is angry against injustice in the world especially that of "repressing the truth" (WV), and particularly the truth about God.

1. 19–20. Men are able by their reason alone (i.e. without revelation) to know for certain the Existence of God. This is DE FIDE (i.e. it is an article of our Faith), and proclaimed as such by the Vatican Council in A.D. 1870 (Denz., 1785 and 1806). This text and Wisdom 13. 9, "If they (the pagans) were able to know so much as to make a judgement of the world, how did they not more easily find out the Lord thereof?", support the declaration. St Thomas in I 2. 1 and 2

[1] Liddell and Scott.

proves the same thing, and in art. 3 proceeds to give the famous "quinque viae" by which the Existence of God is demonstrated by reason. This was therefore possible to the pagans, wherefore, says Wisdom 13. 8, "They are not to be pardoned", or as St Paul puts it (probably he knew the passage), "they are inexcusable".

1. 21–23. They have known God (by reason), but they have not glorified him as God. Instead they have turned to foolish idolatry, and have "changed the glory of the incorruptible God into the likeness of the image of a corruptible man (the Greek gods), and of birds and of four-footed beasts (the many animal-gods of the East), and of creeping things (such as the scarabs of Egypt)".

1. 24–32. As a result they have turned to all kinds of shameful sins, first of all of impurity, even sins against nature, and then every other kind of malice (there is a mighty list in vv. 29–31); and all this because they "worshipped the creature rather than the Creator" (v. 25), and "having known the justice of God, did not understand" (v. 32). And he adds that just as bad are those "who applaud others who practise" these things (v. 32 WV).

2. 1–11. But God will judge these things, not man. To those whom in his mercy he leads to penance, he will show "the riches of his goodness, and patience, and longsuffering" (v. 4), but to the impenitent he will show his wrath and just judgement (v. 5). God will judge justly, and "will render to every man according to his works" (v. 6). This is a quotation from Ps. 61 (Heb. 62) 13, which is also used by Our Lord in Mt. 16. 27. To the just he will give eternal life, glory and honour; to the wicked, wrath and indignation, tribulation and anguish: in both cases to the Jew first (because he had the revelation and so has the greater responsibility) and then to the Greek.

God's perfect justice and his perfect mercy are a mystery, but St Thomas (I 21. 4) gives us the wonderful explanation

that both his justice and his mercy are manifest in all his
works, since his every work of justice presupposes, and is
rooted in, his mercy, for every right of a creature to justice
depends ultimately on God's free gift (an act of mercy) to the
creature of everything including its very existence.

2. 11. "There is no respect-of-persons (προσωπολημψία)
with God": this is a purely NT word (used again in Eph. 6.
9, Col. 3. 25 and by St James in 2.1, and a cognate word in
Acts 10. 34—Peter's vision of the sheet) aptly translated
"favouritism" by Dr Wand in Eph. and Col., but in James,
where it is a human quality (with a delicate distinction),
"snobbishness".

2. 12–16. "Not hearers of the Law, but doers, are just
before God" (v. 13), cf. the end of the Sermon on the Mount
(Mt. 7. 21), and the same idea in James 1. 22. Jews, who have
the Law of Moses to guide them, will be judged by that. But
Gentiles have their consciences and "having not the Law, are
a law to themselves" (v. 14). By this standard Christ will
judge them. Of course, every man has a natural conscience
which guides him to right and wrong, but it is the Law which
emphasizes right and wrong and shows him that to do evil is
an offence against God. St Paul develops this idea in the
next part of the Epistle, especially 5. 20 sq. and 6. 15 sq.

ii. What is the sin of the Jews   *to Jewish-Christians*

2. 17–24. If you "bear the name of 'Jew' " (v. 17 WV), you
claim to know God's will, and be "a guide of the blind, light
in darkness, an instructor of the foolish, a teacher of infants"
(vv. 19–20), yet you do not practise what you preach. In this
way "through you the name of God is blasphemed among the
Gentiles" (v. 24, quoting Isaias 52. 5). This is a thing that we,
Catholics, should also bear in mind. The same thing can be
said of us. As Catholics we are expected at least to claim to
know what is right and wrong, and therefore we are expected
to live up to it. If we fail to do so, we are scorned, and in this

way God's name is blasphemed, for they scorn us as claiming to be his followers.[1]

2. 25–29. "To be a Jew is not to be a Jew outwardly: to be
circumcised is not to be circumcised outwardly, in the
flesh" (v. 28 RAK). The point of circumcision was to show
membership of the People of God, and to be, therefore, a
sign of justice. If a circumcised man is not a just man, he is
no better than an uncircumcised Gentile, and if a Gentile is a
just man, he is as good as circumcised. It is a matter of the
heart and the spirit, not of the letter of the law. "Circumcision
indeed profiteth if thou be a doer of the Law" (v. 25 WV).

3. 1–8. "Of what use is it then to be a Jew?" (v. 1 RAK).
"Much every way, because the words of God were committed
to them" (v. 2), i.e. they had the whole Old Testament to
guide them. We, Catholics, again should take these words to
heart. But if some Jews are faithless, does that "do away with
the faithfulness of God?" (v. 4 WV). μὴ γένοιτο: an emphatic
No (often translated "God forbid!", and the other translations, "It is not to be thought of" RAK, "Indeed no" Wand,
"By no means" USA, etc., all lack the forcefulness of the
plain Greek, which simply means "may it not be"). "God is
true and every man a liar" (v. 4) (the second part comes from
Ps. 115. 11) is finely paraphrased by RAK, "God must prove
true to his word, though all men should play him false".

3. 9–20. *Before Christ's revelation* everyone was "under
sin", and so we Jews are not "in worse case" (v. 9 WV), and
there follow many quotations from the Old Testament (for
the benefit of Jewish readers) to show the power of sin in the
world before Christ.

3. 20. What was the function of the Law of the Old Testa-

---

[1] The Pharisees who were so sternly rebuked by Christ were clinging
to, and relying upon, "the Law" and its material observance to "justify"
them. They lived upon traditional observances and made a fetish of it.
This pharisaic vice, with its consequent self-rig...eousness, is one to which
the Catholic, knowing the unique treasure he possesses, is especially prone
if he fails to put the love and service of God before all things.

ment? "To give us full consciousness of sin" (RAK), i.e. to explain to us not merely that sin is evil, but that it is against God's law. Its function was not to "justify"us, paraphrased by RAK: to make us to "become acceptable in his sight".

3. 21–26. *But now it is otherwise.* *"Justification from God is displayed apart from the Law"* (v. 21 Spencer).

3. 22. Here is the central teaching of the Epistle, in its original beautiful terse Greek[1]

δικαιοσύνη Θεοῦ διὰ πίστεως Ἰησοῦ Χριστοῦ εἰς πάντας τοὺς πιστεύοντας· οὐ γάρ ἐστι διαστολή.

Literally: "Justification of God, through faith of Jesus Christ, to all the believing-ones, for there is no distinction": Fr Spencer's translation remains very literal: "Justification from God by means of the faith of Jesus Christ, for all and upon all who believe—for there is no distinction". RAK's paraphrase is very helpful: "God's way of justification through faith in Jesus Christ, meant for everybody and sent down upon everybody without distinction, if he has faith."

3. 23. "For all have sinned", Jews and Gentiles alike, and need to be "justified", i.e. to be transferred from a state of sin to a state of grace (i.e. of friendship, of being a "persona grata", with God).

3. 24. This justification is effected δωρεάν or "gratis", i.e. by free gift of God, "through the redemption that is in Christ Jesus".

3. 25. For Christ, by his death, has become a "propitiation", i.e. a sacrifice, a "means of reconciliation" (RAK). This whole argument is taken up again in c. 5.

3. 27–31. Since Justification is a free gift to all, Jewish-Christians (remember that all this section is addressed to them) have no cause for special boasting. "Do we therefore nullify the Law? No, we corroborate it" (cf. v. 31 Spencer).

---

[1] In this, as in many other passages, a student with only a very small knowledge of Greek can easily understand enough to profit by looking at the original text.

4. 1–25. But what about Abraham? An acute problem to every Jewish-Christian: how was he justified? The argument turns on the text (quoted in v. 3) from Genesis 15. 6, "Abraham believed God, and it was reckoned to him as δικαιοσύνη."[1] Of course, Abraham is the "father of circumcision", i.e. patriarch of the Jews, but because of his faith he is father of all believers (v. 12), so that in the Mass we also speak (in the prayer "Supra quae" after the consecration) of the sacrifice "Patriarchae nostri Abrahae". God did, after all, promise to Abraham (in Gen. 17. 4) that he should be the "father of many nations" (v. 17), which refers to us, Jewish and Gentile Christians alike (vv. 23–24). It was Abraham's faith that brought him Justification, as it is our faith that brings it to us. And this means faith in Jesus Christ. The Fathers of the Old Testament believed in the Redeemer to come,[2] we believe in the Redeemer that has come.

4. 25. This faith means an understanding that Christ by his death redeemed us from sin, and by his resurrection he opened heaven for us, which is the completion of the work of Justification.

II. THE CHRISTIAN IS JUSTIFIED BY FAITH
to all Christians

5. 1–11. The argument is now resumed apart from the context of Judaism. We all through sin "were enemies" of God, but now have been "reconciled to God by the death of his Son" (v. 10). The basis of this reconciliation is our faith in Jesus Christ. "Whosoever believeth in him may not perish, but may have life everlasting" (Jn. 3. 15–16, to Nicodemus); "Being justified therefore by faith" (Rom. 5. 1).

[1] This is the word of the LXX. The Hebrew probably more simply means "righteousness".
[2] St Thomas, in II–II 2. 7, explains that the "majores" or greater men of the OT understood explicitly the prophetic significance of the sacrifices and laws of the OT, while the others, accepting their observance in obedience to God, expressed thus an implicit faith.

These texts (especially from Rom.) were used by Luther to support his erroneous Protestant doctrine of "Justification by faith alone", which is expressed in art. XI of the XXXIX Articles, drawn up by the Archbishops and Bishops of the Church of England in 1562 and printed as an appendix to the Book of Common Prayer. In this article we read that "We are accounted righteous before God, only for the merit of Jesus Christ by Faith, and not for our own works or deservings: wherefore that we are justified by Faith only is a most wholesome doctrine, and very full of comfort". The operative word is that we are "accounted" righteous, i.e. we are not ourselves made just (the true meaning of "justified"), but there is merely an imputation of Christ's justness to us. And secondly, we are justified "without our own works or deservings".

The above errors are first of all contradicted by the texts from St James: "Faith without works is dead" (2. 20) and "By works a man is justified, and not by faith alone" (2. 24),[1] and then also by St Paul's own words in the earlier Epistle I Cor., "If I should have all faith, so that I could remove mountains, and have not charity, I am nothing" (13. 2).

The Council of Trent, in 1547 combating these very errors of Luther, laid down clearly (Denz., 821): "Si quis dixerit hominem justificari vel sola imputatione justitiae Christi, vel sola peccatorum remissione, exclusa gratia et caritate, A.S."[2] and (Denz., 819): "Si quis dixerit sola fide impium justificari ... et nulla ex parte eum suae voluntatis motu praeparari atque disponi, A.S."[3] The preceding explanations of Trent

---

[1] Because of these passages Luther called this Epistle an "Epistle of straw" (quoted e.g. in Pope, V, 292). His original words are quoted on p. 234.

[2] "If anyone says that man is justified either by the mere imputation of Christ's justness or by the mere remission of sin without reference to grace or charity, let him be anathema."

[3] "If anyone says that the sinner is justified by faith alone ... and is in no way prepared or disposed by any movement of his own will, let him be anathema."

(Denz., 797–801) follow the teaching of St Thomas on the subject in I–II 113. 6, where he says that four things are required for Justification (i.e. being brought from a state of sin to a state of grace):

1. God's free gift of grace (the main thing)—Sanctifying grace.
2. The Free-will's acceptance of God's truth—Faith.
3. The Free-will's turning away from sin—Contrition.
4. God's forgiveness of sin—Redemption.

So that Justification begins by our being "made holy" (sanctified), and is perfected by our sin being blotted out, so that we are truly just and not merely "accounted righteous".

The completion of Justification is the flowering of the life of grace on earth into the life of glory in heaven, for as St Augustine said, "Gratia est semen gloriae" (and cf. the famous passage infra, Rom. 8. 29–30). The perfection of eternal life involves the resurrection of the body, referred to above in 4. 2, and which is constantly spoken of in I Cor. 15, e.g. 15. 20 of Christ as "the first-fruits of them that sleep", for Christ has preceded us and led the way to the risen life of heaven.

We should observe here in passing that the Assumption of Our Lady is only an acceleration of what will happen to all the justified, in that her body was straightway raised from the grave, so that in her case the work of Justification was completed at once.

5. 3. Since Christ's Passion and death has arisen a new attitude to suffering: the Christian is able to "glory in tribulation" for Christ died for us: "the special quality of God's love for us is seen in the fact that it was while we were still sinners that Christ died for us" (vv. 8–9 Wand).

5. 12–21. Christ is the Second Adam: "By one man (Adam) sin entered into this world. . . . The grace of God by one man, Jesus Christ, hath abounded unto many" (v. 12, 15). Sin and death are equated, and here St Paul gives us the doctrine of

Original Sin: "So death passed upon all men, in whom (Adam) all have sinned" (v. 12). Cf. I Cor. 15. 21–22.

One thinks, of course, of passages from two great oratorios: the Chorus "Since by man came death" (n. 46) (on the text of I Cor. above) in Handel's *Messiah;* and the great Chorus (the fifth choir of angelicals) in Cardinal Newman's *Dream of Gerontius* which was set to music by Elgar:

> O loving wisdom of our God!
>   When all was sin and shame,
> A second Adam to the fight
>   And to the rescue came.
>
> O wisest love! that flesh and blood
>   Which did in Adam fail,
> Should strive afresh against their foe,
>   Should strive and should prevail.[1]

5. 13–14. Three periods of the history of man's relation with God: (1) Adam to Moses: sin. (2) Moses to Christ: consciousness of sin (for the Law was there to bring this consciousness). (3) Christ: the blotting out of sin: grace.

6. 1–11. The Christian man, who is "justified", is now presented under a new figure. We are baptized into redemption, which came by Christ's death, and so we are "buried together with him" in order to rise with him a new man (v. 4). "Our old man is crucified with him" in order that our corrupt nature ("the body of sin") may be destroyed (v. 6). (This idea of the "old man" and the "new man" is considerably developed in St Paul's later thought in Eph. 4. 22, 24 and Col. 3. 9, 10.)

6. 12–23. "Let not sin therefore reign in your mortal body" (v. 12): You were formerly slaves of sin, now you are to be slaves of God's grace, of justification, of holiness (vv. 16–20). Sin (and therefore also the Law, which brings consciousness of sin) leads to death, while grace leads to life everlasting (vv. 15, 21–23).

[1] Also used as a hymn (Westminster 186, old edition 56

F

The next section, 7. 1–8. 8, is addressed to Jewish-Christians, as 7. 1 shows. By now the main doctrinal points of the Epistle have been stated, so that our study can now proceed with much less detail.[1]

7. 1–13. The idea of the death of the "old man" applied to Jews: the Jew who has become a Christian has died in respect of the "old man" who was under the Law of Moses. He was like a man married, and only death dissolves the marriage (vv. 1–3) (WV entitles this section "Christ our spouse in place of the Law"). His baptism was the death of the "old man": "And I died" (v. 10). In this sense the Law of Moses led to death, but in itself was something good and holy (v. 12); it was through the Law that sin could be "seen as sin" (v. 13 WV).

7. 14–25. This is an important section on human psychology: even though the Law pointed out sin to me, there is "another law in my members, fighting against the law of my mind (i.e. my own conscience)" (v. 23). This other law, my human inclination towards sin and concupiscence, this other motive that impels my actions, causes me "to do not the good which I will, but the evil which I hate" (v. 19). This is the experience of every sinner: we knew it was wrong, but yet we did it. What can we do about it? "Who is to set me free from a nature thus doomed to death? Nothing else than the grace of God, through Jesus Christ our Lord" (vv. 24–25 RAK).

8. 1–8. "No judgement stands now against those who live in Christ Jesus" (v. 1 RAK): i.e. no death-sentence, for they have died and are now risen again with Christ. They "have the mind of Christ" (as he wrote shortly before in I Cor. 2. 16), and are no longer "of the flesh", i.e. living on a purely natural plane: for "to live the life of nature is to think the thoughts of nature; to live the life of the spirit is to think the thoughts of the spirit" (v. 5 RAK for "they that are according

---

[1] Lagrange in his commentary has an interlude of twenty-eight pages on Justification.

to the flesh, mind the things that are according to the flesh, etc.").

The rest of this section seems to be addressed to all Christians.

8. 9–11. "But you (Christians) are not in the flesh": you have died to sin, and live by Justification.

8. 12–17. Another new figure: the Christian's heirship. They are sons who are going to inherit the good things of God; they are not merely servants,[1] but joint-heirs with Christ: "the spirit of adoption of sons, whereby we cry (to God): Abba (Father)" (v. 15). Note the introduction of the Aramaic word אבא: St Paul uses it in a similar context in Gal. 4. 6, and it appears on the lips of Christ in the Agony in Mk. 14. 36. It seems likely[2] that it was an ejaculatory prayer used by the first Christians in Palestine, like "Maran atha" (I Cor. 16. 22), and that from there it spread to other Christian communities. Gal 4. 5–7, 22–31 contains the same argument of heirship applied to the distinction between Jews and Christians.

8. 18–28. St Paul returns to the Christian's attitude to suffering, a subject that was raised in 5. 3–9: "The sufferings of this time are not worthy to be compared with the glory to come" (v. 18): for "to them that love God, all things work together unto good" (v. 28). Furthermore, all creatures are awaiting their adoption as sons of God (vv. 19–23).

8. 29–30. A summary on Justification, from the first gift of God's foreknowledge and choice to the final glorification in heaven. This text is always quoted in a theological treatise on Predestination.

Predestination is a part of God's merciful providence. Since eternal life and the grace that leads to it are both a pure gift of God, it follows that there is a design in God's mind according to which a man is to receive the gift of heaven and

---

[1] Cf. Jn. 15. 15: "I will not now call you servants . . . but I have called you friends".
[2] Lagrange on this passage.

the means to attain to it (cf. St Thomas I 23. 1). This design (ratio) is called Predestination. Already the Council of Valence in A.D. 855 (Denz., 322) had laid down as an article of Faith that "God predestines the elect to (eternal) life, and the wicked to (eternal) death; but in the case of the elect, God's mercy precedes any merit of theirs, while in the case of the damned their evil deeds precede the just judgement of God". (The suggestion that God should predestine anyone to be damned apart from any evil action on their part is a horrible heresy contradicting the doctrine that Christ died to redeem all men: Calvin maintained that Christ died only for the predestined.) The Catholic teaching of the Council of Valence is elaborated by St Thomas in I 23. 5.[1]

St Paul summarises his teaching on Justification:[2]

God foreknew (from all eternity)
> predestined (i.e. his design to bring the man to heaven)
> called (and the man responded)
> justified (i.e. blotted out sin)
> glorified (i.e. brought to the glory of heaven).

8. 31–39. "Si Deus pro nobis, quis contra nos?" (v. 31, powerful in the Latin version). He lists all possible tribulations, but "we overcome, because of him that loved us" (v. 37), and nothing "shall be able to separate us from the love of God" (v. 39).

III. THE JEWISH QUESTION   *to unconverted Jews*

9. 1–5. His sorrow about the position of Jews, his "kinsmen according to the flesh", who have not accepted what should be their natural inheritance, i.e. the grace of Christ.

---

[1] We do not propose to go into the matter of the theological disputes that arose in the sixteenth century between the Thomists (Dominicans) and the Molinists (Jesuits) in connexion with this doctrine on the main lines of which, as given here, all are agreed.

[2] See note above on Rom. 5. 1. The doctrine reappears in Rom. 9. 6–24 and especially Eph. 1. 4–11.

9. 6–24. He returns to the question of Predestination: God's free purpose, his merciful design that precedes any human merit (as the Council said, above), when they "were not yet born, nor had done any good or evil, that the purpose of God according to election might stand" (v. 11), is the source of Justification. The whole passage is a working-out of the doctrine, with especial reference to the Jews. The Gentiles are called equally with the Jews (v. 24).

9. 25–29. Quotations from the Old Testament to show that although Gentiles will become God's people, yet a remnant of Israel will be saved. He returns to this theme in 11. 5.

9. 30–33. The key-passage of this section. The Gentiles, who were not seeking Justification, have found it; while Israel, who had the Law, has not reached its proper conclusion, which is Justification.

10. 1–13. Why has it happened so? "They did not recognise God's way of Justification, and so they tried to institute a way of their own, instead of submitting to his" (v. 3 RAK excellently). They relied upon "works", i.e. human things, such as their traditions and their Israelite birth. As usual in the sections written for Jews, there is much quotation from the Old Testament.

10. 14–21. To be saved Israel must call on the Lord—therefore they must hear—therefore they must have a preacher—therefore he must be sent. All this has indeed been done, but "Who hath believed our report?" (Isaias 53. 1 quoted v. 16).

11. 1–12. "Hath God cast away his people? μὴ γένοιτο." There is a remnant, though the rest have been blinded (vv. 5–7), and yet, "by their office, salvation is come to the Gentiles" (v. 11).

The rest of this chapter is addressed to Gentile-Christians, as 11. 13 shows, to explain the problem to them.

11. 13–15. A touching reminder to the Gentiles that although he, Paul, is indeed their Apostle, yet he is a Jew and

hopes that his preaching may somehow save some of his brethren.

11. 15. "If the losing of them has meant a world reconciled to God, what can the winning of them mean, but life risen from the dead?" (RAK). The last phrase is difficult and the meaning quite uncertain though the words are plain enough. It is one of the very few textual difficulties in this Epistle. The Greek text has ζωὴ ἐκ νεκρῶν "life from dead", and the meaning may be (i) that the conversion of the Jews will be the signal for the general Resurrection at the end of the world. This is the more usual interpretation, although the usual words for the resurrection do not occur. Or (ii) that their conversion will cause a spiritual resurrection among all Christians. Or (iii) that their conversion will be a triumph even greater than the triumph, achieved through their failure, of the conversion of the Gentiles, and that "life among the dead" is simply a phrase conveying the idea of something unspeakably glorious. This interpretation provides the best rhetorical balance to the first sentence of this verse. When studying this verse, one has to ask oneself what one could expect as an apodosis.

11. 16–24. Israel is like an olive tree: the root is holy, but some of the branches are broken (the unbelieving Jews), and wild olives have been grafted in (the Gentiles). But these engrafted wild olives must not despise the root (Israel), for even if the original branches are now broken, it is possible for God sometime to graft them in again (the conversion of the unbelieving Jews), for after all the root of believing Israel is their natural root. It is a very beautiful figure, and we see Paul's tenderness to those of his own race who are blind (cf. v. 7).

11. 25–32. "I would not have you ignorant of this mystery . . . that blindness in part has happened in Israel," but that it is not to be for ever. Their conversion will come, but only when "the full number of the Gentiles be entered in" (v. 25

WV). This is a mysterious prophecy, but St Paul is insisting on it: "so all Israel should be saved" (v. 26).

11. 33–36. The great peroration: all is in the hands of God: "O the depth of the riches of the wisdom and of the knowledge of God! How incomprehensible are his judgements and how unsearchable his ways!" (v. 33—one of St Paul's most wonderful passages).

IV. PRACTICAL PROBLEMS   *to all*

12. 1–2. In general the Christian is to consecrate to God his very body, he is not to be "conformed to this world", but on the contrary he is to be conformed to "the perfect will of God". We think of our constant prayer, "Thy will be done", for to live in accordance with the will of God is one of the most elementary principles of the spiritual life.

12. 3–8 (i). Peace is to be kept in the community: there is to be no rivalry with regard to the various gifts that each one receives from God, for "we being many, are one body in Christ" (v. 5). This is the same teaching as he gave shortly before to the Corinthians, especially in I Cor. 12. 11–30.

12. 9–21. This peace and concord is attained by simple moral principles, such as "hating that which is evil, cleaving to that which is good" (v. 9), and "loving one another with the charity of brotherhood" (v. 10). In the following verses are several admonishments that remind us of the Sermon on the Mount, especially those on revenge, such as "To no man rendering evil for evil" (v. 17) and "Be not overcome by evil, but overcome evil by good" (v. 21).

13. 1–7 (ii). Obedience to the civil power, since all power comes from God and the ruler is God's minister. This was Christian teaching from the beginning: we find it again in St Peter (I Pet. 2. 13–17), and we should bear in mind that both letters were written under Nero. Admittedly no great persecution had yet taken place, and so far the Roman power had declined to condemn the Christians (cf. Gallio in Acts

18), but the matter is stated as a principle, one must obey not merely out of fear, but for conscience's sake (v. 5).

13. 8–10 (iii). "He that loveth his neighbour hath fulfilled the law" (v. 8).

13. 11–14. To sum up: "Let us cast off the works of darkness (all kinds of sin, v. 13) . . . and put on the Lord Jesus Christ" (vv. 12, 14), cf. Col. 3. 10 where they are to "put on" the new (Christian) man.

14. 1–23 (iv). The matter of eating food that might cause offence to someone. The argument is the same as that about idol-offerings in I Cor. 8 and 10. 14 sq. The chief concern here seems to be about "clean and unclean" meat (v. 14), though the word "meat" in Rh is simply of food in general. Flesh-meat is mentioned in v. 21 (where abstinence is recommended if any scandal might arise[1]) and v. 2 (where it is recommended rather to be a vegetarian than offend one's conscience). The reference may be to idol-meats, but "clean and unclean" rather suggests possible scruples of a Jew. St James had proposed at the Council of Jerusalem (Acts 15. 19–20) that Gentiles not only avoid idol-offerings, but avoid causing offence to Jews to whom it was revolting to eat meat other than כָּשֵׁר (Kôsher), i.e. white meat from which the blood had been drained (as in our pork and poultry).

15. 1–13 (v). A final admonishment to patience, especially that the Jewish and Gentile Christians should be understanding one to another, for Christ is the Lord of all: he has fulfilled the promises made to the Israelites of old, and he has shown mercy to the Gentiles.

CONCLUSION

15. 14–21. He again gives his reasons for writing to them, which he mentioned at the beginning: to impart to them "some spiritual grace" (1. 8), and he tells them of his preaching in other parts.

[1] See above on I Cor. 8. 13.

15. 22–29. He explains his travel-plans, which we studied in the introductory paragraphs, and his reasons for not having so far visited Rome, viz. that till now he has only preached in places which had not yet heard the Gospel "lest I should build on another man's foundation" (v. 20).

15. 30–33. He asks for their prayers, especially for three things: (i) that he may not have trouble from unbelieving Jews in Judea (which in fact he did have, and got arrested), (ii) that his scheme for collecting alms for the poor at Jerusalem will succeed, and (iii) that he may be able to come and visit them (which did not come off, since he only came as a prisoner).

16. 1–23. Salutations. Margaret Monro[1] calls this chapter "a picture of friendship". Phebe, specially commended, seems to be commended as if she would be with them soon, so it may be that she was the bearer of the letter (v. 1–2). The chapter continues, vv. 3–16, with greetings *to* people, vv. 17–20 an interruption to remind them of what he has written about, vv. 21–23 greetings *from* people, and vv. 24–27 a prayer and blessing in conclusion. Aquila and Priscilla are now in Rome (v. 3–4). Epenetus is apparently a convert of Paul (from Asia), now in Rome (v. 5). Most of the others are unknown to us. The term "kinsman", applied to six people, probably merely means that they were Jews (cf. Rom. 9. 3). The "households" in v. 11 probably refer to slaves. Herodian, a "kinsman", i.e. Jew, for instance, is in the "household" of Aristobulus, the brother of King Herod Agrippa I, who lived in Rome. Narcissus, who apparently had some Christian slaves, was probably the famous freedman of Claudius, whom Agrippina (Nero's mother) had murdered on her son's accession in A.D. 54,[2] and his slaves still went by his name. The Rufus in v. 13 may be the one referred to (obviously as well

[1] *Enjoying the New Testament*, p. 87.
[2] See Tacitus, *Annales*, 13, 1. Though the Martyrology (Oct. 31st) identifies the Narcissus of this passage with a Christian martyr. (See Appendix B.)

known) in Mk. 15. 21 as son of Simon of Cyrene who carried
the cross of Christ; St Mark was writing for a Roman audience. Rufus' mother ("who has been a mother to me" RAK)
would then be the wife of Simon: a close connexion with the
Passion. She must have been an interesting person to know.
Timothy is still with Paul (v. 21), and in v. 22 we have the
famous reference to the scribe himself, Tertius, who throws
in his own greetings.

(27–28)   THE EPISTLE TO THE
                      GALATIANS

The Problem. The Epistle to the Galatians cannot be ap-
proached in the same way as the other Epistles, because of
the great uncertainty about the time of its composition, with
consequent hesitance about the circumstances of its writing
and identification of events referred to.

Scholars nowadays (both Catholics and non-Catholics) are
more or less equally divided between the two main schools
of thought on the subject. There are those who hold the
Early Date (about A.D. 48, after the I Journey), in which case
it is the earliest of all Epistles, and this opinion, which only
appeared in the nineteenth century, has steadily gathered
adherents. The other view is that of the *Late Date* (either
A.D. 50–52 on the II Journey, or A.D. 54–55 on the III
Journey), which (especially with reference to the III Journey) was the general view until the nineteenth century.
According to this view it is not, of course, the earliest Epistle,
but contemporary with I–II Thess. (on the II Journey) or
with I–II Cor. and Rom. (on the III Journey).

The matter turns on certain key-points in the Epistle, and
one can only arrive at one or the other conclusion by decid-
ing one's view on these key-points. The various conclusions
are summarised in the annexed table (p. 159).

We will take the key-points now in order, and outline the
discussion in each case. On each point scholars are ranged

about equally in the two opposing camps. In each case we will give the names of authors on each side whose books are easily accessible and to whom the student could refer for fuller treatment.

(i) *Who are the Galatians?* Galatia proper is the area in the centre of Asia Minor, which until 25 B.C. was a vassal-kingdom of the Romans. At this date it was absorbed as a province and administered together with the adjacent areas of parts of Phrygia, Pisidia and Lycaonia, in which areas lie the cities, so well known in Acts, of Iconium, Lystra, Derbe and Antioch-in-Pisidia.[1] Galatia proper was peopled by a Celtic or Gallic race (whence the name Galatia).

If Galatia proper is meant (the *North-Galatian* theory), the Galatians he writes to (whom he had visited, e.g. Gal. 1. 8, 11) cannot be inhabitants of places visited on the I Journey, for his movements are followed accurately in Acts 13 and 14, and all the cities are outside Galatia proper. We are left, therefore, to suppose (as all writers until the nineteenth century did) that St Paul visited Galatia proper when we read in Acts 16. 6 that he passed through "the Phrygian and Galatian country" on the II Journey, and in Acts 18. 23 through "the Galatian country and Phrygia" on the III Journey. It remains open to doubt whether the word Phrygia (the same in both texts) is an adjective to be taken together with Galatian, giving the meaning Phrygio-Galatian country (i.e. the whole Roman province), or a noun in contradistinction to Galatia proper. Naturally upholders of the North-Galatian theory incline to the second.

On the other hand, if the Roman Province of Galatia (including the southerly areas of Phrygia, Lycaonia and Pisidia) is meant (the *South-Galatian* theory), the Epistle may be addressed to St Paul's converts of the I (or any other) Journey in those districts to the south of Galatia proper, i.e.

[1] See Geographical Intro., p. 11.

Iconium, Lystra, etc. It is this theory that has therefore made possible the Early Date by linking the Epistle with the I Journey. Upholders of the South-Galatian theory, of course, interpret Acts 16. 6 and 18. 23 of the whole province, including the added territories, and hold that St Paul probably never penetrated into Galatia proper at all. The North-Galatian theory is incompatible with the Early Date.[1]

(ii) *When did St Paul visit the Galatians?* This is closely connected with the above. Only the South-Galatian theory will fit the I Journey. But in Gal. 4. 13 St Paul mentions his preaching to them τὸ πρότερον (Vulgate "jampridem"): WV, USA "formerly", RAK "in the first instance". This rather suggests two visits, one being the "former". (Rh "heretofore", Challoner "therefore"[2] do not make this so obvious.) For the Early Date we have to have recourse to the return on the I Journey to give two visits. If the Epistle belongs to the II Journey, we have to suppose the South-Galatian theory to provide two visits. If it is on the III Journey, the North-Galatian interpretation of Acts will account for two visits. On the other hand the text may merely refer to a visit previous to his writing. Since St Paul visited Iconium, Lystra, etc., on each journey, the South-Galatian theory will fit in with visits on any of the journeys.[3]

(iii) *When was the visit to Jerusalem in 2. 1?* Again the authors are fairly equally divided. All are, of course, agreed that the visit recorded in Gal. 1. 18, three years after Paul's conversion, is the one also recorded in Acts 9. 26, where, however, the lapse of time is not indicated, so that we have to take the "many days" of 9. 24 to be a space of three years

[1] For North-Galatians: Lagrange on Gal., and all the Fathers, Jacquier on Acts 16, Martindale, *St Paul*, pp. 73-4.
For South-Galatians: Pope, Sales, Ramsay (*St Paul the Traveller*), Cornely, WV on Gal. (Fr Keogh, S.J.).
[2] In the small (Vaughan) edition. Other editions (as Arendzen 1947) have "heretofore".
[3] The authors here are distributed according to date of writing of Gal.: see below.

(see the chapter on the Life of St Paul, p. 39), placing this visit in the year A.D. 37.

Paul's next visit was made with Barnabas after he had been fetched from his retreat at Tarsus and brought to Antioch: we find them being commissioned by the Christians of Antioch to bring relief to the famine-stricken community at Jerusalem (Acts 11. 30) and then returning to Antioch (12. 25). Altogether he was at Antioch for about one year (11. 26), i.e. the year before he set out on his first journey. So this visit was about A.D. 47.

Thirdly, on returning from his first journey, he and Barnabas "abode no small time" (14. 27) at Antioch, and they then went together (again Paul and Barnabas) up to Jerusalem to settle the Judaizing question that had just arisen (15. 2). This was the Council of Jerusalem, A.D. 49.

Now, the question is this: Is the visit recorded in Gal. 2. 1–9, when Peter and Paul defined their respective apostolates (Peter to the Jews, Paul to the Gentiles) to be identified with the famine-relief visit of A.D. 47, or with the Council in A.D. 49?

Taken quite literally, Paul appears in Gal. 2. 1 to be referring to his very next visit, which would be *the famine-relief visit* of Acts 11. 30. In Gal. 2. 10 he mentions his care of the poor. John is reported to be there ("James, Cephas and John", 2. 9), and Acts does not mention him by name at the Council in c. 15, though "the apostles" are mentioned. If this is the famine-relief visit, it is possible to hold the Early Date, and consider the Epistle to be written after the I Journey, i.e. before the Council-visit had taken place at all. In this case "after fourteen years" means fourteen years from his conversion, since the famine-relief visit cannot be much more than ten years after his first. (Parts of a year can count as a year.)

On the other hand, the business of the visit in Gal. 2. 1, the definition of the apostolates to Jews and Gentiles, coincides strikingly with the that of the Council, so that many scholars identify it with the *Council-visit* in A.D. 49. The famine-relief visit is passed over in Gal., since it was about a purely temporal matter and not concerned with the apostolate. This is perhaps borne out by Gal. 2. 2, "I went up according to revelation", hardly to be applied to a matter of famine-relief. In this case the fourteen years can be reckoned from the visit mentioned just before in Gal., that after his conversion. This identification obliges one to hold a Late Date, at least in the II Journey which began just after the Council. (In our chronology of St Paul's life we have followed this identification.)[1]

(iv) *Was the dispute with Peter in Gal. 2. 11–14 after or before the Council?* The answer to this follows simply from the identification of the visit. The Council, with the voice of Peter (Acts 15. 7–11), decided that Gentile converts were not to be made to submit to the Law of Moses, against the Judaizers (15. 5), who had maintained that they must be circumcised and observe the Law and ritual of Judaism. A proviso was added by James (15. 13–21) that possible scandal to Jewish brethren should be avoided, by asking the Gentiles not to do anything in their presence that would injure their Jewish prejudices.

Now, after Paul's visit to Jerusalem, he met Peter at Antioch, who immediately ate with Gentiles without a scruple; but as soon as some Jewish brethren came from Jerusalem, Peter left the company of the Gentiles "fearing them who were of the circumcision" (Gal. 2. 12). Paul was indignant and reproved Peter for "dissimulating" or giving the impression that Jewish customs among Christians were preferable to Gentile customs.

If Paul had just come from the Council, and the dispute therefore took place *after the Council*, then Paul was accusing

---

[1] Gal. 2. 1 = famine-relief: Pope, WV Gal., Ramsay.
  Gal. 2. 1 = Council: Lagrange (on Gal.), Jacquier (on Acts), WV Acts (Fr Lattey, S.J.), Vosté, O.P. (*Theses in Act.*), Sales.

Peter of "putting the clock back" and denying the newly-proclaimed equality of Jewish and Gentile Christians.

If, however, the Council had not yet taken place, and the dispute took place *before the Council*, then it was no more than part of the discussion that led up to the Council, and we know from Acts 15. 2 that Paul and Barnabas had "no small contest" already then with those who wished to impose on all Christians the Law of Moses.[1]

(v) *Connexions with other Epistles.* The difficulty of dating Galatians not unnaturally turns our attention more notably to other Epistles with which it might be grouped. Two Epistles come to mind at once. Gal. is to a great extent autobiographical, in that Paul is explaining the divine origin of the teaching which he puts forward and is vindicating his own apostolate. And, of course, *II Cor.* is much concerned with the same contention. In both Epistles we find the tone of sharp rebuke to those who allowed themselves to be led away from the Gospel as Paul had preached it to them, e.g. Gal. 3. 1: "O senseless Galatians, who hath bewitched you, that you should not obey the truth?" and 2. 9: "If anyone preach to you a gospel, besides that which you have received, let him be anathema", cf. II Cor. 11. 4: "If he that cometh preacheth another Christ, whom we have not preached, etc." The other obvious connexion is with *Romans*, for both in Rom. and Gal. St Paul is insisting that Justification or Salvation is not to be found through the Jewish Law, but by Faith in Christ (Gal. 3–5 and Rom. 7–11), and, further, in both Epistles the case of Abraham receives special attention (Gal. 3 and Rom. 4). But there is an important difference between Rom. and Gal. in the approach to the same problem. The parts of *Rom.* which deal with this problem are clearly addressed to *Jews*, who pride themselves on their Jewish birth and observance, while *Gal.* is dealing with *Judaizers*, who do not merely want their own privilege, but are wishing to impose their obser-

[1] The authors, of course, are grouped as above.

vances on Gentile Christians, e.g. Gal. 5. 12–13: "They constrain you to be circumcised". The doctrine is the same, but the emphasis is different. Furthermore, as Lagrange points out (Gal. Intro. p. lxiii), while *Gal.* is expressly directed to correcting the error of the Judaizers and so to explaining the relation of the Law to Faith in Christ, *Rom.* is really a treatise on the Christian life and the entry to it by Faith, and the Jewish attitude comes in only as an element in that exposition.

Naturally upholders of the Late Date give prominence to the connexions with these later Epistles, and although Lagrange would place the Epistle just before II Cor. and from Ephesus (III Journey), he admits that Rom. and Gal. represent so much "the same preoccupations and the same thoughts, resulting in similar expressions" (Gal. p. xxviii), that Gal. may well have been written at the same time as Rom., from Corinth (which is the view we took in our chronological table of the Epistles, p. 50). Upholders of the Early Date, of course, stress the differences and maintain that Gal. (written before the Council) alone among the Epistles deals with the Judaizing crisis which was settled once and for all at the Council.

This matter must be taken in connexion with the other points, and it must remain an open question whether the decrees of the Council, promulgated to Antioch, Syria and Cilicia (Acts 15. 23) had effect as far afield as Galatia (especially North-Galatia!) when (on the Late Date theory) even Peter himself was tempted not to enforce them. (The problem still existed at Philippi in the Captivity Period, as Phil. 3 shows.) This question alone shows how closely linked all the problems of this Epistle are.

Summary on the Date. The older North-Galatian theory supposes a Late Date (III Journey), to allow for two visits to Galatia proper. The South-Galatian theory is necessary for an Early Date and for a Late Date (II Journey), but it can be used for any dating.

A TABLE OF THE OPINIONS ON GALATIANS

EARLY DATE	LATE DATE	
48	50–52 or	54–55
after I Journey from Antioch (Acts 14. 27)	on II Journey from Corinth (Acts 18)	on III Journey from Ephesus or Corinth (Acts 19–20)
(the first Epistle)	(with I–II Thess.)	(with I–II Cor.: Ephesus, or Rom.: Corinth)
		to North Galatians (or South Galatians)
to South Galatians	to South Galatians	
previous visits = I Journey and return (Acts 13–14).	previous visits = I and II Journeys (Acts 13–18, incl. Acts 16. 6).	previous visits = II and III Journeys (Acts 16.6 and 18. 23) (if S. Gal. all journeys.
1st visit to Jerusalem (Gal. 1. 18) = visit three years after conversion (Acts 9. 26), A.D. 37		1st visit to Jerusalem (Gal. 1. 18) = visit three years after conversion (Acts 9. 26), A.D. 37.
2nd visit (Gal. 2. 1) = famine-relief visit (Acts 11. 30), A.D. 47, fourteen years after conversion.		2nd visit (Gal. 2. 1) = visit for Council (Acts 15. 2), A.D. 49, fourteen years after previous visit.
(The Epistle was written before the Council, so of course it cannot come in.)		(The famine-relief visit is passed over, being only about temporal affairs.)
Dispute with Peter (Gal. 2. 11–14) before the Council, while at Antioch before (Acts 13. 1) or after (Acts 14. 27) I Journey.		Dispute with Peter (Gal. 2. 11–14) after the Council, when Paul returned to Antioch (Acts 15. 30) before starting II Journey.

Note (i) Dates given here are according to the chronology used in this book, and do not necessarily accord exactly with those used by the authors quoted as holding the various opinions.

(ii) Parts of a year can always be reckoned as a year.

(iii) While not wishing to impose on the student any of the theories about Galatians, we must for practical purposes adhere to one date in this book (as also in Vol. IV of the series, cf. there pp. 139, 203), and we take it that Gal. was written from Corinth (together with Rom.) on the III Journey in A.D. 54–55, and we incline to the traditional North-Galatian theory, although the South-Galatian will fit the date equally well.

The Early Date means that the visit of 2. 1, the Dispute with Peter, and the Epistle itself were all *before* the Council, and that the Judaizing crisis was cleared up at the Council. The identification of the visit of 2. 1 with the Council necessitates a Late Date (i.e. *after* the Council) and therefore supposes that the Judaizing question persisted at least in Galatia.

The Late Date emphasises the connexion with Rom., even to the extent of supposing Gal. and Rom. to be contemporary (from Corinth); while the Early Date dissociates Gal. from Rom., asserting that Rom. is a much later treatise with a different approach to the same problem, and that Gal. was the first of Paul's Epistles to be written, being a rapid *ad hoc* treatment of the particular error of the Judaizers.

The South-Galatian theory first appeared in 1825, when it was proposed by the Danish scholar Mynster and became well known among Roman historians, especially through Perrot (1867). It was taken up for the dating of the Epistle, principally by Sir William Ramsay, in 1890. Before the nineteenth century a North-Galatian theory and late date were universally held.[1]

Argument. The theological teaching of this Epistle, that Justification is by Faith in Christ and not by observance of the Jewish Law, has been carefully studied in Rom. This Epistle has no preamble, St Paul goes *in medias res* at once: he would rescue them from the error of Ἰουδαΐζειν (Paul's own word to Peter in 2. 14), i.e. compelling Gentiles who become Christians to observe the Law of Moses. The argument is quite clear and consecutive.

Address (1. 1–5).
Paul (and the brethren with him) to the churches of Galatia. (He adds a prayer to the mention of peace from Christ.)

I. His purpose in writing (1. 6–10).
His converts are "so soon removed" from the

[1] Obvious sources for further detailed opinion are:
For Early Date (after I Journey): Pope, WV Gal. (S.–Gal.).
For Later Date (II Journey): Ramsay, Cornely, Sales (S.–Gal.).
For Late Date (III Journey): all traditional sources, including Challoner's note, USA, Lagrange, Prat, Holzner, Martindale.

Gospel that he preached to them. They must return to what he taught them. They are not to listen to the Judaizers.

II. His Apologia for his own Apostolate (1. 11–2. 14).
    i. His gospel was revealed to him by God, and was not learnt from other men (1. 11–12).
    ii. In proof of this he tells them his story:

After his conversion he did *not* go to Jerusalem, but into Arabia, and then back to Damascus (1. 13–17).

After three years his *first* visit to Jerusalem (1. 18–24).

Then after fourteen years his *second* visit (2. 1–10).

And then, far from merely getting his ideas from other men, he even "withstood Peter to his face" on the Judaizing matter (2. 11–14).

III. The Argument against the Judaizers (2. 15–4. 31).
    i. We are not justified by the Law, but by Faith in Christ (2. 16), as a Christian I am "dead to the Law, that I may live to God", in fact, "I live, now not I, but Christ liveth in me" (2. 20). They are "senseless Galatians" to want to live under the Law, now (3. 1) (2. 15 -3. 5). Cf. Rom. 5–8.
    ii. Abraham (before the Law of Moses) was justified by his Faith in God, so that, since all Christians share this Faith, Abraham is thus the father of all (3. 6–14). Cf. Rom. 4 (especially v. 16).
    iii. The promises made by God to Abraham are like a man's will which cannot be altered: the Law of Moses did not alter them (3. 15–18).

iv. Before Christ we were like children, and the
    Law was "our pedagogue in Christ" (3. 24):
    now, however, we are like grown-up heirs.
    A child, like a slave, must simply obey his
    pedagogue. Now that you are grown-up,
    would you return to that slavery? This is
    what the Judaizers would have you do (3. 19–
    4. 10).

(*Digression:* a personal appeal: they received him so
    well, would they now abandon his teaching? 4. 11–
    20).

v. The idea of the free heir and the slave is taken
    up in the figure of the sons of Abraham:
    Ismael was born of a slave-woman (Gen. 16),
    but on the birth of Isaac of a free-woman,
    Ismael was at once disinherited (Gen. 21).
    Now that Christ has come, his followers are
    (as it were) born of the heavenly Jerusalem,
    and the Jews who do not recognise him, the
    sons of the earthly Jerusalem, are disinherited
    and remain in slavery (4. 21–31).

IV. Practical Advice (5. 1– 6. 10).
    i. The consequences of Judaizing: the observance
       of the Law now, cuts men off from the grace
       of Christ (5. 1–6).
    ii. Warning therefore against such teachers (5. 7–
        12).
    iii. They have been called to the liberty of the
         spirit, i.e. Faith in Christ, and should no
         longer be under the bondage of the Law. All
         the Law is fulfilled in the command (of
         Christ, Mt. 22. 39, which comes from the
         OT, Lev. 19. 18): "Thou shalt love thy
         neighbour as thyself" (cf. Rom. 13. 8). From

this comes the whole idea of Christian fraternal charity, explained in many examples (5.
13–6. 10).

Concluding remarks in Paul's own handwriting (6.
11–18).

Some passages that should be noted[1]

1. 11. "The gospel which was preached by me": this means
either that he received by revelation the whole of the Gospel,
or else perhaps it here refers to his particular teaching on the
the matter of the relations of Christians to the Old Law. In
I Cor. 11. 23 and 15. 3 he tells how he "received" of the Lord
what he teaches. (See note on I Cor. 11. 23.)

2. 2. "Seemed to be something" is the literal translation of
an obvious colloquialism, used in 2. 6. Here, however, the
infinitive and pronoun are omitted, and the phrase is still
more colloquial. It seems clear that Peter and the other
Apostles are intended.

"Run in vain": not that Paul doubted his own revelation
and apostolate, but it was a question of getting his sphere and
that of the Apostles in Jerusalem defined, and of working
together with them.

2. 9. "Seemed to be pillars": famous phrase of the Apostles
at Jerusalem. James, the local bishop, Cephas or Peter (probably on a visit to Jerusalem, if he really was by this time in
Rome),[2] and John. Peter's primacy is very obviously suggested in these verses (1. 18 Paul comes specially to see him,
2. 2 "in vain" unless planned together with Peter as in 2. 7, 8:
see Lagrange on these verses).

"Gave me and Barnabas the right hands of κοινωνία,
sharing fellowship, communion," expressing the unity of the
Apostolate. Although these things are here written to prove

---

[1] Only important passages not hitherto noticed in the Introductory
pages.
[2] See Intro. to Rom., p. 131

that Paul did *not* get his knowledge of Christ's revelation from other Apostles (but from Christ himself), yet they are of the utmost value in establishing the nature of the Apostolate at the very beginning.

2. 19. "With Christ I am nailed to the Cross": the same idea as in Rom. 6. 4., "We are buried together with him by baptism," and 6. 6, "Our old man is crucified with him": with Christ the old sinful man dies, and with Christ the new Christian man rises from the dead. That is the context of the famous phrase: "I live, now not I, but Christ liveth in me" (2. 20).

3. 13. "Christ . . . made a curse for us", cf. II Cor. 5. 21, "Him, that knew no sin, (God) for us hath made sin": Paul has deliberately not said "accursed" or "a sinner", which would be a blasphemy. But he has explained how Christ offered himself as a sacrifice, taking on himself the curse of sinful humanity, identifying himself with us in his love for us. Cf. also Rom. 5. 18: Justification comes to all men "by the justice of one", i.e. Christ; and the later Epistle Eph. 5. 2, "Christ hath loved us and hath delivered himself for us, an oblation and a sacrifice to God" (cf. St Thomas III 48. 3).

3. 20. "A mediator is not of one, but God is one." The mediator in the context (v. 19) is Moses, by whom, as intermediary, the Law was delivered. Dr Wand then paraphrases, "It is obvious that an intermediary acts for more than one party; in this case the other is God." But our text is a literal translation of the Greek, and perhaps we should understand the two parts of the verse in opposition: we could then paraphrase, "Of course the giving of the Law was a contract between God and the People, and so required an intermediary (Moses); *but* the promise to Abraham (before the Law) was an entirely free gift so that there was only *one* party involved, God the giver, and no intermediary required" (cf. WV note).

4. 5–7. The Christian is the son and heir, joint heir with Christ: cf. Rom. 8 12–17 where the Aramaic word "Abba" is

also introduced. The argument is the same, but here there is the special application to the Jews.

4. 13. "On account of a physical infirmity I preached the gospel to you formerly" (USA), lit. "weakness of the flesh", cf. the "thorn for the flesh", of II Cor. 12. 7. Unlike II Cor. (which is a very vague expression) this passage taken literally certainly means illness. Upholders of the North-Galatian theory (e.g. Lagrange) readily see an illness that held up Paul's journey and caused him to stay in Galatia, which he would otherwise have passed by, so that his falling ill was the cause of his preaching there. The reference to eyes in 4. 15 and "big letters" of 6. 11 have suggested a semi-blindness, and all sorts of ailments such as malaria have been suggested. It is obvious that he was very grateful for the care he received from the Galatians, when they might have considered him a burden (4. 14). But (as in II Cor.) troubles such as persecution and temptation have been suggested here. RAK is unwilling to commit himself to an illness and paraphrases, "Because of outward circumstances which were humiliating to me": see also his note. 4. 15 "give your eyes for me" may be merely a hyperbolic expression for their goodness to him.

4. 21. "You that desire to be under the Law" shows the influence of Judaizers working among them, as also 5. 10 and 12.

6. 11. "See with what large letters I am writing to you, with mine own hand!" (WV). The passage is studied in the introductory chapter on St Paul's letters (p. 47) among the various handwritten conclusions to the Epistles. This example stands somewhat alone.

6. 15–16. A summary of the business of the Epistle in Paul's postscript: the observance of the Jewish Law (typified in circumcision) or its non-observance makes no difference now; what matters is to be the "new man" by Faith in Christ. This is the true Israel.

6. 17. "From henceforth let no man be troublesome to me

(on this matter which I hope I have settled in this Epistle); for I bear the marks of the Lord Jesus in my body": the word "marks" is both in Greek and in Latin "stigmata", which is the reason why this word is used for the miraculous marks on the hands, feet and side of some of the Saints (beginning with St Francis of Assisi), which appeared as a manifestation of their devotion to Our Lord's Passion. The exact meaning here is uncertain: (i) the scars of the injuries he received in persecution during his apostolate that are a witness to his work for Christ, or (ii) speaking symbolically as if he were a slave of Christ, with Christ's mark branded on his body (for Roman slaves were often thus branded with their master's mark).

Note. This brings us to the end of the period of St Paul's "Missionary Epistles", written in the course of his various journeys. The succeeding phase, that of the "Epistles of the Captivity", represents a development in St Paul's thought and vocabulary, and the needs of the Churches are new. For the new phrases and ideas, see especially Prat, I, 37 and 271 sq., WV, III, liii, and Intros. in Pope to Eph., Phil., and Col.

(From his 1st Captivity: Eph., Col., Philem., Philipp.)

(29–31)   THE EPISTLE TO THE
                    EPHESIANS

A. Time and place. At the conclusion of his III Journey, St Paul arrived in Jerusalem (Acts 21. 15–18), bringing the funds (24. 17) he had collected with so much trouble in Asia Minor (I Cor. 16. 1), Macedonia (II Cor. 8 and 9, Rom. 15. 26) and Greece (I Cor. 16. 1, II Cor. 8. 1, Rom. 15. 26); the visit was a pilgrimage: he had made an effort to reach Jerusalem by Pentecost (Acts 20. 16), and he fulfilled the requirements of the seven days' pilgrimage of prayer in the temple (20. 26–27). It was the year A.D. 55. Just then some Jews "that were of Asia" raised a riot against Paul with the accusation (monstrous enough when we know his teaching on Jewish customs for Jews, and Gentile customs for Gentiles among the Christians) that he was teaching against the Law, and bringing a Gentile friend, Trophimus of Ephesus, into the temple (which is about the last thing that Paul, of all people, would do: to impose a Jewish pilgrimage on a Gentile) (20. 28–29). There was a general riot, and Paul was rescued by the Roman soldiers and taken into custody (20. 30 sqq.). After three days (22. 30, 23. 11–12, 23) he was removed to the prison at Caesarea, where he was kept for two years (24. 27) without condemnation. Apparently he was allowed visitors, for the centurion was commanded "that he should be easy, and that he should not prohibit any of his friends to minister unto him" (24. 23). Probably Luke was for some of the time one of these, for when St Paul, after his appeal to Caesar (25. 11), was shipped to Rome, Luke was with him, for he uses "we" when they set sail in 27. 4. It was now about September A.D. 57 (27. 9, "the fast" before the Day of Atonement in September). After the shipwreck they stayed in Malta for three months (28. 11), and eventually reached Rome, where "Paul was suffered to dwell by himself with a soldier that kept him" (28. 16). This must have been early in A.D. 58. "And he remained two whole years in his own hired lodging" (28. 30), i.e. A.D. 58–60. Here he received many people: for instance, "he called together the chief of the Jews" (28. 17), "there came very many to him unto his lodgings" (28. 23).

In our introduction to Philemon (p. 52, at the very beginning of our exegesis of St Paul's Epistles), we observed how all four so-called "Epistles of the Captivity" have much in common: they all have references to the writer's captivity, Col. and Philem. contain the names of several people at both ends and all those in Philem. are also in Col., and it is evident that both Col. and Philem. were sent to Colossae (Onesimus, the runaway slave of Philemon, is "one of you," Col. 4. 9). Now the bearer of Col. is Tychicus (Col. 4. 7–9), who is also the bearer of Eph. (Eph. 6. 21), and it is reasonable to suppose that both letters were delivered on the same journey, since the normal route to Colossae would be through Ephesus. Thus Eph., Col., and Philem. are closely bound together. Phil.[1] stands apart if only for the fact that it is written not to Asia with a single dispatch, but to Philippi in Macedonia. But the references to imprisonment (Phil. 1. 7), the presence of Timothy in the openings of Phil., Col. and Philem., the references to his work for the Gospel even while a prisoner (Phil. 1. 13, "my bonds are made manifest"; Eph. 6. 19, "that I may open my mouth with confidence, to make known the mystery of the gospel"), all the contacts with visitors (as the lists of names show), and finally the clear expectation of release in the near future (Phil. 2. 24 and Philem. 22), all these things together point to Phil. being written at much the same time as the other three. (In our study we have placed the other three in a group first, because of their close connexion, but there is no direct evidence whether Phil. was written after or before the other three, which were obviously written and dispatched together.)

All this is apart from the unity of thought, style and vocabulary of all four[2] and the almost universal tradition that they belong to the same period of captivity.

The same tradition has almost always held that these Letters were written from St Paul's Roman Captivity, from "his own hired lodging" (Acts 28. 30), A.D. 58–60, where it is evident from Acts that he was able to receive many visitors. This is also in itself the most probable, although it cannot be definitely proved from the text, apart from the two references in Phil. 1. 13 to the "praetorium" and 4. 22 to "Caesar's household", which are almost explicit references to Rome.[3] The tradition that Mark lived in Rome with Peter offers confirmation, when taken with the references to Mark being near Paul in Col. 4. 10 and Philem. 24.

[1] The student's attention should be called to the usual abbreviation Phil. for Philippians, as distinct from Philem. for Philemon, which is, however, further recognisable by having a verse number only.
[2] Cf. e.g. WV, III, liii.   [3] Texts studied in intro. to Philem., p. 53.

Yet, it should be observed that some authors hold that the reference is to his captivity at Caesarea (where, however, the only visitors permitted were "friends to minister unto him", Acts 24. 23, and he can hardly have had hope of an immediate release), or even on the III Journey at Ephesus (taking the references in II Cor. 1. 8–10 to mean something as serious as imprisonment under threat of death). On these theories the "praetorium" and "Caesar's household" have to be understood as meaning garrisons of the Imperial Guard. The presence of Onesimus as far away as Rome is regarded as *a priori* likely or unlikely, according as one accepts or rejects the tradition of the Roman captivity. The assignment of all four Epistles to the Roman captivity is by far the most general opinion.

B. To whom? Reference was made to the Church of Ephesus in the introduction to I Cor. (p. 72) and to the geographical position at the head of the great road into Asia Minor in the Geographical Introduction (p. 9). St Paul had visited Ephesus twice, first on the II Journey for a short stay (Acts 18. 19–21), and then on the III Journey for a two-year residence (Acts 19), which ended in the riot of the silversmiths. The Church of Ephesus was therefore the one that had the privilege of having Paul's longest visit in the course of his missionary journeys. This was in A.D. 52–54, i.e. about four years before the Epistle to the Ephesians. But he did see some of the Ephesians in between: it was on his way back from Corinth to Jerusalem that his ship put in at Miletus, and Paul had decided not to visit Ephesus again lest he should be detained, "for he hasted, if it were possible for him, to keep the day of Pentecost at Jerusalem" (Acts 20. 16). So he summoned the "ancients" or presbyters, or clergy of Ephesus to come to see him at Miletus, about thirty miles distant. Here he delivered to them that famous and moving address (Acts 20. 18–35), in which he bids them farewell, warns them against false teachers, and urges them to keep the true doctrine of Christ. "And when he had said these things, kneeling down he prayed with them all. And there was much weeping among them all; and falling on the neck of Paul, they kissed him, being grieved most of all for the word which he had said, that they should see his face no more. And they brought him on his way to the ship" (Acts 20. 36–38). These verses, more than any perhaps, show Paul's relations with the Christians of Ephesus.

But there is a difficulty about the address to Ephesus: (i) two of the oldest MSS (ℵ and B) omit the words "at Ephesus" from 1..1, (ii) the heretic Marcion (second century) read the words "at Laodicea" in their place,[1] (iii) everybody wants to know the meaning of Col. 4. 16, "When this epistle (Col.) shall have been read with you, cause that it be read also in the Church of the Laodiceans (about eleven miles from Colossae): and that you (at Colossae) read that which is of the Laodiceans". What is this Epistle to the Laodiceans?

The vast majority of existing MSS and versions include the words "at Ephesus" in the address, yet St Jerome is at pains to explain the phrase that seems to hang in the air, "the saints that are", which is to be understood to mean "those that are saints *par excellence*." This points to the words "at Ephesus" *not* standing in the early texts. Yet early tradition almost universally held (on traditional and not on textual grounds) that the Epistle *was* written to the Ephesians.

This encourages most modern scholars to understand that the letter was an Encyclical or circular letter, sent first to Ephesus (the capital of Asia, and the principal Christian community) to be then circulated round the Churches of Asia Minor, including of course Laodicea and Colossae. Since Paul was writing anyway to Colossae (to Philemon about the affair of Onesimus), he wrote a letter to the community there, but instructed them to get hold of the circular letter (Eph.), when it should come to the neighbouring town

[1] Tertullian, *Adversus Marcionem*, V, 11 and 17.

of Laodicea, and they might as well, in return, read the one he had sent to Colossae.

On this theory the absence of the words "at Ephesus" in the MSS is the most accurate text, but their insertion by scribes is also the most natural thing (since everyone knew the letter was sent there), and further, the insertion of the words, "at Laodicea" in Marcion's copy is not surprising (especially if it should happen to have been a copy made at Laodicea—Marcion was from Pontus), and it also saves us from supposing an otherwise unheard-of Epistle to the Laodiceans. Lastly it should be noticed in support of the theory of the Encyclical that in spite of the obviously intimate relations of Paul with Ephesus, the Epistle is entirely lacking in the personal messages (Tychicus, the messenger, alone is named, 6. 21) or in advice for a concrete situation or crisis (as in most of the preceding Epistles), and that more than any other Epistle (except Heb.) it is a general treatise on Christian theology.

So it happens that scholars are divided on the matter of the address of Ephesians,[1] but since the letter has now circulated all through the Christian world, it is not of prime importance to know for whom it was first of all intended.

C. Argument. The teaching of this Epistle is certainly in St Paul's sublimest manner. Although certain of the elements are familiar to us from earlier Epistles, the general presentation of Christian teaching represents a new turn in St Paul's thought. The dominant idea is *the union of the Christian with Christ*, with the consequent *unity among Christians*. The idea may be summed up in the phrase "In Christ", which occurs no less than twenty times in Eph. There are certain new words also that St Paul uses frequently in the Epistles of the Captivity and not before. In some cases they are

[1] Various opinions may be found, for instance:
Eph. =Encyclical: Pope, Prat, I, 7, Martindale, 222.
Eph. =to Laodiceans: Knabenbauer, S.J., Vosté, O.P.
Eph. really to Ephesians: Cornely, Sales, WV.

words actually coined by St Paul. For instance, there is the
striking use of compounds invented with σύν (e.g. Eph. 2.
5–6: "hath *quickened* us *together* in Christ ... *raised* us *together* ... *made* us *sit together*", in each case it is one compound Greek word). Then there is the word ἐπίγνωσις
"super-knowledge" of Christ, which is the secret of the
Christian life (Eph. 1. 17); which occurs in all four Epistles
(also in the Pastorals and II Peter), but only twice before
(Rom. 1. 28, 10. 2). The great word πλήρωμα "fullness,
plenitude, perfection" occurs rarely elsewhere, but has acquired a special meaning in Eph. 1. 23, 3. 19, 4. 13 and Col.
1. 19, 2. 9.

I. Dogmatic Teaching on being one with Christ (c. 1–3).
    i. God has predestined us to be adopted as his
        sons, through Christ (1. 3–14).
    ii. May he therefore give you the true knowledge of
        Christ, for Christ is the head of the Church,
        his body (1. 15–23).
    iii. We, who were dead, have been quickened to-
        gether with Christ (2. 1–10).
    iv. So you are no longer strangers but fellow-
        citizens; you are part of Christ's building, of
        which he is the corner-stone (2. 11–22).
    v. Wherefore I (and here is the famous parenthesis,
        v. 2–13), I pray that Christ may dwell in your
        hearts (c. 3).

II. Moral Teaching (following from union with Christ)
    (c. 4–6).
    i. Be therefore careful to keep the unity of the
        Spirit: one Lord, one Faith, one Baptism, etc.
        (4. 1–16).
    ii. Put off the "old man" and put on the "new man"
        (4. 17–24).

   iii. This means getting rid of all kinds of vice (4. 25
      to 5. 20).

   iv. It means being patient and kind: advice to
      wives, husbands, children, servants (5. 21 to
      6. 9).

   v. Put on "the armour of God", and pray (6. 10–18)
Conclusion (6. 19–24).

Exegesis

Address

   1. 1–2. Paul to the saints (at Ephesus ? see above), grace and
peace.

1. On being one with Christ.
   i. God's predestination and adoption of us.

   1. 3–6. The idea of Predestination is familiar from Rom.
8. 29, and also that of our adopted sonship from Rom. 8. 12
and Gal. 4. 5.

   1. 7–8. God has not only predestined us, but redeemed us
by the Blood of Christ.

   1. 9–10. Our redemption is the manifestation of the mystery of God's Will: "his loving design" (RAK).

   1. 10. "To re-establish all things in Christ": this is, of
course, translated from the Latin Vulgate "Instaurare omnia
in Christo",[1] and this translation has become a tradition (it is
preserved in USA). The Greek word, however, is ἀνακεφαλαιώσασθαι (a very important word to which St Paul has given a
special meaning). St Jerome said it should be translated
(literally) "recapitulare", i.e. to gather under one κεφάλαιον,
caput, heading or chapter. It was thus used for "to sum up",
hence "recapitulate" or repeat afresh. (It is possibly from
this meaning that the traditional "re-establish" has come, but
it is difficult to see exactly how the Latin reading came about.)
WV has "to bring all things to a head in Christ"; RAK

---

[1] The motto taken by Pope Pius X (1903–1914).

permits himself to say "by resuming everything in him, all
... summed up in him". The general meaning is plain:
everything that is, now that Christ has come, has a new
meaning, a new life, in Christ (is summed-up, or re-estab-
lished, in him); and this was to happen "in the dispensation
of the fulness of times", i.e. God made "all history work out
towards one culminating moment" (Wand), the moment of
Christ's redemption.[1]

1. 11–14. Continuation of the idea of predestination to
sonship.

ii. The need of true knowledge of Christ

1. 15–16. As so often, St Paul tells them of his prayer for
them.

1. 17. His special prayer is that God will give them wisdom,
and the revelation or understanding of Christ, and ἐπίγνωσις
or "super-knowledge" of him. This is after all the one thing
that really matters, and Paul writes in Philippians the
famous passage: "I count all things to be but loss, for the
excellent knowledge of Jesus Christ my Lord" (Phil. 3. 8).

1. 22–23. St Paul's teaching once more on Christ's Mystical
Body, which is the Church, and of which Christ himself is the
head. He had worked out this teaching in I Cor. (especially
2. 16, 6. 15, 10. 17 and 12. 12 sq.).

1. 23. But here he introduces the new word in this connexion: the Mystical Body is the πλήρωμα "complement"[2] or
completion or fullness of Christ himself. WV note: "The
Church is the extension of the Word Incarnate. Without the
Church, the Incarnation is unmeaning, as a head without a
body". The doctrine of Christ as head of the Mystical Body
is proclaimed as an article of Faith by the Council of Trent:
"Christ Jesus himself as 'the head to the members' (cf. Eph.

---

[1] On ἀνακεφαλαιώσασθαι see especially Prat, II, 92, and Vosté.
[2] In English, as in classical Greek, the word is used of a ship's "complement".

4. 15) and 'the vine to the branches' (cf. Jn. 15. 5) gives strength (virtutem influat) unceasingly to the justified, and this strength always precedes, accompanies and follows upon all their good works" (Denz., 809), and cf. St Thomas III 8 1.[1]

iii. Before Christ was death, now, in Christ is resurrection

2. 1–7. The equation of sin and death, as opposed to redemption and resurrection, together with the idea of the "old" (heathen) man who is to die, and so become the "new" (Christian) man who rises from the dead (the old and new man come here in c. 4) is familiar to us after reading Romans, especially c. 6 and 7 (e.g. 6. 3, "Baptized in his death"; 6. 4, "Buried together with him . . . walk in newness of life; 6. 6, "Our old man is crucified with him"; 7. 10, "And I died," etc.), comparing of course the passage in Gal. 2. 19–20, "With Christ I am nailed to the cross . . . but Christ liveth in me". We should, however, observe the new emphasis in Eph. on this new life with and in Christ, the idea that dominates this new period of St Paul's writing (this is about four or five years after Rom. and Gal.). In Rom. and Gal. he already had the compound words "buried with", "crucified with", etc., but there are many more in the Epistles of the Captivity,[2] especially here in 2. 5–6.

2. 8–10. Our salvation is through Faith in Christ, and not through purely human works: again material from Romans (and see notes on Rom. 5. 1–11), and cf. the Decree of Trent quoted above on 1. 23. Here St Paul tells us (v. 10), "For we are his handiwork, created in Christ Jesus for good works, which God hath prepared beforehand that therein we may walk" (WV). It was the heresy of Pelagius (the only notable English contributor to the list of heresies) which maintained

[1] For πλήρωμα see especially Prat, II, 283.
[2] List in Pope, V, 165.

G

that although the Grace of God admittedly made it easier to
obey God's commands, yet it was possible to achieve this
without it. This teaching was declared heretical at the
Council of Carthage in A.D. 418 (Denz., 105).

iv. Pagans have now become God's citizens

2. 11–12. Paul explains to Gentile readers that the Jews
(the circumcised) call them the Uncircumcised, and reminds
them that after all they did not have the advantage that the
Jews had before Christ, for the Gentiles, who were aliens to
the commonwealth[1] of Israel, had no promise of a Redeemer,
and were, in fact, living without a God altogether.

2. 13. "But now in Christ Jesus, you, who sometime were
afar off, are made nigh by the blood of Christ."

2. 14–16. "He himself is our peace. He has broken down
the dividing wall that separated Jew from Gentile. He has
abrogated the Law with all its detailed regulations. And he
has made the two races one. Out of two distinct individuals
He has, so to speak, by uniting both with himself, created one
new man. Thus he has established peace and has put an end
to the old hostility by reconciling both to God through the
offering of His own body on the cross" (Dr Wand's singularly
beautiful and very exact translation).[2]

2. 17–19. The Gentiles are therefore no longer strangers,
but are become citizens as much as those who possessed the
revelation from the beginning.

2. 20–22. The figure of the city or commonwealth is replaced with that of the building (cf. I Cor. 3. 9–15, "You are
God's building"). All are "built upon the foundation of the
apostles and prophets" (an important passage for the apostolic tradition), "framed together" and "built together"
(compound verbs expressing unity) into a habitation of God.

[1] πολιτεία translated "conversatio" in Vulgate, followed by Rh "conversation", as also in Phil. 3. 20.
[2] It will be noticed how modern English requires short sentences: Eph.
more than other Epistles is written in chains of dependent clauses.

v. Paul's prayer for them

3. 1. It is here that we have Paul's long parenthesis apropos of his ministry of preaching: the parenthesis that lasts for twelve verses. The thread is resumed in v. 14, only to be laid aside again for a brief parenthesis in v. 15. The pattern of this chapter can be understood in this way:

> v. 1. *"For this cause"* (i.e. your incorporation as citizens), I, Paul, prisoner for the sake of you Gentiles
>
> v. 2–13. (If yet you have heard . . . of the grace given to me . . . to preach among the Gentiles . . . etc.)
>
> v. 14. *For this cause* (as I was saying), I bow my knees to the Father of Our Lord Jesus Christ,
>
> v. 15 (Of whom all paternity is named)
> *I pray*
>
> v. 16. (i) that he grant you strength;
>
> v. 17. (ii) that Christ may dwell in your hearts;
>
> v. 18. (iii) that you may comprehend the breadth, length, height, and depth;
>
> v. 19. (iv) that you may know Christ's love for us;
> (v) that you may fulfil the πλήρωμα of God;
>
> v. 20–21. (To whom be all glory.)

3. 3. "The mystery had been made known to me": Paul speaks here several times of "the mystery", which is the Greek word, originally signifying something whose knowledge is hidden, and in the New Testament used of God's counsels revealed to men. Hence RAK's rendering in 3. 4, "Christ's secret".

3. 5. The mystery before was unrevealed, but now is made known through the Apostles.

3. 6. The mystery is this: that the Gentiles (as much as the Jews who knew before of God's promises) have become "coheirs and concorporate and comparticipate in the promise" (WV: following the Rh of 1582 in coining these compound words).

3. 14–15. I pray to God the Father "from whom all father-hood in heaven and on earth receives its name" (USA).

3. 17. The main point: "That Christ may dwell by faith in your hearts", that you may be "rooted and grounded in love" (USA).

3. 18–19. That you may be able "to grasp in all its breadth and length and height and depth the conception of the love of Christ. That is a subject of knowledge which surpasses knowledge" (Wand). And in this way you will fulfil the πλήρωμα of Christ, by truly being members of his Body.

3. 20–21. A "doxology"[1] or prayer of praise concluding this part of the Epistle.

II. THE CHRISTIAN VOCATION

i. Unity

4. 1–3. The first consequence of being one with Christ is that Christians should be one among themselves, "careful to keep the unity of the Spirit in the bond of peace". Rightly Ephesians has been called the Epistle of Unity.

4. 4–6. The principles of unity among Christians: one Body (the Mystical Body of Christ), one Spirit (which gives life to the Body), one Hope (in Christ's promises of eternal life[2]), one Lord (Christ), one Faith (in Christ, the faith by which we are saved), one Baptism (by which we are all made sons of God), one God and Father of all.

4. 7–16. Each one of us receives his special gifts from Christ: each one contributes to the One Body, as do the various members of the human body. This idea was worked out in much detail in I Cor. 12. 4–30 (e.g. 12. 11, "all these things [gifts] one and the same Spirit worketh, dividing to every one according as he will") and in less detail in Rom.

[1] This word, from δόξα "glory", is used by the liturgiologists for the Gloria Patri added to a psalm, or similar verse concluding a hymn. The last verse of a hymn is regularly cast in Gloria Patri form.

[2] The point of the Act of Hope: "Oh my God, I hope in thee, because of thy promises to me."

12. 3-8 (e.g., 12. 5, "So we being many, are one body in Christ"). Once more the doctrine is presented again in Eph., but special emphasis on Christ himself as the unifying principle.

4. 8-11. St Paul is teaching that Christ's heavenly gifts come to us just because Christ ascended into heaven. St Thomas (III 57. 6) explains that Christ's Ascension is part of his work for our salvation, (i) To prepare for us the way to heaven (cf. Jn. 14. 2, "I go to prepare a place for you"); (ii) Christ's human nature now in heaven is in itself an intercession for us; and (iii) Christ from heaven sends us heavenly gifts (cf. Jn. 16. 7, "It is expedient to you that I go: for if I go not, the Paraclete will not come to you: but if I go, I will send him to you"). Paul's argument is based on the text from Ps. 67 (Heb. 68) 19, where, however, the Hebrew text reads: "Thou didst mount the height, thou didst lead captives captive, thou didst receive gifts from men" (WV Lattey), of which the context is God's working of historical victories of the OT. Paul follows the LXX text, with, however, the alteration of "gave gifts to" instead of "received gifts among". Paul's text is used several times in the Ascension liturgy.

4. 13. "Until we all attain to the unity of the Faith and the deep knowledge (the one word ἐπίγνωσις) of the Son of God to perfect manhood, to the mature measure of the fulness (πλήρωμα) of Christ" (USA). The "mature measure" is the "measure of the ἡλικία" which means maturity in either age or stature (cf. the problem about Mt. 5. 27: "Add to his stature one cubit" or "to his age one span"). The figure is of the mature manhood of the Mystical Body of Christ when all Christians are spiritually full-grown members of it.

ii. Put off the "old man" and put on the "new man"

4. 17-24. Paul's now familiar figure: the "old man" with his pagan vices and the "new (Christian) man". See notes on 2. 1-7.

iii. This means getting rid of various vices

This and the remaining sections, consisting of moral advice, are straightforward without any difficult passages. (Cf. Rom. c. 12.) We should, however, observe one or two phrases:

4. 26. "Be angry and sin not" is quoted from Ps. 4. 5 (familiar to us from Compline), in the LXX version. The Hebrew reads, "Tremble and sin not" (WV). "Let not the sun go down upon your anger" has become a famous saying.

4. 32. "Forgive one another, even as God hath forgiven you", cf. the converse in the Our Father, when we ask God's forgiveness on the understanding that we forgive others.

5. 5. "Which is a serving of idols" as in Col. 3. 5, though here the Greek has "Which (or Who) is idolatrous". The pursuit of pleasure is as a false god.

5. 10. "Proving what is well pleasing to God": i.e. "testing" (USA).

5. 16. "Making the most of your time" (USA).

iv. Patience and kindness

5. 21. USA entitles this section "The Christian Home": wives, 5. 22; husbands, 5. 25; children, 6. 1; servants, 6. 5.

5. 23. "The husband is the head of the wife", cf. I Cor. 11. 3 (in connexion with women's headdress at worship).

5. 25. "Husbands, love your wives, just as Christ also loved the Church, and delivered himself up for her" (USA). An *important passage*, since here for the first time we have the parallel drawn between the love of married people and the love between Christ and the Church, the idea of the Church as the "Sponsa Christi", the idea that gave a classical interpretation to the Book of Canticles.[1] The husband's devotion to his wife is to include readiness to "deliver himself up for her". St Paul has suggested the parallel in II Cor. 11. 2,

---

[1] The II Council of Constantinople (A.D. 553) declared the literal interpretation of the Canticles as a mere love-song, to be "nefanda christianorum auribus".

"that I may present you as a chaste virgin to Christ", but there the Corinthian community is likened to a bride, while here a wife is likened to the Church. The figure is carried on to the end of the chapter, and in v. 32 he calls it a "mystery", translated by the Vulgate "sacramentum", i.e. a figure or symbol with a sacred meaning.

6. 1. Children are to be obedient: with the corollary, "Fathers, provoke not your children to anger" (Dr Wand writes, "Be careful not to exasperate your children").

6. 5. Slaves are to be obedient to their masters "as to Christ": with the corollary that masters are to act in the same way, i.e. on a basis of the service of Christ, not of men.

v. Final exhortation

6. 10–17. "Let all alike realise the strength they possess in the Lord and in the power of his might. Arm yourselves with the full equipment that God has provided to enable his soldiers to hold their own against the tactics of the Devil" (vv. 10–11, Wand). Armour, girdle, breastplate, boots, shield, helmet and sword are mentioned in turn as symbols. WV note: "St Paul, constantly under guard, had abundant opportunity of noticing military equipment".

6. 18. An urgent exhortation to prayer.

Conclusion

6. 19. They are to pray also for him: "that I may open my mouth with confidence": this may refer either to the preaching he was doing to his visitors, or else to the trial which was to end his present imprisonment, the trial before the Emperor for which he had appealed at Caesarea and been brought to Rome.

6. 21. Tychicus, the messenger, who also carried the letter to Colossae (Col. 4. 7, almost identical words) and accompanied Onesimus (Col. 4. 9) who carried the letter to his master Philemon (Philem. 12 and 17).

6. 23–24. The Epistle ends with a general salutation to the brethren.

(32)   THE EPISTLE TO THE COLOSSIANS

A. Time and place. All this has been studied for the contemporary Epistles to the Ephesians and Philemon. The letter was written from Paul's Roman Captivity A.D. 58–60.

B. To whom? Colossae (Κολοσσαί in Greek, though Rh has "Colossa" and AV "Colosse") was on the main road eastwards about 150 miles from Ephesus. Laodicea, about eleven miles nearer Ephesus, but in the same valley of the Lycus, had already grown to be a more important city, and apparently the Christian community there was stronger, since in Apoc. 2 and 3 it is among the "Seven Churches", and Colossae is not. The probable reason why the Colossians got a letter of their own is that Paul was writing there anyway, about Onesimus. The Encyclical (Ephesians) would, of course, reach Laodicea first, and the Colossians are bidden to get it from them when it arrives: meanwhile they are to let the Laodiceans see the letter he wrote to them (Col. 4. 16).

It appears that Paul had never been to Colossae or Laodicea himself, which "have not seen my face in the flesh" (Col. 2. 1), but he cares very much about them. Their own preacher had been Epaphras, who was at the moment in Rome and had told Paul all about affairs at Colossae (1. 7–8, 4. 12–13). He had worked also at Laodicea and at Hierapolis (about ten miles further on from Laodicea) (4. 13). The fact that Epaphras had been to see Paul in prison was, of course, another reason for Paul to write. Philemon of Colossae, however, seems to be a convert of Paul's: "Thou owest me thy ownself also" (Philem. 19), perhaps at Ephesus.

For the greetings sent in this Epistle, see on Philem. 23–24. In Col. we have the addition at the Asian end of Nymphas, and at the Roman end of Mark and a certain Jesus Justus.

Little is known of the Church of Colossae. They obviously met at the house of Philemon (Philem. 2). The Martyrology tells us that Philemon and Appia were killed by pagans who invaded their assembly when all the rest of the congregation had fled (Nov. 22nd), and that Epaphras was appointed by St Paul as Bishop of Colossae, and eventually died there, a martyr (July 19th).

C. Argument. The teaching of Col. is an application of that of Eph. to certain particular matters. Epaphras had evidently told Paul of the difficulties at Colossae, and so Paul writes to them the thoughts that are in his mind, with special remarks for their assistance. The principles involved are those expounded in Ephesians.

Address (1. 1–3)

Preamble (1. 3–14)

> "We give thanks . . . hearing of your faith . . . as you learned of Epaphras" (vv. 3–7). "We pray . . . that you may walk worthy of God" (vv. 9–10), "who hath translated us into the Kingdom of the Son of his love" (v. 13).

I. Christ (1. 15–3. 4)

   (i) He is the image of God (1. 15), the Head of the Mystical Body (1. 18), he has reconciled us (1. 20) (1. 15–23).

   (ii) Paul is his minister (1. 24–2. 6).

   (iii) Life in Christ: "rooted and built up in him" (2. 7), "buried with him and risen again" (2. 12, 20; 3. 1). Christ has overcome the things of this world, be they pagan mystery-cults (2. 15, 18) or the claims of the Jewish Law (2. 16): wherefore "quae sursum sunt sapite, non quae super terram"[1] (3. 2) (2. 7–3. 4)

II. The Christian Life (3. 5–4. 6) (cf. Eph. 4. 29–6. 9)

   (i) Vices to be renounced (3. 5–17).

[1] Epistle for Holy Saturday.

G2

   (ii) The Christian home (wives, husbands, children, fathers, servants, masters) (3. 18–4. 1)

   (iii) Prayer (4. 2–6).

Concluding messages (4. 7–18).

Certain phrases to be noted. (Note that many phrases are identical with those of Eph., but we specially note those proper to Col.)

1. 15. Christ is "the *image* of the invisible God": the point about an image is likeness, and a son is "the image of his father" especially in so far as he partakes of the same (human) nature. So in God, God the Son has the same (divine) nature as God the Father, and can therefore quite correctly be called his "image" (St Thomas I 35. 1). We have in these verses some of St Paul's most developed theology about Christ. This verse is really an affirmation of Christ's divine nature.[1] Further, the invisible Godhead is manifested to us in the Son of God, his image.

1. 16–17. "*In him* were all things created": cf. Jn. 1. 3, "All things were made through him (the Word)" (USA), and Heb. 1. 2–3, ". . . His Son . . . by whom also he made the world". And in the Creed we say, "Per quem omnia facta sunt": for God created the world through his wisdom, his thought, his Word, his λόγος (St Thomas I 45. 6).

1. 18. "He is *the Head* of the Body, the Church", cf. Eph. 1. 22–23.

1. 20. Through him God has "*reconciled*" all things to himself. Cf. Rom. 5. 10. These four points are the main elements in a complete Christology.

1. 24. A difficult verse: Paul's own sufferings "fill up those things that are wanting of the sufferings of Christ." Since all Christians are members of the Mystical Body of Christ, their sufferings are identified with Christ's sufferings, and "I fill

[1] Bishop Lightfoot, in his elaborate note on this passage, remarks that already Philo (cf. Hist. Intro. *f*, p. 34) used the word "image" of the λόγος of God.

up", i.e. "I add my measure" (St Thomas's commentary). This is the usual interpretation, and any suggestion is avoided that Christ's own sacrifice is not all-sufficient to redeem the world, which would be a blasphemy. The whole Christian ascetical tradition has held to the value of suffering and of mortification when these sufferings are united to those of Christ, so that by them we are able, in a sense, to share in the sufferings of Christ. Ordinary human experience shows us that the pain of someone we love gives rise in us of a desire to have their pain, not, of course, that we can thereby physically alleviate their suffering, but spiritually we can thereby share the burden and so bring consolation to the sufferer. In this very phrase Paul shows how great a lover he was of the Suffering Christ.

2. 14. "Blotting out the handwriting", i.e. the evidence of our sin, or else the now abolished document of the Mosaic Law, "fastening it to the Cross", thus "cancelling" it (USA, RAK). This may be a metaphor taken from the Roman military practice of hanging the "trophies" taken from the vanquished on a cross-like pole. Christ, by the Sacrifice of the Cross, has blotted out our sins, so that we become truly just (justified) and not merely accounted so (see note on Rom. 5. 1–11).

2. 15. Christ has overcome the things of this world: the "principalities and powers", which probably refer to pagan mystery-cults with their beliefs in various hidden powers in nature, or to the intermediate beings or Aeons of the Platonic system (cf. on Philo, p. 35), which were by many Jews of the time identified with angels. These are referred to in v. 18.

2. 18. False religions which venerate such beings, and which are based upon the "mind of the flesh", i.e. purely "human speculation" (RAK).

2. 20–21. "Through your unity with Christ you have already died to the elemental crudities of this world. Why then do you lay down pettifogging rules for yourselves as if

you were still living for this world, such as 'Touch not! Taste not! Handle not!' " (Wand).

3. 11. The only mention in the New Testament of Scythia, as of typical barbarians. Scythia lay north of the Black Sea.

4. 10 sq. Aristarchus (who may be the same one who in Acts 20. 4 set off with Paul from Greece towards Palestine, a Thessalonian), Mark (cousin of Barnabas) and the unknown Jesus Justus are all "of the circumcision", i.e. Jews (v. 11). From which it is sometimes inferred that those in vv. 12–14 were Gentiles: Epaphras (of Colossae), Luke, the evangelist, and Demas. This is some support for the opinion that St Luke was a Gentile.

THE EPISTLE TO THE
PHILIPPIANS

A. Time and place. From the Roman Captivity of St Paul A.D. 58–60, either before or after the group of Epistles Eph., Col., Philem., dispatched together to Asia Minor with Tychicus (see Intro. to Eph.). We are placing it after, in view of 2. 23–24 (see note).

B. To whom? The Church of Philippi was founded by St Paul on his II Journey, in A.D. 50. He arrived in Macedonia and went straight to Philippi from Troas, in company with Silas (Silvanus), Timothy (since Lystra), and Luke (since Troas). He had come in answer to the request made to him in a dream while at Troas. The party stayed there "some days". (All this is in Acts 16. 8–12.) They stayed with a lady called Lydia, after her conversion. At Philippi occurred the incident of the girl with the "pythonical spirit" who was cured by Paul, whereat her masters "seeing that the hope of their gain was gone" reported the matter to the authorities. A riot ensued and Paul and Silas were put in prison. Paul wrote shortly afterwards (I Thess. 2. 2) that they were "shamefully treated". At midnight there was a miraculous earthquake, which freed the prisoners and converted the gaoler. But Paul and Silas did not run away: on the contrary they demanded an explanation of the "magistrates" (i.e. the officers in charge of the Roman colony) for the treatment that had been (quite illegally) given to men that were Roman citizens. The officers had to come in person and bring them out of the prison with apologies. They returned to Lydia's house, but then thought it wiser to leave the city. (The story is beautifully told, at length, in Acts 16. 13–37). Luke stayed behind, for he ceases here to use "We".

St Paul's next and last visit to Philippi was about five years later on the return journey from Greece to Palestine (III Journey). Because of a plot against him, discovered in time, he decided not to sail straight to Palestine, but to go overland as far as Philippi, and sail from there (Acts 20. 3–6). At Philippi Luke joined him again ("We sailed", v. 6). It does not seem to have been a long visit this time. This was round Easter ("the azymes") A.D. 55.

So now Paul was writing to the Philippians about nine years after his first visit, and about four years after his last visit. The Epistle shows him to be on very affectionate terms with them. Philippi is the oldest foundation among the individual Churches to which St Paul addresses an Epistle.

C. Argument. In contrast to the other Epistles of the Captivity, Phil. has a strong personal note. Not only does Paul speak much of himself and his correspondents, but also of several people by name. More, perhaps, than any other Epistle (in proportion to its length), Phil. is concerned with practical affairs and personal news.

Address (1. 1–2). "Paul and Timothy."
Preamble (1. 3–11).
He gives thanks, and prays for them. He expresses his gratitude for their help "from the first day till now" (1. 5), i.e. remembering his early ministry among

them. He prays especially that they may grow in the
love of God (1. 9).

I. News of himself (1. 12–26).

His imprisonment, but the progress of the Gospel in
Rome: everything has "fallen out to the furtherance
of the Gospel" (1. 12). He is still uncertain of his fate
(1. 20, cf. 2. 23–24), but has a hope of acquittal (2. 24).
He hardly knows which to hope for: death ("to be dissolved and to be with Christ", 1. 23), or life, to continue working for them.

II. Exhortation to Unity and Humility (1. 27–2. 18).
  (i) "Be of one mind" (1. 27–2. 2).
 (ii) Let everything be done in humility, with the ex-
      ample of Christ's humility before us (2. 3–15).
(iii) This will show me that my labours have not been in
      vain (2. 16–18).

Digression (prompted by the mention of himself) (2. 19–
30).

He proposes to send Timothy to them, whom they
know well, for he was with Paul on both his visits to
Philippi (Acts 16. 1–2, 12; 20. 4–6), and Paul cannot
think of anybody who could be better (2. 20).

But now he is sending back Epaphroditus ("your
apostle", 2. 25), who had brought gifts to Paul from
Philippi (2. 25 and 4. 18). He had been dangerously
ill during his stay in Rome, but he recovered and has
been so useful to Paul (2. 27–30).

III. Warning against false teachers, apparently Judaizers
(c. 3).

Far from Judaizing, we Christians are the true circumcision "who in spirit serve God" (3. 3, cf. Rom. 2. 29,
"circumcision is that of the heart").

Digression on this point: if there is any glorying in being
a Jew to be done, Paul is able to glory as well as any-

one (cf. II Cor. 11. 2, "They are Hebrews: so am I, etc.") (3. 4–6).

Further Digression: it is not the Law which justifies, but the knowledge of Jesus Christ (cf. Eph. 1. 17, and of course for the whole argument cf. Rom. 5–8 and Gal. 2. 15 sq.); the important thing is therefore (3. 14) to "press towards the mark, to the prize of the supernal vocation of God in Christ Jesus". (3. 7–16).

The warning is now continued against the "enemies of the Cross of Christ" (3. 17–21).

IV. Again he urges Unity (4. 1–9).

  (i) There were apparently quarrels among some of the ladies of the parish: "I beg of Evodia, and I beseech Syntyche, to be of one mind in the Lord" (4. 2). These things, presumably reported by Epaphroditus, will, he hopes, be put straight by him on his return (the "sincere companion" is probably Epaphroditus himself) (4. 1–3).

  (ii) The fruits of this unity will be joy (4. 4) and "the peace of God, which surpasseth all understanding" (4. 7).

  (iii) They are to hold to the doctrine which he taught them (4. 8–9).

V. He thanks them for their kindness (4. 10–20).

It has made him so happy to hear from them again; not that they had forgotten him, but they "were busied" (4. 10). He is not in want, for they so often had looked after him in the past, and now, through Epaphroditus, once again.

Concluding greetings.

Some texts to be noted. (Since Phil. is principally occupied with moral advice, there are few passages of doctrinal importance, apart from the "kenotic" passage in 2. 6–8.)

1. 1. This Epistle alone includes the "bishops" in its

address. The original meaning of the word ἐπίσκοπος is, of course, an "overseer" (from ἐπί over, and σκοπέω look), which came to be used of a bishop (and the English word is simply a corruption of the Greek). The meaning here is almost certainly the more elementary one of an "overseer" or person in charge in the Church. The same thing should be said of men who were "bishops" at Ephesus in Paul's speech in Acts 20. 28.

1. 8. The "bowels" as the seat of the emotions. It was a phrase of Paul's at this period, occurring no less than three times in Philemon (vv. 7, 12 and 20).

1. 13. The passage about the "praetorium", a fairly sure indication that the letter was written in Rome (see Intro. to Philem., p. 53).

1. 16. "I am set for the defence of the Gospel": κεῖμαι, lit. "I lie", used similarly in I Thess. 3. 3 where it is translated "I am appointed" (as USA does here). RAK: "I am here to defend the Gospel."

1. 21-22. His dilemma: "to live is Christ, and to die is gain." "But what if living on in this mortal body is the only way to harvest what I have sown?" (RAK).

2. 6-8. The famous "kenotic" passage, so called from St Paul's use of the word ἐκένωσε "he emptied" himself. It is a famous difficult passage, chiefly because it has been misinterpreted by heretical writers both of antiquity and of the present time.

First of all let us observe that our Rheims-Challoner text represents very accurately the Greek. We will take the phrases in this passage in order: (i) *Being in the form of God:* for the Greek philosophers the "form" means what a thing *is,* hence its "nature". We saw in Col. 1. 15 how St Paul insists on Christ's divine nature: "consubstantialem Patri, of the same nature as the Father" as we say in the Credo. (ii) *Thought it not robbery to be equal with God:* i.e. being of the same (divine) nature, claimed equality in divinity with

God the Father, as a right and not a robbery. This shows the Vulgate interpretation; but the Greek may equally be translated "thought it not a thing-to-be-clung-to" (rather than a thing robbed), which is the rendering of USA (and the meaning reflected in WV and RAK). This latter translation emphasises Christ's humility, which is the context of the passage (an exhortation to humility, imitating Christ's humility). (iii) *But emptied himself:* Vulgate literally "semetipsum exinanivit", which the old Rheims (of 1582), maintaining that this is a theological technical term, translated "exinanited himself". Many heretics (beginning with the Arians in the fourth century) held that the incarnate Christ is not "of the same (divine) nature as the Father", and interpreted this passage in that way. But of course the *kenosis* or "emptying", in view of Christ's Divinity, can only mean that he stripped himself, not of his divine nature (for no one can strip himself of what he *is*), but of the rights of that nature, i.e. divine honour.[1] The whole passage turns on the fact of the two natures, divine and human, in Christ, affirmed at the Council of Chalcedon in 451. At the Incarnation Christ assumed human nature, without emptying himself of divine nature. (iv) *Taking the form of a servant:* human nature, as distinct from the nature or "form of God" of v. 6. (v) *In likeness . . . and in habit (or appearance) of a man:* because Christ *was* a man (having human nature), he had the appearance of a man. It is a false exegesis to suppose that his humanity was only apparent and not real (the oldest heresy of all, of the Docetists). On the contrary: "Blessed be Jesus Christ, true God and true Man."

2. 17. Even if Paul is not acquitted at the coming trial, and has to die, let it be an occasion of congratulation.

2. 23–24. Yet he expects soon to know the verdict, and has a reasonable hope of a good one, "that I myself shall come to

[1] For full treatment of this matter, and of the heretical doctrines, see Prat, I, 316 sq.

you shortly." This perhaps points to the latter part of the two years' imprisonment awaiting trial at the Emperor's court, and is a reason for placing Philippians last among the Epistles of the Captivity.

3. 2. The "concision", of the Judaizers, i.e. those who cut; St Paul deliberately reserves the word "circumcision" for the "spiritual Israel" in the next verse (WV note).

3. 8. The famous verse: "I count all things (including the Old Law, and all human institutions) to be but loss, for the excellent knowledge of Jesus Christ my Lord."

3. 11–14. Paul's hope of the future glory of heaven, but "not as though I had already attained, or were already perfect".

3. 20. "Our citizenship is in heaven" (USA). See note on this word on Eph. 2. 12.

4. 3. The "sincere companion" is unidentified, unless it be Epaphroditus, the bearer of the letter, who would be there when it is read. Clement, the third successor of Peter as Bishop of Rome, is mentioned only here in the New Testament.

4. 4. "Rejoice in the Lord always": the text for the Introit of the 3rd Sunday of Advent, whence its name "Gaudete Sunday". The passage has been fortunate in its musical settings, for the plainsong of this Sunday is particularly beautiful, and one of Purcell's loveliest anthems begins with these words.

4. 5. "The Lord is nigh": this is probably no more than a common exclamation among the early Christians, cf. "Maran atha" with similar meaning at the end of I Cor. (16. 22). (See RAK's note.)

4. 10. I quite understand that you could not write before, for "you were busied", Vulgate "occupati autem eratis". But the Greek means literally "you had no time", or opportunity. So Dr Wand, "But there was nothing you could do."

4. 22. "Caesar's household": usually regarded as an indication that the letter was written from Rome (see Intro. to Philem. and Eph.).

Note. From the "Epistles of the Captivity" we pass into a new period in St Paul's Epistles, that of the "Pastoral Epistles". These are characterized by being written to a single person, and by having a quite definite common theme, the exposition of the duties of a Bishop. The vocabulary of the Pastorals is also quite distinctive, as indeed was that of the Captivity-period distinct from that of the Missionary Epistles.[1] Of the three Pastorals, two (I Tim. and Titus) were probably written during the period of liberty after Paul's acquittal in 60, and the other (II Tim.) during his last captivity.

Period of Liberty: I Tim., Titus, Hebrews

(33)   THE FIRST EPISTLE TO TIMOTHY

A. Time and place. There is no precise indication in the text of the time and place of the writing of either *I Tim.* or *Titus.* But it is possible to infer certain things. (i) It is not possible that they were written during the missionary journeys, for on the occasion that Paul left Ephesus for Macedonia (Acts 20. 1), far from leaving Timothy at Ephesus (as he says, I Tim. 1. 3: "I desired thee to remain at Ephesus, when I went into Macedonia"), on the contrary he sent him to Corinth ahead of himself (I Cor. 4. 17); and further, Timothy is with Paul when he writes II Cor. (1. 1), and Rom. (16. 21) and on the return journey (Acts 20. 4). Similarly, there is no place on the missionary journeys for a visit to Crete (Tit. 1. 5) or to Nicopolis (Tit. 3. 12). Therefore, some other period of St Paul's life must be sought. (ii) This period cannot be the Captivity Period 58–60, for this followed immediately on the missionary period, and the remarks about proposed travels, in I Tim. 3. 14, "Hoping that I shall come to thee shortly," 4. 13, "Till I come," and Tit. 3. 12, "Make haste to come unto Nicopolis, for there I have determined to winter," are remarks not of a prisoner merely with some hope of release (as for instance, Phil. 2. 23–24 and Philem. 22), but of a free man making definite plans. (iii) Therefore we are left with the supposition that they were written after Paul's

---

[1] Particularly good on the teaching and vocabulary of the Pastorals is the chapter in Pope, V, 218 sq.

acquittal about A.D. 60, when he had resumed his travels.[1]
It is generally believed that he was arrested again about the
year 65 after the First Persecution had broken out.

It is possible that I Tim. 1. 3, "I went into Macedonia,"
refers to a recent move, and therefore that Paul had only just
left Timothy at Ephesus. In this case the Epistle might have
been written from Macedonia. But there is no closer indication. There is no indication at all in Titus.

The Authenticity of the Pastorals (I–II Tim. and Titus).[2]
Apart from a few early heretics (such as Marcion), the whole
tradition of the Church has always accepted the Pastorals as
genuine Epistles of St Paul. It was only in the early nineteenth century that some non-Catholics began to cast doubts
on the fact, and the opinion gathered weight outside the
Church either that they were documents written about a
century later, or, at best, collections of fragments of Pauline
writings. The Pontifical Biblical Commission[3] in 1913 considered it worth while making a declaration on their authenticity, i.e. that they are true Epistles of St Paul. There have,
of course, been attacks on the genuineness of other Epistles
of St Paul, but none apart from this one and that on Hebrews
have been considered of sufficient importance to warrant a
declaration on the subject. For this reason we have not in
this book even bothered to mention them.

[1] The tradition is strong that after his acquittal Paul visited Spain (as he
had hoped in Rom. 15. 24). Pope Clement, writing to Corinth in about
A.D. 96, says (I, 5) that "he came also to the bounds of the West", i.e.
further west than Rome, and the Muratorian Fragment (c. 200) says so
plainly.
[2] Excellent in Pope, V, 220 sq., which we follow here.
[3] The Biblical Commission is a committee set up by Pope Leo XIII in
1903, which is (i) to guide biblical studies among Catholics, (ii) to defend
(when necessary) the authority of the sacred Books, and (iii) to give (where
necessary) a true Catholic interpretation of a difficult passage. The decrees
of the commission are intended for the guidance of the faithful, and especially to prevent the teaching of error. The fifteenth such decree was issued
in 1943. The commission is composed of "Consultors", who are Catholic
scholars from all over the world. Mgr Barton represents England on the
commission.

The doubts were raised on four points: (i) They cannot be fitted into the life of St Paul as given in the Acts. This is obvious, and has been discussed above. (ii) The vocabulary is different. But so is that of the Epistles of the Captivity, and the subject-matter is new, and certain typically Pauline words recur. (iii) The heresies referred to in the Pastorals, it is claimed, suggest a later age. If this is so, it only shows how far back their roots go, but the heresy of the Judaizers, familiar to St Paul, seems to show itself again here. (iv) The position of the Bishop shows a later development of the idea of the hierarchy. This is indeed true, and only goes to show that the hierarchy as understood by St Ignatius of Antioch (A.D. 107) goes right back to Apostolic times.[1]

The decrees of the Biblical Commission on the matter may be summarised as follows:[2]

I. In view of tradition should it be held that the Pastorals are genuine letters of St Paul?   YES.

II. Has the "fragmentary theory" weakened this position?   NO.

III. Have the doubts (outlined above) weakened it?   NO.

IV. Can we safely affirm that the Pastorals were written between Paul's liberation from his first captivity, and his death?   YES.

B. To whom? Timothy was described by Fr Hugh Pope[3] as "the greatest of the secondary characters of the New Testament story". He was the son of a Gentile father, and had a Jewish mother and grandmother named Eunice and Lois (II Tim. 1. 5), at Lystra, where he was picked up by St Paul on the II Journey (Acts 16. 1–3), and remained his constant companion for many years, as we have seen. He joined Paul in writing many of the Epistles, and was with Paul during his

---

[1] See last chapter in *The Church in the NT*, Vol. IV of this series.

[2] The full text may be read in Pope, V, 227–8, and the Latin original in I, 336–7.

[3] V, 235.

first Roman captivity, as the titles of Phil., Col. and Philemon
show. He was appointed by Paul as Bishop of Ephesus, having
been ordained by Paul himself (II Tim. 1. 6, "by the imposition of my hands"). More than once he was sent on a mission
by St Paul (I Cor. 4. 17 and Phil. 2. 19, where he receives the
highest commendation). That he was among Paul's dearest
friends is frequently evident, but especially in II Tim. That
he was the first Bishop of Ephesus is given by Eusebius
(III, 4) as a recorded fact. The Martyrology for January 24th
records his martyrdom by stoning at Ephesus.

C. Argument. The Epistle is so much like an ordinary
letter, in which one topic leads easily to another, with natural
digressions and casual remarks; it has nothing of the nature
of a theological treatise. The following plan, therefore,
merely outlines the general argument.

I. Timothy's work at Ephesus (c. 1).

> The main thing is the Love of God (1. 5), he is
> to avoid unsound teaching ("fables and genealo-
> gies" 1. 4, "vain babblings" 1. 6), chiefly appar-
> ently with reference to Judaizers.
>
> (*Digression* on thanksgiving for his own ministry,
> 1. 12–17).

II. Practical directions (c. 2).

> The first thing is Prayer (2. 1–8).
> A special note about women in church, cf. I Cor.
> 11. 1–16 (2. 9–15).

III. The Episcopate and Diaconate (c. 3).

> (*Digression* on his proposed visit, 3. 14–16).

IV. Warnings against heretics (4. 1–11).

> Especially occult worship (4. 1) and false asceti-
> cism, which is strongly discouraged "for every
> creature of God is good . . . sanctified by the word
> of God and prayer" (4. 3–11).

V. Personal advice (4. 12 to 6. 16).
         For his own life and for guiding others, old and
    young, widows, priests, servants.

    P.S. 6. 17–21. On guiding the rich, and at the end a sum-
mary: "O Timothy, keep that which is committed to thy
trust . . . avoiding knowledge falsely so called."

Some texts to be noted:

    1. 4. "Genealogies": a speciality of the Jews!
    1. 15, 3. 1, 4. 9. "A faithful saying": the phrase is proper to
the Pastorals, occurring again in Tit. 3. 8 and II Tim. 2. 11.
Does it refer to a current saying, or is Paul merely emphasising a remark of his own?
    1. 17. This beautiful doxology after Paul's thanksgiving
to God for what he has been enabled to do himself is well
known to all the clergy, who recite it almost daily at Prime
(Capitulum).
    1. 20. The excommunication: "I have delivered up to
Satan", cf. I Cor. 5. 5 (where see note).
    2. 7. "Doctor Gentium": Paul's own title for himself,
which has become so famous.
    4. 8. "Bodily exercise" (Greek "gymnasia") means rather
"bodily training" (WV, USA), i.e. an asceticism which
dwells on corporal mortification, which is "profitable to
little" compared to the training of the spirit in piety. But we
know St Paul's ideas on the true asceticism and discipline of
the body from I Cor. 9. 27, "I chastise my body and bring it
into subjection, etc.," and his idea in Col. 1. 24 of "filling up
the sufferings of Christ".
    4. 12. It was not more than about fifteen years ago (per-
haps less) that Timothy first joined Paul in A.D. 49 (Acts
16. 1), and his father and mother were still alive then. He
must have been quite young then, if he is still young now in
A.D. 60–65. Paul, now aged about 60–65, is clearly writing to

a young man, as his manner also shows. He calls him often "my son".

4. 14. The grace of the priesthood. He returns to this in II Tim. 1. 6. "Don't forget to use the grace you actually possess, which was given to you, when, after consulting the prophets, the presbyters laid their hands upon your head" (Wand).

5. 23. Among points of personal advice, Paul recommends moderation in ascetic practices: "You need no longer be a total abstainer" (Wand), a rendering which suggests the simplicity of the Greek.

6. 10. "The desire of money is the root of all evils."

THE EPISTLE TO TITUS

A. Time and place. As for I Tim.

B. To whom? Titus was "left in Crete" by Paul, presumably on some visit there after his acquittal. We first hear of him being taken by Paul to Jerusalem as a living example of Paul's work among the Gentiles (Gal. 2. 1–3). If this visit is to be identified with the Council of Jerusalem, it would be in the year 49 (about fifteen years before this Epistle). We then next hear of him as an emissary of Paul to Corinth (II Cor. 2. 13), when Paul had hoped to meet him at Troas, but, failing to do so, had happily found him in Macedonia with the good report from Corinth (II Cor. 7. 5–7). He then sent him on a further mission to Corinth (II Cor. 8. 16).[1] He was obviously a person in whom Paul placed great trust, and for whom he felt great affecton (as the mentions of him in II Cor. and Titus show). The New Testament is otherwise silent about him, except for the final reference in II Tim. 4. 10. The opinion that he was Luke's own brother is mentioned in the note on II Cor. 8. 18–19 (and see also Intro. to II Cor.,

---

[1] If II Cor. 12. 18 belongs to the "stern Epistle" (see p. 124), then it would indicate yet another mission to Corinth.

p. 118*n.*), with the possible explanation thereby of the silence of Acts.[1]

Of his work in Crete nothing is known apart from this Epistle, but his death and burial are recorded in the Martyrology for January 4th. Yet he seems to have been away for a period, for Paul asks him (Tit. 3. 12) to meet him at Nicopolis,[2] which presumably he did. That journey can be linked with the news, written about two or three years later, in II Tim. 4. 10, that Titus had gone into Dalmatia, for Nicopolis on the Adriatic is not far from the province of Dalmatia, and such an extension of the journey is quite likely.

C. Argument. The teaching of this short Epistle is very similar to that of I Tim.

The Address is longer (1. 1–4).

Titus' work in Crete (1. 5 to 3. 11).

> Priests are to be ordained (1. 5), heresies are to be avoided, especially Judaizing (1. 10–16 and 3. 9–11), people are to be guided wisely (c. 2 and 3. 1–8).

Practical matters in conclusion (3. 12–15).

Some texts.

1. 7. Among the qualities of a Bishop is that he should not be "greedy of filthy lucre", a famous phrase that comes into all the old English versions, but has disappeared from the modern (cf. I Tim. 6. 10).

1. 10 and 14 show the Judaizing tendencies, which were still causing trouble. 3. 9 mentions "genealogies" as in I Tim. 1. 4.

1. 15. "All things are clean to the clean": another famous phrase, the context, however, of which is of Jewish ceremonial uncleanness, etc., in the matter of food, cf. I Tim. 4. 4, "Every creature is good".

2. 13–14. Eternal life through Christ's Redemption.

[1] Pope, V, 241–2.
[2] See Geographical Intro., p. 8.

3. 3–7. Through Christ we are "justified" (cf. Romans 5–8), and not through our own "works of justice" (see note on Rom. 5. 1–11, pp. 140–2, on the theology of justification). "The laver of regeneration": Baptism.

3. 8. "A faithful saying": cf. I Tim. 1. 15.

3. 13. "Send forward Zenas and Apollo": lit. "send on", USA "help them on their way", which suggests that they visited Crete on their way somewhere else, and were perhaps the bearers of this Epistle.

(34–36)   THE EPISTLE TO THE HEBREWS

A. Time and place. This Epistle, having no initial address (except the traditional title), no autobiographical observations (apart from 13. 19, "That I may be restored to you the sooner"), no mention of people by name (except 13. 23, "Know ye that our brother Timothy is set at liberty: with whom [if he come shortly] I will see you"), and no place-names (apart from the enigmatic "The brethren from Italy salute you" in 13. 24), gives us hardly any clue to when or where it was written. If we knew when or where Timothy was ever in prison, it would be helpful. But it seems clear that until the end of Paul's first captivity in Rome, and when he receives I and II Tim., Timothy is a free man. Then Paul indeed speaks of travels, and so presumably he is a free man himself; although it may only be the hope of a prisoner, and indeed some of the ancient codices (notably ℵ, the oldest of all) have τοῖς δεσμοῖς μου in 10. 34, i.e. "you had compassion on *my bands*" (in place of τοῖς δεσμίοις "the prisoners"), though again this may refer to the past.

So there is only room for conjecture, and the most usual supposition is that the Epistle was written (like the Pastorals) during the years of liberty following Paul's acquittal in A.D. 60, when he was a free man, and travelled again, and that Timothy had some spell of imprisonment during that period.

This period is further suggested by the fact of persecution troubling the readers: 10. 34, "Being stripped of your own goods"; 12. 11, "Chastisement for the present"; 13. 3, "Remember them that are in bands." Now in Palestine there were some anti-Christian riots in A.D. 62, between the death of the procurator Festus and the arrival of his successor Albinus, in the course of which James the Less was killed by the Jews (Eusebius, III, 23 and Josephus, *Ant.*, XX, 9, 1). And in Rome in A.D. 64 the First Persecution broke out under Nero.

B. To whom? The title "to the Hebrews" was known from the beginning, but the meaning is not precise. From the argument of the Epistle it is clear that Christians of Jewish race are intended. The only indication of place is the phrase in 13. 24, "The brethren from (ἀπό) Italy salute you," and this can of course be interpreted in opposite ways: either "the people here, i.e. Italy, send greetings to you, who are elsewhere", or "the Italians resident here, in this place, send their greetings to you who are in their homeland, i.e. Italy". The other place is usually presumed to be Palestine. The interpretation that it is written from Italy to Palestine is supported by the frequent mention of temple-ritual and sacrifices, while the known presence of Italian detachments in Palestine, such as the "cohors italica" to which Cornelius belonged (Acts 10. 1), supports the view that the letter was written to Italy from elsewhere, perhaps Palestine. Opinion is divided: there is evidence for persecution in both places, but since the letter is written to an exclusively Jewish-Christian community, such as was to be found perhaps only at Jerusalem, the view that it was written from Italy to Jerusalem has the greater probability. But the matter must remain uncertain.

The Literary Problem. (i) The Question of Canonicity. The earliest Ecclesiastical writers, such as Clement of Rome A.D. 96 (*Ep. to the Corinthians*, 36. 2–5), the Pastor of Hermas A.D. *c.* 150 (Vis. II, 3, 2; III, 7, 2) and Justin (*Apol.*, I, 63, *Dialogue*, 33), all witness to the canonicity of Heb. The Chester Beatty Papyrus (P. 46) of *c.* A.D. 200 includes Heb.

Between A.D. 200 and 400, however, although the whole of the East remained firm, the Epistle came to be rejected in the West and especially at Rome itself, so that Eusebius, writing in A.D. 311–325, tells us that Caius, a learned man in Rome (*c.* 210), mentions "only thirteen Epistles, not reckoning that to the Hebrews with the rest; as there are, even to this day, some of the Romans who do not consider it to be the work of the apostles" (VI, 20). The Muratorian Fragment (*c.* 200 in Rome) does not list Heb. among the Epistles. The reason for these doubts is probably to be found in the misuse of certain passages (especially Heb. 6. 4–8 on penance) by heretics (especially the Novatians in the third century).[1]

But the Decree of Pope Damasus in A.D. 382 (Denz., 84) lists Heb. with the Epistles of St Paul. This is the first official "Canon" or list of the Books of the Bible. But there is still a sign of the old hesitation in the list drawn up by the Council of Carthage in 397 (Denz., 92), which reads "Pauli Apostoli epistolae tredecim, ejusdem ad Hebraeos una".

(*ii*) *Doubts about Authorship.* Some early writers, again in the West, while accepting the canonicity of Hebrews, denied that it was by St Paul, or, at any rate, mentioned it unconnected with the Pauline Epistles. (For instance, Tertullian in *De Pudicitia* 20, *c.* A.D. 220.) Eusebius says that "it was disputed, as not being one of St Paul's Epistles" (III, 3), and St Jerome, writing in A.D. 392, states of this Epistle that "even today among the Romans it is not regarded as being by St Paul" (*De Viris Illustribus*, 59). The Greek writers, on the other hand, remained firm in the opinion that it was by St Paul.[1]

---

[1] Many more details and references to these sections in the notes on Hebrews, in Pope, V, Prat, I, 473 sq., and Höpfl, *Introductionis Compendium*, III.

(*iii*) *The reasons for these hesitations.* Apart from the matter of misuse by Western heretics, there remains the fact that Hebrews differs from the other Epistles of St Paul in several important respects: (i) the customary inscription with Paul's name is absent, (ii) various familiar features (see under *A.*) are all but absent, (iii) the style is notably different and many usual phrases of Paul are absent, and there are 140 words in Heb. not found elsewhere in the NT. Further, the syntax of Heb. is very exact, while we know well Paul's usual manner of breaking off sentences and arguments with parentheses and digressions, (iv) the manner of quoting Scripture with the phrase "He saith" or something similar (e.g. 1.5, 6, 7, 13) is foreign to St Paul's usual style (e.g. often in Rom., "It is written," or something precise such as, "Isaias saith, Moses saith," etc.). The phrase in Heb. is rabbinic.

(*iv*) *The proposed Solutions* (already outlined in the Introduction to the Epistles, pp. 47–8). There are three main views:

(1) Heb. is not by St Paul at all. This opinion was, as we have seen, already found in the third to fourth centuries. The Epistle was ascribed to Barnabas (by Tertullian), Clement of Rome, or even Luke (see Eusebius, VI, 25). But few of these doubts persisted beyond the year 400. The view, however, is very common among non-Catholics today that the author is quite unknown.

(2) The ideas of the Epistle are Paul's, but they were "written up" by someone else, unknown, which accounts for the different style and diction. This was first proposed by Origen (†254/5), quoted in Eusebius, VI, 25. This is the commonest view among Catholics.

(3) "It may well be that Paul . . . had written in Hebrew like a Hebrew—that is, in fluent fashion and in his own tongue. What, then, they found eloquently written in Hebrew they translated still more eloquently into Greek. This, therefore, may have been the reason why this Epistle seems to differ from the rest of Paul's Epistles." This was the view

of St Jerome (*De Viris Illustribus*, 5): it both safeguards the
Pauline authorship and explains the difficulties.

Hebrew was still the liturgical language of the Jews and
was the theological language of the Rabbinic schools,[1] which
Paul had attended under Gamaliel. Rabbinic Hebrew would
be as familiar to him as Ecclesiastical Latin is to those who
have studied at, for instance, the Roman colleges of today. If
the letter was written to the community at Jerusalem, it
would be a very natural medium of expression, and of course
the Roman letter-form would be absent. For the benefit of
Jewish-Christians in the rest of the Empire, it would of
course have to be translated into Greek, which would presumably have been done very early. The drawback to this
theory is the complete lack of evidence of any such process.

(*v*) *The Biblical Commission.* Decrees on this matter were
issued in 1914, in view of the current denial of Pauline
authorship. They can be summarised as follows:[2]

 I. In view of tradition is Heb. to be counted canonical
    and by Paul? YES.

 II. Do the differences in style, etc., disprove this? NO.
     Do the similarities of thought show it? YES.

 III. Need we say that they are Paul's actual words? NO
      —saving a further decision of the Church.[3]

C. Argument.[4]

Main thesis: the Superiority of the new (Christian) dis-

[1] See Hist. Intro. *e*, pp. 27 sq.
[2] Full text in Pope, V, 267–8, Latin original in I, 337–8.
[3] This is the only case of a reply of the Commission in these terms.
[4] Much of the proof of the argument of Heb. is from texts of the OT,
and a full exegesis would require a knowledge of the OT, and its exegesis, of
a depth that we can neither presuppose nor provide here. We shall therefore (contrary to custom) present the outline of the argument, without
proof, but with considerable annotations, and afterwards give "excursus"
on particular points. The special circumstances of Heb. (I think) justify
a special treatment. The divisions are based on those excellently arranged
in USA. With this plan before him, the student should be able to grasp
at a quick reading of the text the general trend of the argument. Details
can be studied later.

pensation over the old (of the Jews) (1. 1–10. 18).

For we have

I. *A superior Mediator* (Christ).

(i) Superior to the angels, i.e. to any intermediate beings between God and man: be they angels whom some were identifying with the Platonic Aeons (as Philo did, see p. 35, and cf. Col. 2. 15–18), which were intermediaries in the work of creation; or the angels by whom Rabbinic tradition supposed the Law was given to Moses (2. 2, cf. St Stephen in Acts 7. 53). In this way Paul was taking into account both the philosophical and Rabbinic outlooks among the Jews (*c.* 1–2).

(ii) Superior to Moses (who brought the Hebrews into the Promised Land, while Christ brings us to the Promised Land of Heaven) (3. 1–4. 13).

II. *A superior High Priest* (Christ), who is a priest "according to the order of Melchisedech", which means a priest that is

(i) Superior to Abraham (who was blessed by Melchisedech).

(ii) Superior to Levi (whose tribe was superseded by that of Juda, from which Jesus came) (Melchisedech was a type of Christ: his priesthood was independent of the Jewish priesthood. But see "excursus" on this) (4. 14–7. 28).

III. *A superior Covenant* (or Testament or Agreement).

(i) The Mediator of the Old Testament was Moses, minister of a tabernacle made by man, on earth.

(ii) The Mediator of the New Testament is Christ, who dwells in the true tabernacle made by God, which is Heaven itself.

(The Old Covenant, with the promise to bring the people to their homeland, was abandoned by the people, and is replaced by the New Covenant based on "better promises") (*c.* 8).

IV. *A superior Sacrifice* (the Sacrifice of Christ himself).

Christ's one, perfect Sacrifice brings eternal redemption; and replaces the many, imperfect sacrifices of the Old Law, which only brought ceremonial "cleanness". These were but a type of Christ's Sacrifice to come (9. 1–10. 18).

Running through these thoughts are the *practical moral conclusions* that are derived from them:

I. If Christ is superior to the angels, by whom the Old Law (which we observed so scrupulously) was given, how careful we should be to observe what he now commands (2. 1–5).

If Christ is superior to Moses, by whom came the promise of "rest" in the home-land, how much more should we "hasten to enter into that rest" which Christ has promised to them that believe (4. 1–11).

II. If Christ is a High Priest superior to the High Priest of the Old Law, we must guard against the danger of apostasy, as befell the Jewish people in the past. This would be "to crucify again the Son of God" (6. 4–8).

III. The New Covenant (as Jeremias said) will be written on the heart (8. 10–12).

IV. Since Christ has redeemed us by the Sacrifice of his Blood "let us draw near with a true heart in fulness of *faith* . . . let us hold fast the confession of our *hope* . . . let us provoke unto *charity*" (10. 19–25).

These verses (10. 19–25) are a *turning-point* in the argument of the Epistle and should be looked at in some detail. Verses 19–21 sum up the foregoing main thesis of the Epistle: verses 22–25 give the plan of the latter part of the Epistle, which is the moral application of the thesis.

Since we have confidence

I. to enter the Holies—the *New Covenant* (10. 19).
II. in virtue of the Blood of Christ—the *New Sacrifice*, (10. 19).
III. since Christ is the *New High Priest* (10. 21).

IV. and has given us a new way through the veil (i.e. the veil that hung before the Holy of Holies in the Jewish Tabernacle, thus dividing men from God and requiring an intermediary, the High Priest), for the place of this veil is taken by Christ's flesh, i.e. the Incarnate Christ is now the intermediary—the *New Mediator* (i.e. the living Christ, true God and true Man, is himself the "new and living way") (10. 20).

Let us draw near in the spirit

I. of *Faith* (which is the theme of the rest of c. 10, and c. 11).

II. of *Hope* (which is the theme of c. 12).

III. of *Charity* (which is the theme of c. 13) (10. 22–25).

The rest of the Epistle (10. 22–13. 17) is a *working out of these themes* of moral instruction.

I. *Faith* is necessary (as St Paul has so often shown before, especially in Romans—see note on Rom. 5. 1), and this means a "heart sprinkled" (i.e. cleansed by the Blood of Christ, as foreshadowed in the sprinkling with the blood of sacrificial victims in the OT), and a "body washed with clean water" (i.e. baptized) (10. 22).

Three motives are given for holding to the Faith, and avoiding wilful sin "after having the knowledge of the truth":

(i) God's terrible judgement on those who are unfaithful, who have refused Christ's Redemption, who have "trodden under foot the Son of God", who have "esteemed the Blood of the testament unclean" and so "offered an affront to the Spirit of grace" (10. 29). This is the horror of mortal sin, turning the back on Christ, rejecting with full knowledge his gift (10. 26–31).

(ii) The value of afflictions and persecutions received on account of the Faith: even if we are "stripped of our own

H

goods", we know that we have "a better and a lasting substance". Patience is required, "for yet a little and a very little
while, and he that is to come, will come". Apparently a
reference to the παρουσία or Second Coming of Christ (cf.
I Thess. 5 and II Thess. 2), till the unknown date of which is
but "a little time" compared to eternal life (10. 32–39).

(iii) The example of the heroes of the Old Testament: the
whole of this chapter is occupied with examples of Faith in
the Old Testament (c. 11).

II. Our *Hope* is raised, not merely by the thought of this
"cloud of witnesses" to encourage us, but by "looking on
Jesus . . . upon him that endured such opposition from sinners against himself; that you be not wearied" (12. 2–3).
Wherefore persevere, lest any be rejected (12. 1–17).

A reason is added why they should have no fear: the Old
Sinai was terrifying, but not so the New Jerusalem of Heaven,
of which Jesus is the Mediator. "See therefore that you
refuse him not that speaketh" (12. 25) (12. 18–29).

III. Let *Charity* abide in you[1] (13. 1–17).

Under this heading are included various exhortations: the
honour of marriage, avoidance of avarice, obedience, avoidance of strange doctrines; in general, "do good" (13. 16).

Once more a distinct reason is added, reminding them of
the previous teaching: our Christian altar is far superior to
that of the Jews. And as in the OT the bodies of the sacrificial
victims were burned outside the camp, so Christ consummated his sacrifice outside the city. We should go forth to
him, for we have here "no abiding city" (WV[2]), but are
looking forward to the home-land that is to come, i.e.
Heaven.

The Conclusion of the Epistle (13. 18–25).

[1] It should be noted that these are only convenient divisions: here Hope
and Charity are not theological virtues. Hope here means rather Constancy
and Perseverance, while Charity is φιλαδελφία, or Brotherly love and
kindness.
[2] This precise rendering (proper to WV) has received special popularity
through the title of Fr Bede Jarrett's book.

Excursus on special points.[1]

I. *Christ the Mediator.* This is the theme of *c.* 1–3 although the word itself does not occur until 8. 6 (and again in 9. 15 and 12. 24). St Paul himself in Gal. 3. 20 (where see note) said that a Mediator is one who stands between two. In our context, of course, it is of the intermediary between God and man. In I Tim. 2. 5 he had written (perhaps at very much the same time as Heb.): "One Mediator of God and men, the man Christ Jesus, who gave himself a redemption for all". And in Rom. 5. 10 the great passage, "When we were enemies, we were reconciled to God by the death of his Son" (cf. II Cor. 5. 19). The point is that the only perfect mediator between God and man is the Incarnate Christ, true God and true Man. The mystery of Christ's Mediation is one with the mystery of his Incarnation. Others (angels, Moses, high priests, etc.) have been mediators, but only of a very imperfect kind, since they do not partake of the two natures, and Christ became the Mediator precisely in virtue of his becoming Man for our salvation. (St Thomas III 26. 1 and 2.)

When Paul is about to speak of Christ's superiority over the angels he begins (1. 1–3) with that wonderful opening which has been likened[2] to the opening of St John's Gospel, and indeed conveys some similar ideas: the Son being "the brightness of his glory, and the figure of his substance" corresponding to "the Word was with God, and the Word was God, the same was in the beginning with God", and to the words of the Creed, "ex Patre natum ante omnia saecula". But in particular we should notice Paul's "By (διά) whom also he made the world" and John's "All things were made by (again διά "through") him, and without him was made nothing that was made" and the Creed's "Per quem omnia

---

[1] It is not possible in a school course like the present to attempt a verse by verse commentary of Hebrews, or even (as in other Epistles) to explain at least every obvious difficulty. We must content ourselves with the outline of the argument and the closer examination of certain important texts. Detailed studies of most of these points will be found in Prat, I, 367 sq.

[2] Sales, in loc.

facta sunt" (and cf. Col. 1. 16, on which see note). One element therefore of Christ's Mediation is the fact that all things were created through him, as λόγος or Wisdom of God (St Thomas I 45. 6). But even in this respect his Mediation is far superior to that of any angels, who can be no more than ministers of God in his control of the world (cf. St Thomas I 110. 1) and can in no way share in the work of creation, which belongs to God alone (St Thomas I 65. 3), whatever the Platonists believed about Aeons, or the Gnostic heretics about demi-urges, etc. But this notion of Creation through the Son, although here deliberately mentioned by St Paul, is not included in the meaning of Christ's Mediation as a theological technical term, which refers to his redemptive work only.

Note. In what sense do we say that the Blessed Virgin Mary is Mediatrix?[1] Principally in virtue of her free consent to become the Mother of God and thus to co-operate essentially in the redemptive work of Christ the one Mediator; and, further, in so far as she was made by Christ to be the Mother of all men (Jn. 19. 27, "Behold thy mother") and is the Queen of Heaven, so that she is our principal intercessor.

II. *The "New Testament"*. Christ is called the "Mediator of the New Testament" in 9. 15 and 12. 24, and the "Mediator of a better testament" in 8. 6. The phrase "The New Testament", now used for the whole Christian dispensation, and in particular for the Book which contains it, goes back, of course, to Christ himself at the Last Supper (Mt. 26. 28 with Mk. 14. 24; and Lk. 22. 20 with I Cor. 11. 25, and see note on this and v. 24). In Gal. 4. 24 Paul explains the allegory of the sons of Sara and Agar in terms of the "two Testaments". Already in II Cor. 3. 6 he speaks of the "ministers of the New Testament". But it is in Hebrews that the idea is worked out to the full.

The Old Testament was that made between God and Jewish people. The word "testament" is διαθήκη for ברית

[1] The Mass and Office of Our Lady Mediatrix of all graces first appeared in 1921, and were extended throughout the Church in 1939 (Feast, May 31st).

(berith) in Hebrew, which means a covenant or agreement between two. The mediator is the minister of the covenant between two (cf. Gal. 3. 20). But St Paul shows in Heb. 8. 8 how already Jeremias (31. 31) had prophesied that God would "make a new convenant with the house of Israel . . . not according to the covenant which I made with their fathers . . . the covenant which they made void".

This is now the new covenant, the covenant made by Christ, "established on better promises" (Heb. 8. 6), "by means of his death for the redemption of those transgressions, which were under the former testament" (9. 15). The better promise is that of "eternal inheritance" (ibid.). But just as the old covenant was established by blood (the blood of the sacrificial victims sprinkled on the people by Moses, saying, "This is the blood of the covenant,"[1] Ex. 24. 8), so also the new covenant is established in the Blood of Christ (Heb. 9. 18–23), as he himself said, and the words are preserved in the words of the Consecration at Mass, "Calix Sanguinis mei, novi et aeterni testamenti".

But here St Paul brings in the other meaning of διαθήκη (the original, classical usage), a "testament" in the sense of a last will and testament of a dying man. (This meaning is not applicable to the old covenant or to the Hebrew word used for it.) For this new covenant or agreement (διαθήκη) is also the last will and testament (διαθήκη) of the dying Christ, which (like all wills) comes into force at the testator's death. Hence the New Testament (in both senses) begins with the redemptive death of Christ (Heb. 9. 16–17).[2]

III. *Melchisedech*. A shadowy figure who, coming as if from nowhere, suddenly appears in the story of Genesis, and as quickly disappears again. Gen. 14. 18–20: "Melchisedech, the king of Salem (= ? Jerusalem), bringing forth bread and

---

[1] Our Bible uses "covenant" in the OT and "testament" in the NT.
[2] Gal. 3. 15–18 uses the figure of the will and testament, but of the promises made to Abraham, which cannot be altered.

wine, for he was the priest of the most high God, blessed
him (Abraham) . . . and he (Abraham) gave him the tithes of
all." St Paul refers to him in Heb. 5. 6, 10, quoting the
Messianic psalm 109 (Heb. 110) 4, "Thou art a priest for
ever, according to the order of Melchisedech," i.e. a priesthood independent of that of the Levites. The idea is worked
out in c. 7. Melchisedech became the type of a priesthood
that was at once older and more lasting than that of the old
covenant with Moses and Aaron. The offering of bread and
wine connected him at once with the Christian priesthood.
St Paul, in virtue of the mysteriousness of the figure of Melchisedech in Genesis, refers to his priesthood having (like
Christ's) no human beginning, and no end, "without father,
without mother, without genealogy" (7. 3). And further,
Abraham (standing for the Jewish people) offered him tithes
and received his blessing, showing that he regarded Melchisedech as his superior, just as the Jewish priesthood should
recognise the superiority of that of Christ.

IV. *The Priesthood of Christ*. The first notion of the priesthood is the office of Mediator, one who is "ordained for men
in the things that appertain to God" (Heb. 5. 1), and principally to offer men's gifts to God and then to bring God's
gifts to men (St Thomas III 22. 1). Now since Christ is the
perfect Mediator, he also is the perfect priest. The Hebrew
high priest did indeed "offer up gifts and sacrifices for sins",
but he was "compassed with infirmity" (5. 1–2), and was
only a type of the perfect priesthood of Christ, for Christ did
indeed "have compassion on our infirmities" and was
"tempted in all things like as we are, without sin" (4. 15).
Christ, the perfect priest, offered the perfect sacrifice, which
was himself, obtaining thereby "eternal redemption" (9. 12).
This is the gift of God he brings to men, being a "high priest
of the good things to come" (9. 11). Because the gift he brings
is an eternal gift, his dispensation of it is eternal, and he
"hath an everlasting priesthood" (7. 24), even though the

sacrifice which he offered was consummated on the Cross, for death did not put an end to his priesthood, but "he continueth for ever . . . always living to make intercession for us" (7. 24–25) (St Thomas III 22. 5).

The Greek word in all these passages for "high priest" is ἀρχιερεύς, i.e. archpriest, but the Latin consistently translates this by "pontifex" (the title of the high priest of the Roman pagan cult, a title afterwards used by the Bishops of the Church). This word was generally supposed by Latin writers to mean originally a "bridge-maker" (pontem facere —like artifex, e.g., from artem facere) and hence a mediator between the divinity and mankind, a supposition anyway which helped the exegesis. A boy attending a class on Christ's priestly mediation in Heb. 9. 11, wrote in his notes the following simple sentence which is worthy of record: "Christ made a bridge between God and man—a bridge of pain."

The Christian priesthood is nothing but a sharing in the priesthood of Christ, for priests are "the ministers of Christ (in the offering of his Sacrifice) and the dispensers of the mysteries of God" (I Cor. 4. 1).[1] It is, of course, in virtue of the mediatorship and priesthood of Christ that priests have the power to forgive sins.

V. *Christ's one Sacrifice.* The sacrifices of the Old Law, "the blood of goats and of oxen . . . sanctify such as are defiled" (9. 13), and because of the recurrence of ceremonial defilement, it was necessary to repeat the sacrifices: "for it is impossible that with the blood of oxen and goats sins should be taken away" (10. 4), and "the Law . . . by the sacrifices which they offer continually can never make the comers thereunto perfect" (10. 1).

But now, "we are sanctified by the oblation of the body of Jesus once" (10. 10), for "he entered once into the Holies,

[1] Pius XI's Encyclical on the Catholic Priesthood, 1935. At the same time was issued the Votive Mass of Christ the Priest, of which the Epistle is from Heb. 5. 1–10.

having obtained eternal redemption" (9. 12). Christ's one Sacrifice is all-sufficient to bring eternal redemption. No longer now will "every priest stand daily ministering, and often offering the same sacrifices, which can never take away sins" (10. 11). That was the situation under the old covenant. On the contrary, Christ, "offering one sacrifice for sins, for ever sitteth on the right hand of God" (10. 12).

The Christian priesthood is a sharing in Christ's priesthood: "Christus autem est fons totius sacerdotii" (St Thomas III 22. 4), the priest is an "alter Christus, cum ejus gerat personam" (Pius XI in his Encyclical): the Christian Sacrifice, the Mass, offered by priests, is therefore Christ's own Sacrifice, "one and the same Victim, who offered himself on the Cross, now offering himself by the ministry of priests, the only difference being the manner of offering" (Council of Trent, session xxii, Denz., 940, cf. St Thomas III 83. 1). The identity of the Sacrifice goes with the identity of the Priesthood.

In Christ's Sacrifice, he is at once Priest and Victim: he "offered himself unspotted unto God" (9. 14) (cf. St Thomas III 22. 2).

VI. *Apostasy and Penance*. The admonishments in this letter are chiefly to perseverance, and warnings against apostasy. An important passage is 6. 4–6, "It is impossible for those who were once illuminated, have tasted also the heavenly gift, etc. (i.e. the Faith) . . . and are fallen away, to be renewed again to penance, crucifying again to themselves the Son of God, and making him a mockery."

It has been the constant teaching of the Church that those who fall into grave sin after Baptism can always return to grace through the Sacrament of Penance, for Christ said: "Whose sins you shall forgive, they are forgiven them" (Jn. 20. 23). As far back as Ignatius in A.D. 107 we find teaching like this: "God forgives all who repent" (*To the Philadelphians*, 8), and there is the famous likeness of the Sacrament of Penance to a "second plank after shipwreck" (the first being Baptism itself), first described by Tertullian (c. A.D. 200) in his *De Paenitentia*, c. 4, and then also by St Jerome (e.g. Ep. 130, 9). The teaching of the Novatians and other heretics, that a fall from grace after Baptism is irreparable, is condemned. Penance is open to all (e.g. St Leo in A.D. 452, Denz., 146, and of course, later, at Trent, Denz., 807, 894–5). The heretics taught that the sin of apostasy especially was irreparable, and they invoked this passage of Hebrews.

Of orthodox exegesis there are two views:

(i) (the commoner among the Fathers). The passage refers to the impossibility of returning to grace through another Baptism. We enter into the fruits of Christ's Crucifixion by Baptism: so another Baptism would mean another Crucifixion ("crucifying again . . . etc."). The "second plank" is not Baptism again, but the Sacrament of Penance.

(ii) (commoner among modern writers). It is impossible, i.e. morally impossible, i.e. so difficult and improbable so as to be almost impossible, having fallen away, to be renewed to penance. This is rather borne out by the passage on final impenitence in 10. 26 and 29, where we read that nothing but God's punishment awaits those who have rejected Christ's Redemption, and have "trodden under foot the Son of God, etc." Such a one is unlikely to return, when he has gone as far as that, and has "made a mockery" of the Son of God. In this sense he is "crucifying him again". The sin of apostasy is not, of course, of itself irreparable, but in point of fact is rarely repaired. This would be the sense of St Paul's warnings.[1]

VII. *The Definition of Faith in* 11. 1. "Faith is the substance of things to be hoped for, the evidence of things that

---

[1] The exegesis of this difficult passage is well explained in the commentary of Sales. Opinions are divided:
  (i) Rebaptism: most of the Fathers, St Thomas, Challoner, Sales, RAK.
  (ii) Moral impossibility: St Jerome, WV (Canon Boylan), Prat, USA.

are not seen" (USA). That is, we cannot accept on Faith either what we already possess, or what we can already see for ourselves (cf. St Thomas II–II 1. 4). What we accept by Faith, we accept on the authority of God "who can neither deceive nor be deceived" (Catechism, n. 10).

The word "substance" (ὑπόστασις) properly means "that which underlies" and came to have a technical philosophical meaning. WV goes back to the more original meaning, and translates "assurance", i.e. that which underlies what we hope for. (RAK conveys this, but still retains the word "substance": "that which gives substance to our hopes.")

VIII. *The phrase in* 5. 7. The reference is to Christ's agony and humiliation: he prayed, "to him that was able to save him from death, and was heard *because of reverence*." This is the literal translation, and the word, originally meaning prudence, had come in later Greek to mean piety or godliness. It is an unexpected word to find used of Christ, and is only found here and in 12. 28 (of men) in the New Testament. WV "devout submission", USA "reverent submission", RAK "piety".

(From the Second Captivity: II Tim.)

(37–38)   THE SECOND EPISTLE TO TIMOTHY

A. Time and place. Tradition, as shown by Eusebius (II, 22), has always held that II Tim. was written from Paul's last captivity, shortly before his death. In contrast to the Epistles of the first captivity, there are no travel plans, no hope of a speedy release; on the contrary, it is now only a matter of waiting for the end: "I am even now ready to be sacrificed, and the time of my dissolution is at hand" (4. 6). This imprisonment was a different business altogether: the previous one was merely to await trial in Rome after his appeal made at Caesarea. At the time of his appeal, the Roman authorities could find nothing against him: "This man hath done nothing worthy of death or bonds" (Acts 26. 31), and indeed, as the visiting King Agrippa said, he "might have been set at liberty, if he had not appealed to Caesar" (Acts 26. 32). So he felt fairly sure that the court in Rome would not take the accusations of the Jews very seriously, and therefore that he would eventually be released. This time, however, it was different. In A.D. 64 Nero had started a systematic persecution of Christians,[1] and Paul's second arrest was as a result of this. It was no use hoping for acquittal this time, and Paul evidently knew it. In II Tim. he refers, in contrast, to his previous trial: although he had to defend himself entirely alone ("At my first answer no man[2] stood with me"), yet he was "delivered out of the mouth of the lion" (4. 16–17).

As in the Epistles of the Captivity, he refers to his chains (1. 16, 2. 9), and this time he is imprisoned "as an evildoer" (USA, RAK "criminal") (2. 9), and not in "his own hired lodging" as last time (Acts 28. 30). In II Tim. 2. 9 he refers clearly to Rome. These things, combined with the tone of the letter which suggests certainly approaching death, confirm the tradition that the Epistle was written from St Paul's last captivity. It is thus the last writing we have of the great Apostle, and with our study of this Epistle we bid farewell to St Paul, having fittingly devoted more than half our year's work to an examination of his writings.

B. To whom? Timothy (see on I Tim.) was apparently still at Ephesus. This is indicated indirectly in this Epistle: 1. 18, "Thou very well knowest" things that happened at Ephesus; 4. 13, Timothy is to call at Troas on the way, and Troas is on a likely route from Ephesus to Rome; 4. 19, greetings are sent to Prisca and Aquila, last heard of in

[1] See Hist. Intro. *d*, p. 25 (Suetonius, *Nero*, 16).

[2] Not even Luke, apparently, though he was present for part at least of Paul's first captivity (Col. 4. 14; Philem. 24). If he was already away from Rome before the trial, his finishing of Acts while Paul was still awaiting trial, and so before his own departure, becomes the more understandable.

Rome (Rom. 16. 3), though they did at one time live at
Ephesus (I Cor. 16. 19, Acts 18. 18, 26) and may well have
now returned there. On the other hand the information
"Tychicus I have sent to Ephesus" (II Tim. 4. 12) suggests
that the reader was not there. So it is impossible to say
exactly where Timothy was when this letter was sent to him,
although Ephesus is the more obvious suggestion, in view of
I Tim. 1. 3.

 C. Argument. (Paul's familiar letter style.)
    Address (1. 1–2).
    Preamble (1. 3–5).

 I. Exhortation to
    Courage (1. 6–12; 2. 1–14) and to
    Sound Doctrine (1. 13–14; 2. 14–26).
    Digression on certain people (1. 15–18).

                 c. 1–2

 II. Certain Dangers (3. 1–9)
    and their remedies:
     (i) He is to hold to Paul's teaching (3. 10–14).
     (ii) He is to study the Scriptures (3. 15–17).
     (iii) He is to preach "in season and out of season"
       (4. 1–5).

                 c. 3–4

 III. Personal matters:
     (i) News of himself (4. 6–8).
     (ii) News of others (4. 9–18).
    Concluding salutations (4. 19–22).

(The matter of the canonicity of this Epistle was studied
under I Tim.)

Exegesis
Preamble
 1. 3. As so often Paul tells his correspondent how he prays
for him.

1. 4. "Mindful of thy tears," probably Timothy's sadness when Paul left him at Ephesus: I Tim. 1. 3, "I desired thee to remain . . .", obviously it was a hard thing for the young man. They were great friends.

1. 5. Paul's interest in Timothy's family. His mother, Eunice, was "a Jewish woman that believed" (Acts 16. 1), probably a convert of Paul's on the I Journey when he visited Lystra twice (Acts 14. 6–19, 20). From her ("from thy infancy") he had learnt the Scriptures (II Tim. 3. 15).

I. EXHORTATION TO COURAGE

1. 6. "By the imposition of my hands": he was ordained by Paul himself. The principal moment in the ceremony of the ordination of a priest (from the beginning, and in present-day ritual) is when the Bishop (after the Litanies which follow the Gradual or Tract of the Ordination-Mass) in complete silence lays both hands on the head of the man being ordained. It is a most impressive rite. St Paul speaks of "the grace that is in thee" by this ordination. Special grace and special strength is needed for a priest to perform his sacred function (called a "grace of state") and this is one of the effects of the Sacrament of Holy Order. It is an article of Faith (Trent, session xxiii, 3, Denz., 960) that special grace is conferred in this Sacrament, and this text is quoted, thus giving to this passage an authoritative interpretation, al-though the Greek word is χάρισμα, which more usually refers to particular supernatural powers (miracles, tongues, etc., cf. I Cor. 12).

1. 9. God "has called us by his holy calling, not according to our works, but according to[1] his own purpose": "vocation" to the priesthood.

1. 13. "Hold to the form of sound teaching which thou hast heard from me" (USA): we should remember that, although the Synoptic Gospels were by now in existence, books were

[1] In the standard small (Vaughan) Rh NT there is a line omitted by misprint in this verse.

few, and books on Christian doctrine almost non-existent,
Instruction therefore depended almost entirely on preaching,
i.e. on an oral tradition, cf. Rom. 10. 17, "Fides ex auditu:
faith cometh by hearing." Paul has insisted before (e.g. Gal.
1. 8–9) that the people to whom he preached should hold to
his divinely-received teaching.

1. 15. A sad note: since Paul is a prisoner again many have
turned against him. Several are mentioned in this Epistle:
here, Phigellus and Hermogenes, in 2. 17 Hymenaeus and
Philetus, in 4. 14 Alexander the coppersmith. Two of these,
Hymenaeus and Alexander, were mentioned in I Tim. 1. 20
as excommunicated. Probably most of these were Ephesians,
for Timothy is told to avoid their company (II Tim. 4. 15).

1. 16. But in contrast, Onesiphorus was good to him and
visited him recently in prison. He prays for God's mercy on
"the house of Onesiphorus" and sends them greetings (4. 19).
This phrase, coupled with the prayer for God's mercy "in
that day" (1. 18) on Onesiphorus himself, has led most
writers to suppose that he was now dead.

2. 3–6. "A good soldier of Christ Jesus," cf. the phrase
often used in connexion with Confirmation (e.g. Catechism,
n. 262). Further, a priest's work is a "whole-time job": he
cannot "entangle himself with secular business", for "they
who preach the Gospel should live by the Gospel" (I Cor.
9. 7–14 where the same analogies of the soldier and farmer are
used).

2. 8. The centralness of the doctrine of Christ's Resurrection, cf. I Cor. 15. 14, "If Christ be not risen again, then
is our preaching vain, and your faith is also vain."

2. 11. "A faithful saying": the phrase typical of the Pastoral Epistles (I Tim. 1. 15, 3. 1, 4. 9, Tit. 3. 8), which introduces (vv. 11–13) what is generally believed (from its quasi-
metrical construction) to be a fragment of an early hymn.

2. 14. Sound teaching is far more valuable than "contro-
versy" (WV).

2. 18. "Saying that the resurrection is past already": the precise nature of this error is not quite clear. Probably it is connected with the idea (later developed by the Gnostic heretics) that the only resurrection is a spiritual one; and in this way, perhaps, they misinterpreted Paul's own teaching (in Rom. 6. 4 and Col. 2. 12, 3. 1) that in Baptism we are "buried" with Christ, in order with him to "rise again". In this way the only possible resurrection would already be past.

2. 19. The seal of true doctrine: two principles—(i) God chooses his own; (ii) Man has his share: he must "depart from iniquity". See the note on Rom. 5. 1–11 (Predestination, etc.).

2. 20. The famous figure of the vessels (used in Rom. 9. 19–23 in a different context, that of God's free choice). Noble vessels, e.g. for the table; common vessels, e.g. for the kitchen. If we will, we can all become noble vessels.

II. DANGERS AND REMEDIES

3. 1. These dangers are still to come, and Paul warns Timothy, especially against false Christians (v. 5) who look pious, but are not.

3. 8. Jannes (or Jamnes) and Mambres (or Jambres)[1] were names given by Hebrew tradition to the magicians of Pharaoh who at first succeeded by magic in reproducing Moses' miracles (Exodus 7. 11, 8. 7), but finally failed (9. 11).

3. 11. "You know the sufferings that came my way, notably at Lystra, your own home-town, where I was stoned when I first came (Acts 14. 18); yet God delivered me. Let this give you courage."

3. 15–16. The famous passage on Scripture and its inspiration. It is Paul's word that has become a theological term.[2]

---

[1] According to different manuscripts.

[2] "Inspiration", both in Latin and Greek, means a "breathing-into", and one of the early writers, Athenagoras, in his *Legatio* 9, takes up the figure, saying that the Holy Spirit breathes into the Sacred Writers as a flute-player into his flute. The word first appears in a decree of the Church only at Trent (Denz., 706).

4. 1–8. The famous passage so often used at Mass on the feast of a Doctor. One of the great remedies is to preach. This is Paul's very last advice. He has spent his life preaching: now Timothy is to carry on the work.

4. 6–8. These are the words of a dying man. His sacrifice is now near, his course is done, his battle is over, and through all "I have kept the Faith". Final perseverance is God's most precious gift. These verses contain what are among the most wonderful words that a dying Christian could utter. Paul knows that God will reward his faithfulness, and in the same way will reward all who are faithful and so can look forward to Christ's coming (in judgement) without fear.

CONCLUSION

4. 8. "Make haste to come to me quickly," before it is too late.

4. 9–10. Demas, who had been with Paul during his first captivity (Col. 4. 14, Philem. 24 mentioned with Luke), has given in, and gone. Of Crescens we know nothing else. Titus, who had gone to Nicopolis to see Paul (Tit. 3. 12, see note there), has continued the journey north to Dalmatia.

4. 11. Luke alone has remained faithful. Paul suggests that Timothy should bring the other evangelist, Mark.

4. 12. Tychicus, a great messenger, has been sent again to Ephesus, whither he had taken the Epistle about seven or eight years previously (Eph. 6. 21), together with that to Colossae (Col. 4. 7–9).

4. 13. Paul wants the old cloak he left behind at Troas (at least this is usual translation of φαιλόνης, though some, as WV, prefer to translate "wrapper", i.e. for the books). Probably the prison-cell was cold and damp, for winter was coming on (v. 21). He also wants some books and manuscript notes (parchments): these were probably also his own, left at Troas. (Does this suggest that he was arrested there, and had to leave in a hurry?)

4. 16–17. His previous trial: see Intro. to this Epistle.

4. 19. A last greeting to his old friends Aquila and Priscilla, who had been faithful since their first meeting at Corinth (Acts 18. 2), way back in the year 52, a good fifteen years ago.

4. 20. "Erastus remained at Corinth," not unnaturally, for it was his own town, and at one time (when Rom. was written about twelve years ago) he had been "treasurer of the city" (Rom. 16. 23). A little before this (if it is the same Erastus: could the treasurer have been away at Ephesus?) Erastus went to Macedonia with Timothy (Acts 19. 22), and probably on to Corinth (I Cor. 4. 17) with him, on Paul's behalf. Trophimus, the Ephesian, whose presence in Jerusalem with Paul prompted the false accusations that led to Paul's arrest (Acts 21. 29).

4. 21. Of Eubulus nothing is known, but Pudens is an interesting character. The Martyrology (May 19 and June 20) records that he was a senator in Rome, instructed by the Apostles, and the father of four saints: Novatus the martyr, Timothy the priest, and Pudentiana and Praexedes the holy virgins. There is a tradition in Rome that the city's oldest church, St Pudentiana's on the Esquiline, is on the site of the house of Pudens and that this was the abode of St Peter.[1] The Claudia mentioned here is believed to be his wife, who is said[2] to have been the daughter of Caractacus the British king who was brought to Rome as a captive in the reign of Claudius, together with his wife and daughter.[3] This is perhaps confirmed by the line of Martial (*Epigram.*, iv, 13), "Claudia, Rufe, meo nubit peregrina Pudenti". Should this legend be true, it

---

[1] See any good guide-book to Rome. Especially good, and critical, is *Romée, ou le pèlerin moderne à Rome* by Noële M. Denis and Robert Boulet, Paris, 1935, pp. 368 sq.

[2] Stated, without reference, by Dr Brownlow in *The Early History of the Church of God*, C.T.S., 1901. Cf. Morton, 408.

[3] The thrilling story, with his courageous speech and the Emperor's subsequent clemency, is told in Tacitus, *Annales*, 12, 36–7.

would mean that one person from this island is mentioned in the New Testament![1]

That Linus here mentioned was the first successor of St Peter as Bishop of Rome was the opinion already of St Ireneus (*Adv. Haer.* III, 3. 3). Here we have what seems to be a clear case of the deliberate silence of the New Testament writers about St Peter being in Rome. If it was not for "security reasons", surely he would have been mentioned here (cf. Intro. to Romans, p. 131).

Note. The material since the suggested pause at Christmas after II Cor. is arranged for about sixteen periods, an average length for a Lent Term.

PART IV. THE CATHOLIC EPISTLES
(39–42)   GENERAL OBSERVATIONS

The term "Catholic" for the seven Epistles (or at least for some of the seven) is a very ancient one. For instance, the "Muratorian Canon", that unofficial list of about A.D. 200, says, "epistola sane iude et superscrictio iohannis duas in catholica habentur"[2] (i.e. Jude and two of John); the term seems to have been fairly general in the East for various of the Epistles standing after those of St Paul. For instance, Eusebius, (II, 25, at the end) speaks of "the seven called catholic epistles" (written A.D. 311–325), clearly referring to a general practice of so naming them. St Jerome (*c.* 400) uses the term in the West (e.g. in *De Viris Illustribus*, 1, 2, 4, etc.), although the more usual term seems to have been "Epistolae canonicae", as is shown in the Decree of Pope Damasus of 382 (Denz., 84). The canon drawn up by the Council of Trent

---

[1] St. Pudentiana's was the titular church of Cardinal Bourne—a further English connexion.

[2] This famous document, which gets its name from its discoverer and first editor (1740 at Milan), the priest L. A. Muratori (see art. in *Cath. Encycl.*), is a source of much delight to those who have difficulty with their study of Latin, since the scribe had no care for gender, number, case or agreement in his Latin. It is presumed to be a very bad translation from a lost Greek text, made in Rome. The text is in Pope, IV, 88–90. It is well to note that the bad grammar makes it often difficult to understand.

does not use the words "Catholic Epistles", but the old Greek name is in general use everywhere now.

The word is derived from the adverbial expression καθ' ὅλου "in general" (from κατά according to, and ὅλος whole). The meaning, as applied to a letter, seems to be an "encyclical", and indeed none of the Catholic Epistles (except perhaps II Jn. and III Jn. addressed to a single person) are clearly addressed to a single community. In this the Catholic Epistles are notably different from most of those of St Paul. The old application of the word "Catholic", or encyclical, to all these Epistles does, however, suggest that even if they are addressed first of all to a particular community or person it is the writer's intention that all should profit by the doctrine contained in them. This is borne out by Eusebius' use of the word "Catholic Epistles" with reference to those of Dionysius of Corinth which were all addressed to various local Churches (IV, 23).

On the matter of the canonicity of the Catholic Epistles there was some hesitation about some of them in the early centuries, until the Decree of Damasus (382), the first official list (where, however, there still persisted the opinion that II and III Jn. were "alterius Ioannis presbyteri", an opinion corrected by Pope Innocent I in the year 405) (Denz., 84, correction 96). Eusebius (III, 25) gives us the position in the early fourth century:

Universally accepted: I Peter, I John.

Disputed: James, Jude, II Peter, II–III John.

Origen (c. 250), in his Homily on Josue (VII, 1), holds to all seven Epistles, but (quoted in Eusebius VI, 25) records the doubts about II Peter and II–III John. It is not easy to see why Eusebius says that James was disputed, since there is witness to this Epistle (at least by quotation) in the earliest times. St Jerome (*De Vir. Ill.*, 1) indicates the reason of the doubts about II Peter. It is the difference in style from the universally recognised I Peter, which he explains by the employment of a different secretary. That Jude and II–III John should not be frequently quoted by early writers is very natural, in view of their brevity. But Jude is already mentioned in the Muratorian Canon. Internal evidence of style (apart from the rather scanty tradition) links II–III John with the universally accepted I John, but the hesitations arose through the superscription, "The Presbyter (or Ancient) to . . .", in II–III, while there is no superscription at all in I John.

The three Johannine Epistles stand apart, but we find close connexions in the other four, James, I–II Peter and Jude, and it is probable that all were written within a few years of each other. Some writers[1] even see in this group a body of Epistles addressed to predominantly Jewish-Christian communities, as a counterpart to St Paul's Epistles to the Churches, addressed to predominantly Gentile communities. This is certainly suggested by the association of Peter and James in the apostolate of the "circumcision" (Gal. 2. 9), as distinct from the apostolate of Paul and Barnabas to the Gentiles, and by their clear association in legislating for the Jewish-Christians at the Council of Jerusalem (Acts 15, especially 13–14, "James saying, 'Simon hath related, etc.' "). (In our view the two texts relate to the same occasion, see p. 160.) Furthermore, Jude seems to be writing *as* the brother of James (Jude 1, and see notes on this Epistle), and his Epistle has very much in common with II Peter. So the little Epistle of Jude makes a strong link between these four Epistles.

But we should observe already here that both James and I Peter (and in consequence II Peter, being written to the same people) do not show themselves to be restricted to Jewish hearers. These matters we shall, however, discuss in their proper places.

The following table shows a conjectural chronology of the Catholic Epistles (and we shall follow this order in our study).

[1] See WV, IV, Intro. (p. xxiv) (Fr Kent).

But in the absence of familiar chronological landmarks (which in the case of St Paul greatly facilitate dating), the dates, which must largely follow on provenance and destination usually only deduced from mere hints in the text, can only be provisional and supply a useful working basis. It is, of course, in the nature of a "Catholic" or encyclical letter not to have a precise destination.

The two longer Epistles (James and I Peter), of the two who occupied themselves specially with the apostolate of the Jewish-Christians, will be studied first, and then the two short ones which have so much common material. We are giving precedence to Jude, on both chronological and critical grounds, as will be explained.

A CHRONOLOGICAL TABLE OF THE CATHOLIC EPISTLES

Epistle	Date	From	Addressed to	Length (chapters)
1. JAMES	before 62 (his death)	Jerusalem (his residence)	"the 12 tribes scattered abroad" (1. 1)	5
2. I PETER	62–64 (after death of James, before Gt. Persecution)	Rome ("Babylon" 5. 13).	Christians in Asia Minor (1. 1)	5
3. JUDE	62–66 (after death of James, before Jewish War)	?	Jerusalem ?	1
4. II PETER	64–67 (during his imprisonment in Gt. Persecution)	Rome (place of his death)	as I Peter (3. 1)	3
5. I JOHN	96–100 (old age)	Ephesus (his residence)	Local Churches	5
6. II JOHN	,, ,,	,,	"The Lady Elect" (a Local Church?)	1
7. III JOHN	,, ,,	,,	Gaius	1

(First Group: James and I Peter)

THE EPISTLE OF ST JAMES

The Author. Not James the Great (so called because the other is called in Mk. 15. 40 "James the Less'), for he was long dead, being the first of the Apostles to die (in Herod's persecution A.D. 42, Acts 12. 2). James the Great was the brother of John the Evangelist and son of Zebedee. (Acts 12. 2 tells us that the one who was killed was the brother of John.)

So we are left with the other James in the lists of Apostles, whom Mark calls "Little James" (probably with reference to his stature, as a convenient distinguishing mark from the son of Zebedee). In that passage (Mk. 15. 40) his mother Mary is mentioned, together with his brother Joseph.[1] The same names come in the parallel in Mt. 27. 56. He is usually identified with "James, son of Alpheus" in the lists of the Apostles in Mt. 10. 3, Mk. 3. 18, and Lk. 6. 15. Luke in 6. 16 gives Jude as "Jude of James", which is usually understood to mean "brother of James" (see on St Jude, p. 248).

"Little James" and his brother Joseph[1] and his other brother Jude are mentioned in Mt. 13. 55 as "brethren" of Our Lord. Since, however, their mother Mary (Mt. and Mk. above) in the accounts of the Passion is not to be identified with the Mother of Jesus (Jn. 19. 25 expressly names the two other Marys at the Cross, Mary Magdalene and Mary of Cleophas—this last is most likely the mother of James, etc.[2]) they cannot be brothers in the strict sense, but must be kinsmen or cousins.[3]

The James who was Bishop of Jerusalem, and played an

---

[1] Or Joses (WV), according to the Greek text, though in Mt. some MSS have "Joseph".

[2] This means either identifying Cleophas and Alpheus (which some scholars are unwilling to do), or supposing a second husband.

[3] This is a complicated matter, which we cannot go into here: Appendix I to WV, IV is devoted to it, and Appendix A to Pope, V.

important part in the Council in Acts 15, is referred to by St
Paul in Gal. 1. 19 as "James, the brother of the Lord". He
appears as the important person in the Christian community
at Jerusalem in Acts 12. 17: Peter says, "Tell these things to
James and the brethren" (James singled out), Acts 15 (the
Council, and Acts 21. 18: Paul goes to visit "James, and all
the ancients (or presbyters) were assembled".

There is little hesitation in tradition in ascribing this
Epistle to James (the small one), Apostle, son of Mary and
Alpheus (=Cleophas?), brother of Jude, cousin of Christ,
Bishop of Jerusalem. But it should be observed that scholars
are not agreed upon the identification in fact of all these
titles with one man.

His death. Fortunately we have three independent accounts
of the martyrdom of St James. All three were collected by the
invaluable historian Eusebius: the first is that of Josephus
(written *c.* A.D. 80–100) in his *Antiquities* (XX, 9. 1) (Eusebius, II, 23[1]), the second is that of the early Christian writer
Hegesippus (*c.* A.D. 180), in a passage in an otherwise lost
work, preserved in Eusebius, II, 23, and the third is that of
Clement of Alexandria (*c.* 200) in a passage also only available to us in Eusebius, II, 1.

The gist of the story is that when the procurator Festus[2]
died and before he was succeeded by Albinus in A.D. 62,[3] the
high priest illicitly summoned the Sanhedrin and condemned
James to death by stoning. Josephus says that this illicit
action roused the anger of Albinus on his arrival and he
promptly deprived that high priest of his office. Hegesippus
gives details of the martyrdom, how they cast him down from

[1] Note that Eusebius also records a sentence not found in the usual
text of Josephus.
[2] The same Festus who arrived in Palestine in 57 while Paul was still a
prisoner at Caesarea (Acts 25. 1). He only held office for five years.
[3] The date is learned from Josephus (*Wars*, VI, 5, 3), i.e. Albinus was
already procurator "four years before the war began (in 66)". This is
confirmed by Eusebius' *Chronicle* (P.G., XIX, 543), which dates James'
death in "the seventh year of Nero" (i.e. from Sept., 55).

the temple, and, on seeing that he was not yet dead, began to hurl stones on to him until they saw that he was praying aloud. Then someone finished him off with a fuller's pole.

Date of the Epistle. The date 62 gives us the latest date, of course. But there is no clear evidence how long before this it was written. The probability is that it was not before Paul's arrest in 55, and, if one maintains that James is correcting false interpretations of St Paul's Epistle to the Romans, then his Epistle will have been written for certain after A.D. 55.

To whom? The Letter is addressed to "The twelve tribes, which are scattered abroad". But the meaning of this is not certain.

(i) (the most obvious, and also the most likely) To *Jewish-Christians* scattered abroad. No mention is made of the observance of the Mosaic Law, since this would be taken for granted. Further, we know from Acts 15 and Gal. 2. 12 (some strict observers of the Law "came from James") that James had particular charge of the Jewish-Christian section of the Church in Palestine. And Abraham is called "our father" in 2. 21.

(ii) To whole of the "Israel of God" (Gal. 6. 16), i.e. *all Christians*. The very fact that there is no specific teaching on the matter of the Law, together with the fact that the teaching of the Epistle is general Christian ethics, suggests that it was not intended for Jewish-Christians only. As for Abraham, he is "the father of us all" (Rom. 4. 16). There is hardly any more quotation from the Old Testament than St Paul often uses to a mixed audience.

(iii) It has been held, in view of the absence of direct theological teaching on the Person of Christ, that the Epistle was written simply to *Jews*.

(iv) It has also been supposed that the Epistle was written to the community at *Antioch*, which was a centre of Jewish-Christians, as we see from Acts 15 and Gal. 2, and in constant touch with Jerusalem.

Argument. This Epistle is principally concerned with practical affairs: it might almost be called a treatise on "Christian commonsense". It reflects notably the fundamental teaching on Christian Ethics which is contained in the Sermon on the Mount (which, after all, James had actually heard). There are very many well-known texts dealing with Christian behaviour.

The argument is quite plain and straightforward and the Epistle makes very easy reading—perhaps the easiest of all the Epistles. As often as not a new section is introduced with "My brethren". The simple figures that James uses to press home his points are particularly colourful: e.g. the wave of the sea (1. 6), the man who looks at himself in a mirror (1. 23–24), the bridle (3. 3), the rudder (3. 4), the fountain, the fig-tree, the vine (3. 11–12), the business man (4. 13), and the moth-eaten garments (5. 2). There is deliberate humour, e.g. in his description of snobbishness[1] in 2. 2–3, of the unhelpful friend in 2. 16, and of the precious objects that decay in 5. 2–3.

    I. On Patience (1. 2–18).
   II. On practising what we preach (1. 19–27).
  III. On Christian equality and fraternal charity (2. 1–13).
  IV. On Faith and works (2. 14–26).
    V. On bridling the tongue (c. 3).
  VI. On peace and charity (c. 4).
 VII. Advice on various practical matters (c. 5).

Short Exegesis

I. ON PATIENCE

1. 3. "The trying of your faith worketh patience."

1. 4. "Let patience have its perfect work" (USA, closer to the Greek).

---

[1] Dr Wand's lovely translation of προσωπολημψία (respect of persons) in 2. 1. A non-classical word, so the non-classical English is quite legitimate. See note on Rom. 2. 11.

i. 12. "Blessed is the man that endureth temptation", a well-known text used in the Mass and Office of a martyr.

i. 17. God, "the Father of lights, with whom there is no change, nor shadow of alteration": the figure is of the heavenly bodies, which turn (hence AV "shadow of turning"), get eclipsed, or wax and wane.

II. ON PRACTISING WHAT WE PREACH

i. 19. "Let every man be swift to hear, but slow to speak and slow to anger": an elementary principle of Christian behaviour: not to leap to criticism or rash judgement.

i. 21. "Naughtiness": one of the words borrowed by Challoner from the AV. WV and USA have gone back to "malice" of the original Rheims. The Greek is simply κακία.

"Receive the ingrafted word": RAK "Cherish that word implanted in you", i.e. the Gospel of Jesus Christ.

i. 22-24. "Be ye doers of the word, and not hearers only" (cf. Rom. 2. 13, "For not the hearers of the Law are just before God, but the doers"—the same ideas, but the wording is quite different. It is worth remarking here that the argument for literary dependence of James on Romans is not very conclusive).[1]

i. 23-24. Otherwise he is like a man who looks at himself in a mirror (to see himself as others see him, and so to mend his ways), but then goes away, forgets what he looked like, and does nothing about it. "His own countenance" is Challoner's "easing" of the old Rheims "the countenance of his nativitie" which is a literal rendering of the Greek and the Latin (AV has "natural face"). RAK "The face he was born with".

i. 26-27. James' strong practical note again: "If any man think himself to be religious, not bridling his tongue, but deceiving his own heart, this man's religion is vain. Religion

[1] See discussion of this matter in Pope, V, 291-2.

clean and undefiled before God and the Father is this: to
visit the fatherless and widows in their tribulation: to keep
oneself unspotted from this world."

III. ON CHRISTIAN EQUALITY AND FRATERNAL CHARITY

2. 1–4. Dr Wand: "My brothers, do not let your presentation of the faith of our gracious Lord Jesus Christ be spoiled
by snobbishness. If a man comes into your church wearing
jewellery and immaculate clothes, and there comes in also a
poor man very down at heel, and when you see the well-
dressed man you say to him, 'Sit here, this is one of our best
seats,' and you say to the shabby person, 'You can sit here on
the floor,' are you not showing partiality and giving evidence
of a mean discrimination?"

2. 5. "Has not God chosen the poor of this world to be rich
in faith and heirs of the kingdom?" (USA)

2. 8. "The *royal law*: Thou shalt love thy neighbour as
thyself": the law that Christ put next to the Love of God
(Mt. 22. 39, Mk. 12. 31).

2. 10. The point is that transgression of any point of the
law means contempt of the lawgiver. This is the reason of the
sinfulness of breaking any point of God's law, as St Thomas
explains with reference to this passage in I–II 73. 1 *ad* 1.

IV. ON FAITH AND WORKS

The point of this whole section (2. 14–26) is to make it
clear that although we are "justified by faith" (Rom. 5. 1),
i.e. by faith in Christ we enter into the inheritance he has
promised us, this does not mean that there is no need for
good works. Once more it is common-sense, as the example
of the unhelpful friend (vv. 15–16) shows. On the contrary,
"I will show thee, by works, my faith." The whole matter of
Justification requires man's co-operation by his free will (see

note on Rom. 5. 1 for St Paul's teaching and its later formu-
lation by the Church).

It was this passage that caused Luther to write: "Darum
ist Sankt Jacobs Epistel ein recht strohern Epistel"[1] (an
Epistle of straw).

It is this passage also that suggests that James was deliberately correcting (in his easy common-sense way) false
interpretations that had already been put on the words of
St Paul in Rom. (and Gal. 2. 16, Eph. 2. 8–9). Note that here
(2. 21) James is emphasising the good works of Abraham,
while St Paul in Rom. 4. 1 sq. and Gal. 3. 6 sq. is emphasising
his faith. His faith of course was a "living faith" which is
"shown" by good works, i.e. deeds of love or charity. The
theologians speak of Faith being "informed" (i.e. receiving
its "form") by the theological virtue of Charity. This is true
Faith (which justifies us) (Fides formata), distinguished from
the worthless Faith without Charity (Fides informis), of
which St James says (2. 17), "Faith, if it have not works, is
dead in itself." For this distinction see St Thomas II–II
4. 3 and 4.

2. 19. "You believe, you say, that there is one God? That's
good. The demons show that amount of faith and are in
terror because of it" (Wand).

V. ON BRIDLING THE TONGUE

3. 2. This very phrase in English comes from here. "If any
man offend not in word, the same is a perfect man."

3. 2–6. St James then explains that although the tongue is
only a small member of the body, yet it is more powerful to
do good or evil than any other. It is likened to the bit in a
horse's mouth that controls the huge bulk of the horse, to the
tiny rudder that controls a big ship, to the small fire that starts
a conflagration.

---

[1] Quoted in Höpfl on St James, from Grisar, *Luther* III, 443 (2nd ed.).

3. 4. All the old versions had "the governor", except Rh which had "director". The modern versions, naturally, have "helmsman" (WV), "steersman" (RV, USA), or "captain" (RAK).

3. 6. It "inflames the wheel of our nativity", the literal translation. It means, of course, "the circuit of our lives". RAK "this mortal sphere of ours".

3. 7–8. The tongue is further likened to an untamed animal.

3. 9–12. Its power for good or evil. But it should not be so: our tongue will show whether we are good or bad in ourselves. And St James has one of his clearest echos of the Gospel: Mk. 7. 16, "Do men gather grapes of thorns, or figs of thistles?" and cf. a similar phrase in Lk. 6. 44.

3. 13–18. The application of the above to the matter of jealousy. Dr Wand (v. 13), "Have you any wise and erudite persons amongst you? Well, let them show in the gentleness of their manners the modesty of true scholars."

VI. ON PEACE AND CHARITY

4. 1. Wars and contentions come from your own evil desires, greed, lust and pride.

4. 7. What is the solution? Instead of wanting to dominate and possess, "be subject to God". "But resist the devil and he will flee from you."

4. 8. "Draw nigh to God, and he will draw nigh to you"— one of Scripture's most wonderful sayings. The idea comes several times in the Old Testament, notably in Zacharias 1. 3, "Turn ye to me, saith the Lord, and I will turn to you."

4. 11. "Do not speak against one another" (USA). This is the literal translation of the Greek. The Latin has "detrahere", "detract", i.e. take away (the good name of). Detraction has come to mean the revelation, with intent to injure, of someone's misdeed; as distinct from Calumny (or Slander) which means a fictitious accusation of something he has not done.

VII. ADVICE ON VARIOUS PRACTICAL MATTERS

(i) The vanity of riches, 5. 1–3.

(ii) Injustice, 5. 4–6: one of the "four sins crying to heaven for vengeance" is defrauding labourers of their wages (Catechism, n. 327). The crowning injustice was the slaying of the Just One, of him who stood for all Justice.

(iii) Patience in suffering, 5. 7–11: take the example of Job —we know what happened to him in the end, how the Lord is merciful.

(iv) No swearing and unnecessary oaths, 5. 12: another clear echo of Christ's teaching: (Mt. 5. 37, in the Sermon on the Mount) "Let your speech be yea, yea: no, no . . .".

(v) The remedy for sadness is prayer, 5. 13: cheerfulness will manifest itself in song. St Paul also recommended singing in his Epistles written in captivity (Eph. 5. 19, Col. 3. 16).

(vi) In case of sickness fetch a priest, 5. 14–15: a particularly practical piece of advice well known to all Catholics. It is here in the New Testament that we find the reference to the Sacrament of Extreme Unction or Last Anointing. The Council of Trent (session xiv, Denz., 908) declared this to be the authentic interpretation of this passage, which teaches the matter (oil, blessed "in the name of the Lord"), form (prayer while anointing), minister (priest), and effect (comfort and even alleviation, and remission of sins) of the Sacrament.

(vii) Confession, 5. 16: confess sins "one to another". But the context is of the presence of the priest; so the reference is most probably to the Sacrament of Penance, though this interpretation is not laid down.

(viii) Pray for one another, 5. 16–18: "for the continual prayer of a just man availeth much."

(ix) Try and convert those who stray from the truth, 5. 19–20: to do this is a deed that will "cover a multitude of sins". The phrase is used by St Peter (I Peter 4. 8) of fraternal charity.

THE FIRST EPISTLE OF ST PETER

The Author. That this Epistle was written by St Peter, Prince of the Apostles, has practically never been called in question.

St Jerome (*De Vir. Illustr.*, 1) records the tradition that he presided over the Church of Rome for twenty-five years before his death there (crucified head downwards) in the fourteenth year of Nero, i.e. A.D. 67. This means that he arrived in Rome in the year 42, i.e. after the persecution of Herod in Palestine, when James the Great was killed and he was imprisoned, miraculously freed, and then "went into another place" (Acts 12. 17). We have already mentioned (in connexion with Rom. p. 131 and with II Tim. p. 224) the apparently deliberate silence of the New Testament writers on the whereabouts of Peter. The same tradition maintains that after leaving Jerusalem he occupied for a short time the see of Antioch (Feast of "St Peter's Chair at Antioch", Feb. 22), and then passed through Asia Minor, preaching, on his way to Rome (Feast of "St Peter's Chair at Rome", Jan. 18).

The letter sends greetings from "the Church that is in Babylon" (I Pet. 5. 13), which was accepted universally until the Reformation[1] as being a disguise for the name of Rome. Security reasons again. One thing is quite plain: it does not mean Babylon in Mesopotamia, for this great city was at the time (as it is now[2]) no more than a heap of ruins in the desert.[3] It is equally unlikely to refer to the Roman military station in Egypt which went by the name of Babylon.

To whom? ἐκλεκτοῖς παρεπιδήμοις διασπορᾶς, literally "*to the elect* (or chosen—the rest follows in v. 2, "according to the foreknowledge of God the Father, etc."—i.e. Christians) *sojourners of dispersion*" in Pontus, Galatia, etc. (1. 1). The

---

[1] Dr Selwyn, *I Peter*, p. 243.
[2] H. V. Morton, *Through Lands of the Bible*, p. 65. In his *Middle East* there is a photograph of the mere "halt" on the desert railway at Babylon.
[3] Strabo XVI, 15, Pliny, *Hist. Nat.* VI, 26.

word "Diaspora" has led some (e.g. Origen and St Jerome) to suppose this means Jewish-Christians. And this may indeed be so. But since the word has no article, it is more probable that the phrase means simply "dispersed settlers" without any reference to Jewish or Gentile origin. So the Latin "advenis" and Rh "strangers" would not be far off the mark.

Dr Selwyn lays great stress on the exact meaning of the phrase, for he would maintain that the Epistle is addressed therefore to folk who were refugees or "evacuees" in a strange land, and suggests that there must have been many such in Asia Minor who had come from Palestine after the martyrdom of St James in A.D. 62. These (chiefly Jewish) Christians would be in need of special comfort (and who could do it better than he to whom was committed the "gospel of the circumcision"?), since that brief persecution of 62 had made it clear once and for all that Christianity was not merely a department of Judaism, since official Judaism in Jerusalem had cut them off by killing their leader.[1] (At the time of St Paul's trials in Palestine, in 55-7, and at the time of the writing of Acts in 60, Christianity was still regarded as a sect of sedition in Judaism, e.g. Acts 24. 5, and Paul always visited the synagogues, and still worshipped in the Temple at Pentecost 55.)

Further, Peter refers to the sufferings of his readers: (1. 6) "If you must be for a little time made sorrowful in divers temptations"; (3. 14-17) "If you suffer . . . speak evil of you . . . falsely accuse you, etc."; (4. 14) "If you be reproached for the name of Christ". The very terms used indicate petty persecution and railing against Christians, and do not indicate a large-scale persecution. Fr Hugh Pope[2] says that the last text "implies no more than the ordinary treatment meted out to pious folk by the world in general". The nature of the

---

[1] Selwyn, pp. 57, 118.
[2] Pope, V, 303.

persecution enables us to say that the Epistle was written before the systematic persecution of Christians by Nero had begun in A.D. 64. This is confirmed by St Peter's serene teaching about reverence for the government, which is appointed by God "for the punishment of evildoers, and for the praise of the good" (2. 14).[1] He could hardly have said this when Nero's maniacal and palpably unjust treatment of Christians had begun, but he might well have said it after the Roman governor's righteous indignation about the murder of James had become known.

The recipients of the Epistle therefore seem to be Christians (probably chiefly Jewish) in Asia Minor (probably refugees from Palestine), who were undergoing various petty persecutions (or had experienced the unofficial persecution in Jerusalem).

The view should, however, be recorded that the "sojourners" may be taken in the purely spiritual sense that all Christians are only sojourners in this world, having here "no abiding city". In this case we would have a much less precise idea who the recipients are.

Lastly, we should note the question: is St Peter addressing his own converts or not? Information on St Peter's travels after leaving Jerusalem is so scanty that it is impossible to tell whether he visited these Churches in Asia Minor or not. But the tone of this Epistle (as compared to those of Paul to his own converts) seems impersonal, and one therefore inclines to suppose that he was writing to groups he had not visited (at least while they were in Asia Minor), but whose troubles he heard of, and so wrote to comfort them.

Date of the Epistle. The questions of the recipients and of the date are so closely connected that from the above notes we have seen that the Epistle was written before the Persecution of A.D. 64, and, if we follow Dr Selwyn's reasoning about the refugees, that it was written after 62. If we admit

[1] Selwyn, pp. 59–60.

the dependence of I Pet. on certain letters of St Paul, at least
to the extent of having read them (especially Rom. and Eph.[1]),
I Pet. must anyway be later than Eph., i.e. after about A.D. 60.

The position of Silvanus. I Pet. 5. 12, "By (διά) Silvanus
. . . I have written briefly": the most natural explanation is
that Silvanus was at the time Peter's secretary and perhaps
even drafted the letter for him. This may explain the "Pauline" manner of this Epistle, since Silvanus was associated
with Paul in writing I–II Thess. We lose track of Silvanus
(Silas) after the stay at Corinth on the II Journey (Acts 18. 5),
whence I–II Thess. were written in A.D. 51–2. He may quite
well have been in Rome in 62–4.

Argument. The Letter is primarily one of consolation, and
the sections of the argument are clear enough; but exhortation and doctrine are so closely woven together that each
section has a doctrinal basis.

Address (1. 1–2).
Preamble (in the Pauline manner) (1. 3–12).
  He gives thanks to God for them: if trials of faith come
    their way—they have hope in Christ's Resurrection.

  I. A pattern of life: trust in the grace received from
      Christ—through him "you are a chosen generation,
      a kingly priesthood, a holy nation, a purchased
      people" (2. 9) (1. 13–2. 10).

 II. In practice this means obedience and service—Christ
      in his Passion gives us the example (2. 11–3. 12).

III. "If you suffer anything . . . blessed are ye" (3. 14)—
      Christ *died* for our sins (3. 13–4. 19).

IV. Humility and watchfulness (5. 1–11).
      (i) especially for priests (5. 1–4).
      (ii) for younger people (5. 5–11).
    Concluding salutations (5. 12–14).

[1] See Pope, V, 308. At length in Selwyn: Essay II.

Short Exegesis

Address

1. 1. Discussed in the Intro.: the provinces mentioned are all in Asia Minor.

1. 2. Note that the three Persons of the Trinity are mentioned.

Preamble

1. 3. The opening words are identical with the same verse in Eph. and II Cor. The following verses to v. 9 inclusive are a series of clauses (relative and final) dependent on this verse, or subdependent on v. 7; vv. 10–12 are a further parenthesis. This is quite in the manner of St Paul.

1. 6–7. Persecution: "the trial of your faith", cf. James 1. 3 (identical words).

1. 7. "At the revelation of Jesus Christ" (USA), i.e. on the last day, already mentioned in v. 5.

1. 8. "You do not see him (Christ)" (USA): an aorist participle, which has not necessarily got the sense of the past. It does not necessarily imply that those disciples had never seen Christ.

1. 10–12. The parenthesis about the prophets. Cf. St Peter's first sermon (at Pentecost) recorded in Acts 2. 16–39, and later, in Acts 3. 18–25 (after the cure of the lame man). The argument is strikingly similar, showing the continuity of Peter's thought.

I. A PATTERN OF LIFE

1. 18–21. A summary of the Redemption by the Blood of Christ (cf. St Paul often, e.g. Col. 1. 20, "making peace through the Blood of his Cross"). "The mystery which had been hidden from ages and generations, but now is manifested to his saints" (Col. 1. 26): the same idea here, with emphasis on the generation of God the Son from God the

Father from all eternity ("Et ex Patre natum ante omnia saecula", as we sing in the Creed) (cf. St Thomas I 42. 2 for elucidation of the doctrine of the co-eternity of God the Son).

1. 21. Christ's Resurrection is our hope. A constant teaching of St Paul right from I Cor. (15. 14) down to II Tim. (2. 8).

2. 1. This trust in Christ's grace, this hope in his Resurrection, means "laying away all malice, etc."

2. 2–3. We must become as "new-born babes" in innocence, and seek for milk that is "uncontaminated" and "spiritual" (WV) (λογικόν, i.e. pertaining to the mind, whence Vulgate "rationabile", Rh "rational").[1] The milk is, of course, the Gospel (cf. I Cor. 3. 2).

2. 4–7. Christ as "a living stone, rejected by men". St Peter had used this figure before, in his address to the Council (Acts 4. 11). It comes from Ps. 117 (Heb. 118) 22, and was already used by Christ of himself in Mt. 21. 42 (Mk. 12. 10, Lk. 20. 17). This is a striking example of Peter (continuously in Acts and here) using a figure of Christ's.

2. 5 and 9. "A holy priesthood, to offer up spiritual sacrifices" (v. 4): a difficult passage. The most usual (but less enterprising) exegesis is that the priesthood referred to is to be understood of the offering of good works, prayers, penance, etc., and in that way only in a wide sense. But Dr Selwyn[2] maintains that the meaning is essentially *eucharistic*, since the context is that of "Christ, the spotless lamb" (1. 19), and of the temple (the "spiritual house", 2. 5), and of Christ crucified (who is a "stumbling-block", I Cor. 1. 23, surely connected with I Pet. 2. 8), even including the figure borrowed from the Psalms (33. 9), "You have tasted that the Lord is sweet," which is powerful in a eucharistic passage.

The Eucharistic Sacrifice is offered by the Church as a

---

[1] Introit on Low Sunday (for the newly-baptized), with its beautiful music.

[2] Selwyn, pp. 160, 291-8. This commentary, written by the (Anglican) Dean of Winchester and published in 1946, is quite outstanding for its scholarship, balanced judgement and orthodoxy.

whole; as the Levitical priesthood stood between God and Israel, so the Church as a whole stands in relation to mankind. The whole Church, which is Christ, shares in a manner in his priesthood: Christ was "made in all things like unto his brethren, that he might become a merciful and faithful high priest before God" (Heb. 2. 17). The priests ordained to offer the Sacrifice, do so on behalf of the whole Church, as the words of the Mass frequently show.[1] This exegesis of Dr Selwyn is very important in view of the modern teaching (especially in Pius XI's Encyclical "Miserentissimus Redemptor" of 1928)[2] on the "priesthood of the laity".

The phrase "a kingly priesthood" (v. 9) is, together with "a holy nation", quoted from Exodus 19. 6 (LXX, the Hebrew has "a kingdom of priests"). The simplest explanation is that when we share the priestly dignity of Christ, we also share in his royal dignity. But Dr Selwyn is inclined to consider $\beta\alpha\sigma\iota\lambda\epsilon\iota\text{o}\nu$ to be not an adjective (the others follow their nouns, anyway), but a noun, meaning simply "a palace", taking up the figure of house (as in v. 5): "you are . . . a royal building, a priesthood".[3] On the other hand in the Roman Empire royalty and priesthood were closely connected (and emperor-worship had begun to show itself by now), so that, after the safeguard "a holy priesthood" had been made before, there might be a reference to royal dignity attaching to the priesthood.

2. 5. The figure of the Christians as stones, forming a spiritual house, was used by St Paul both early (I Cor. 3. 10–16: Christ is the foundation) and late (Eph. 2. 20: Christ is the corner-stone).

[1] e.g. "meum ac vestrum sacrificium"; "hanc igitur oblationem servitutis nostrae, sed et cunctae familiae tuae"; "tibi offerimus, vel qui tibi offerunt" etc.

[2] Parts of the Encyclical are read in the Breviary during the Octave of the Sacred Heart. The relevant section, including the quotation of 2. 9, "regale sacerdotium," comes in lectio vi on Monday (Roman), on the Octave-Day (Dominican Breviary, ed. 1930).

[3] Selwyn, pp. 165-6.

2. 8. "A stone of stumbling and a rock of scandal": quoting Isaias 8. 14, as did St Paul in Rom. 9. 33. St Peter does not go into matter of the final conversion of the Jews, as St Paul proceeds to do in c. 10–11 (especially 11. 25–26).

II. OBEDIENCE AND SERVICE

2. 12. "Conversation good among the gentiles": another sign of those to whom Peter is writing being "strangers" in a gentile land.

2. 14. The remarks about the government that could hardly have been written after Nero's persecution. "King" = the Emperor.

2. 17. The important principle of "respect and courtesy due to the human personality as such" (Selwyn).

2. 21. Christ's example of patience.

2. 24. "Upon the tree": a phrase used twice by Peter in his speeches recorded in Acts 5. 30 and 10. 39 (Cornelius).

2. 25. "Bishop of your souls": since the Vulgate merely transliterated the Greek and wrote "Episcopus" (see Phil. 1. 1 and note), all the old versions have "bishop". But the meaning here is only an extension of the idea of "shepherd", and so is translated according to its original meaning of "overseer" by USA ("guardian") and RAK. But it is important that it is this word, linked by Peter with Our Lord's title of "shepherd", that became the regular word for a bishop.

2. 18, 3. 1, 3. 7: advice to servants, wives, husbands. Cf. very similar passages in Paul: Eph. 5. 21 sq., Col. 3. 18 sq.

III. SUFFERING

3. 18–22. They are to be comforted in their small trials, by the thought that Christ not merely suffered, but died, and died for our sins.

3. 18. He "died once": cf. Heb. 9. 12, Christ "entered

once into the Holies": the one all-sufficient Sacrifice of
Christ.

3. 19. "In which (i.e. spirit, v. 18) also coming he
preached to those spirits that were in prison": a passage of
celebrated difficulty. It is very natural to take 4. 6 in
connexion: "For this cause was the gospel preached also to
the dead."

Since 3. 19 comes between mentions of the Passion (v. 18)
and of the Resurrection (v. 21) and Ascension (v. 22), it clearly
refers to "He descended into hell" of the Creed. But there are
difficulties of exact interpretation:

(a) "In which" is usually understood of Christ's spirit or
soul in v. 18, separated from his body. That his soul only
descended into the lower world is the usual Catholic doctrine: "descendit in anima, et resurrexit in carne" (Council
of the Lateran IV, Denz., 429). But this is not a usual construction, and the phrase may merely mean "in the mean-
time".

(b) Who are the "spirits in prison"? (i) The usual interpretation (e.g. Fr Holzmeister, and the lexica of Abbott-
Smith and Zorell) is of the souls of the just detained in
Limbo (and RAK's note puts down this interpretation as
"certain"). (ii) But Dr Selwyn claims[1] (although admitting
the possibility of the above interpretation) that the word
πνεύματα (spirits) is always used in the NT of preternatural
manifestations (usually evil spirits, e.g. Lk. 10. 20, I Tim. 4.
1) and never (except for the phrase "the spirits of the just" in
Heb. 12. 23) of the souls of the departed, for which the proper
word is ψυχαί (souls), as in Apoc. 6. 9 and 20. 4 (note that
Apoc. 1. 4 and 16. 3 uses "spirits" of supernatural beings),[2]
and further, that although the earliest writers speak of Christ's
descent into hell, none until Clement of Alexandria (c. 200)
in Stromateis II and VI make use of this passage. This leads

[1] Selwyn, pp. 198 sq. and Essay I, especially pp. 353 sq., and 340-3
(Patristic evidence).
[2] A glance at a concordance will show this at once.

to the other interpretation, that the "spirits" are the evil spirits of the lower world.[1]

(c) In what sense did Christ "preach" to the spirits? (i) If the reference is to human souls, he obviously preached the news of redemption, or else "proclaimed" their freedom. (ii) If the reference is to evil spirits, Christ was proclaiming his victory.

3. 20. "These (i.e. either the men, or the spirits) in times past had been disobedient . . ." (USA).

In the time of Noe "eight souls (ψυχαί) were saved through water".

3. 21. "Its counterpart, Baptism, now saves you also" (USA).

3. 22. "Powers and Virtues being made subject to him" (USA): the terms "Powers and Virtues" are more often in St Paul (e.g. I Cor. 15. 24, Rom. 8. 38, and Col. 2. 15, where see note) used to denote powers hostile to Christ.

4. 3. The depravity resulting from paganism (cf. Rom. 1. 24–32).

4. 6. The interpretation depends upon that of 3. 19. (i) If that passage refers to the souls of the just, this one is to be taken with it, referring to Christ's descent into hell. (ii) If that passage refers to evil spirits, the meaning in this verse is that Christ is indeed appointed Judge of "the living and the dead".

4. 7. "The end of all is at hand": i.e. we should all be ready; this text is commented by St Peter himself later (II Pet. 3. 8): "But of this one thing I would not have you ignorant, my beloved, that one day with the Lord is as a thousand years,

---

[1] Note that although the Church has clearly defined Christ's descent into Limbo after his death, but has never defined that the purpose was to free the souls of the just detained there, nor ever made use of this passage in that connexion, yet the doctrine that at that moment he did in fact free the souls of the just, the "sancti patres" and open Heaven for them, is a part of common Catholic teaching (cf. St. Thomas III 52.5 and Catechism, nos. 64-65).

and a thousand years as one day", and cf. St Paul's warnings in I–II Thess. (see notes there).

4. 8. "Charity covereth a multitude of sins", cf. the last verse of James (5. 20), where the phrase describes the work of converting a sinner.

4. 13. "Beloved, if you are called upon to face a fiery persecution, don't be amazed as if something extraordinary were happening to you. It is sent to test you" (Wand).

4. 18. "If the just man shall scarcely be saved . . .": quoted from the LXX of Prov. 11. 31 (the Hebrew reads, "Behold the just man shall be recompensed on earth").

IV. RECOMMENDATIONS TO HUMILITY AND WATCHFULNESS

5. 1. The "Ancients" (πρεσβύτεροι): the word originally means "older men", and was used in classical Greek for "ambassadors". In the NT it is frequently used for the "elders" of Israel. In Acts 15 (frequently) and 21. 18, and also in I Tim. 5. 17, 19 it is used for those in authority in the Church. In Titus 1. 5 ("ordain priests") and James 5. 14 ("bring in the priests") a priestly duty is more specifically implied. Later (also in Latin "Presbyter") it came to be the usual word for "priest"[1]. USA and RAK leave the word "presbyters" and WV simply translates "priests". John in his Second and Third Epistles styles himself so. Peter here calls himself a συμπρεσβύτερος ("fellow-presbyter" USA).

5. 2–3. Their duty is to "feed the flock" and not to "lord it over the clergy (κλῆροι)": this Greek word, from which ours is derived, meant originally a lot or portion appointed to someone, and so a sphere of work entrusted to someone, here of pastoral care, hence WV and USA "not lording it over your charges", which is more exact than Rh, for the meaning "clergy" is a later one altogether.

---

[1] Cf. the modern word "Presbytery" =priest's house.

5. 5. "Younger men" are to be subject to the "older", the presbyters: there is a play upon the use of the latter word.

5. 8–9. The well-known warning against the devil, which the Church uses nightly (apart from Holy Week) at the beginning of Compline: "Fratres, sobrii estote et vigilate, etc."

5. 12–13. For Silvanus and "Babylon" see Introduction to this Epistle.

(Second Group: Jude and II Peter)

(43)   THE EPISTLE OF ST JUDE

The Author. In the lists of the Apostles in Mt. 10. 3, Mk. 3. 18 and Lk. 6. 16 all the names correspond, except that Lk. (also in Acts 1. 13) gives "Jude of James" while Mt. and Mk. give "Thaddaeus". So that there is no doubt that the same person is intended. Anyway, Thaddaeus in Aramaic תדי (Taddai) has the form of a surname, while Jude is a common first name. Judas Iscariot also used a surname to distinguish him. Apart from these lists the name Thaddaeus is not used again. Jude's own description of himself (v. 1) as "brother of James" has led us to suppose that Lk.'s "Jude of James" means (rather unusually) "brother of James". Jude is mentioned (with James) as a "brother of the Lord" in Mt. 13. 55 and Mk. 6. 3.

The only other thing we know of him from the Gospels is the question recorded by John (14. 22), "Lord, how is it that thou wilt manifest thyself to us, and not to the world?"

Date and Occasion. The brief text gives us no certain information. But he is evidently writing to strengthen his readers against the sudden inroads of false teachers. He says he is "under necessity to write" (v. 3). Can that necessity be the fact, mentioned just before (v. 1), that he is the brother of James who has just been removed by death? This certainly explains the "necessity" why *he* in particular should write. And Hegesippus (in Eusebius, IV, 22) tells us that after the death of James, Simeon, Our Lord's uncle, was made Bishop, but that at the same time a certain Thebutis "began secretly to corrupt" the Church of Jerusalem. This picture of heresy secretly creeping in coincides with the situation envisaged by St Jude. So we are conjecturing that the Epistle was written after A.D. 62 to Jerusalem. Further, one cannot help supposing that some reference to the political turmoil in Palestine would have been made had the Jewish War of 66 already begun. But there is no indication of a war-background at all, so we are supposing the Epistle to have been written before 66.

Argument. Address (1–2).

Reason for writing: warning against heretics (3–4).

  I. Examples of apostasy and its consequences (5–16):
     (i) The faithless people of Israel (5).
    (ii) The fallen angels (6).
   (iii) Sodom and Gomorrha (7–8).
   (iv) The Devil at the death of Moses (9–10).
    (v) Cain, Balaam and Core (11).
   (vi) Enoch (14).

(The examples are interspersed with colourful pictures of what heresy means, 8, 10, 12–13, 15–16.)

Note carefully that (iv) and (vi) above are examples taken from current (apocryphal) legendary literature of the Jews: from books (which have in part come down to us) entitled *The Assumption of Moses* and *The Book of Enoch* respectively. St Jerome (*De Vir. Illustr.*, 4) says that this is the reason why some people in the Early Church rejected this Epistle.

 II. But they are to stand fast (remembering that the Apostles foretold the coming of heresy), "keep in the love of God" (21), and when possible correct those who have erred, "pulling them out of the fire" (23) (17–25).

Relation with II Peter. It may be that other phrases apart from vv. 9 and 14 are taken from legendary literature, which is a possible way of explaining the striking similarity of certain figures and phrases to those in II Peter, i.e. that they are borrowed from a common source. It is rare, however, that there is any prolonged verbal identity (in the Greek) between the two Epistles: both may, however, include vague recollections of the same legends. (The manifest quotations are only in Jude.)

The other obvious possibility is that II Peter borrowed from Jude, or vice-versa. There is no way of proving this one way or the other. Out of the twenty-five verses of Jude, at least eleven contain strong parallels with II Peter.

Apart from chronological grounds (for II Peter was probably written between 64 and 67), it seems to me probable that Jude was written before II Peter: (i) Jude would hardly write so short an Epistle and copy most of it from II Peter: but it is more likely that Peter would incorporate many of Jude's ideas into his sixty-one verses. (ii) The figures where they coincide are usually more colourful in Jude, which suggests they are the original and that Peter, having heard them and liked them, put many of them into his own II Epistle.

(It is Peter's second chapter, a warning against heretics, that contains the parallels with Jude, but in c. 1 and 3 he speaks of other things.)

An example would not be amiss, given in Dr Wand's version, which preserves the vividness of the original:

Jude 12–13. These men are blots on your love-feasts, when they have the audacity to feed with you. . . They are clouds that give no rain, driving all ways before the wind. They are like trees in autumn that bear no fruit, doubly dead, torn up by the roots. Like the raging waves of the sea they cast up nothing but refuse. They are like shooting stars, for which is reserved utter and final darkness for ever.	*II Pet. 2. 13, 17.* They are blots and blemishes on society, using their very love-feasts as an opportunity for revelling, even when you are at the feast with them. . . They are as useless as dried-up springs, or as vague mists driven by the wind. Uttermost darkness awaits them in the end.

THE SECOND EPISTLE OF ST PETER

The Author. We have seen how until the Decree of Damasus in A.D. 382 (Denz., 84) there were doubts about the canonicity of II Peter. No definite citation of Peter as its author is found until Origen, *c.* A.D. 250. All Catholic writers, of course, accept the Epistle as canonical inspired Scripture, but there are several, including no less an authority than M. Chaine in his *Épîtres Catholiques*, who hold that it is not directly Petrine, but is the work of a disciple writing with the authority of St Peter (cf. Hebrews and St Paul), drawing also upon St Jude and to some extent on I Peter and on St Paul.[1] Outside the Church the majority of writers reject the Petrine authorship altogether, perhaps allowing that there are fragments of Peter's teaching in the Epistle.

The original reason for the doubts about II Peter is the difference in style from I Peter, which (as St Jerome already explained) is understandable if Silvanus was no longer there, and Peter used someone else as his secretary to "write up" what he wished to convey. If the secretary had not read Jude, but merely had the images from Peter, it is also understandable that the same images appear in II Peter, but with considerable differences in the words.

In view of the strong tradition that appears first with Origen, though doubts are also recorded, that the author is Peter, and in view of the claims of the text of the Epistle itself, the simplest course is to accept either the direct authorship of Peter, or at least to suppose that it was written for him by a secretary (a different one from that of I Peter).

Time and place. From c. 1 it is obvious that (like II Tim.) this letter is a farewell of one who is awaiting the end: (1. 13–14) "I hold it my duty to keep the memory awake in you, while I am still in this brief dwelling-place (tabernacu-

---

[1] See, for instance, G. Thils, *L'Enseignement de S. Pierre* (Paris, 1943), p. 15.

lum, or tent, in Latin); I am assured, by what our Lord Jesus
Christ has made known to me, that I must fold my tent before
long (tabernaculum again)" (RAK). These phrases suggest
that the writer (as with II Tim.) is awaiting the inevitable
execution of sentence, and it is on these grounds that the
Epistle is dated after 64, the persecution of Nero, and probably close to 67, the traditional date of the Apostle's death.

To whom? 3. 1: "Behold this second Epistle I write to you."
Although I Peter envisages persecution from without, little
had been said about perils from within. Perhaps it was Jude's
denunciation of these perils that made Peter warn the people
he had written to before of the dangers of heresy. Now he
gives them this last warning, implying that even if these
dangers have not yet appeared among them, they are to
expect them ("there shall come deceitful scoffers", 3. 3).

Argument. Address (1. 1–2).
 I. The necessity for Christian virtue (c. 1).
    (i) Because of Christ's own promises (1. 3–11).
    (ii) Peter's claim to authority ("we were eye-
        witnesses of his greatness", 1. 16) (1. 12–18).
    (iii) Because of the prophecies (1. 19–21).

 II. Warning against "false prophets", with examples of
the consequences of apostasy (c. 2).
    (i) The fallen angels (2. 4, cf. Jude 6).
    (ii) The deluge (2. 5, cf. I Pet. 3. 20).
    (iii) Sodom and Gomorrha (2. 6–8, cf. Jude 7–8).
    (iv) Balaam (2. 15–16, cf. Jude 11).

(The examples are, as in Jude, interspersed with pictures
of what heresy means, 2. 10–14, 17–22.)

 III. Warning against false teaching on the Second Coming
of Christ (c. 3).
    He is more concerned with those who deny the
Second Coming altogether, than (as was Paul in
I–II Thess.) with those who expected it at once.

He tells them to expect it (3. 12–14), but not necessarily immediately (3. 8).

Lastly, he tells them to "account the longsuffering of our Lord, salvation, as also our most dear brother Paul . . . hath written to you" (3. 15). (See note below.)

Some important texts

1. 4. "Partakers of the divine nature" by Redemption and God's grace in the soul. Cf. the prayer "Deus qui humanae substantiae" at the blessing of the water in the Mass (Roman Rite): "ejus divinitatis esse consortes".

1. 17–18. Christ's "greatness": he refers to the Transfiguration, "when we (himself and the brothers James, the Great, and John) were with him in the holy mount" (Mt. 17. 1–8, exact quotation of the words they heard; cf. Mk. 9. 1–7, Lk. 9. 28–36).

1. 20. "No prophecy of Scripture is matter for private interpretation" (WV), lit. "is (or becomes) of private interpretation", probably interpretation by the reader, but possibly by the prophet himself, i.e. he does not speak in his own person.

3. 10. "The Day of the Lord shall come as a thief": Our Lord's phrase in Mt. 24. 43 (Lk. 12. 39), used also by St Paul in I Thess. 5. 2 (where see note), and Apoc. 3. 3, 16. 15.

3. 15. "The longsuffering of our Lord" might mean his patience in his Passion, referred to more than once in I Peter (2. 21 sq. and 3. 18, 4. 1), but it would be difficult to see what parallel in St Paul the writer is thinking of. But the word itself ($\mu\alpha\kappa\rho o\theta\upsilon\mu\iota\alpha$) is used by both Peter (I Pet. 3. 20) and Paul (Rom. 2. 4, 9. 22) of God's forbearance or patience with mankind, and so here probably is to be understood of God's allowing time for penance before his Second Coming and Judgement. But it is not at all certain what passage in St Paul is here alluded to, or which of St Paul's Epistles the

readers of II Peter would be already familiar with. I Thess.
5. 1–11 is possible (and having been written about fifteen
years before, would probably be already in circulation).
Eph. (especially 6. 10–18) and Col. (especially c. 3) would
probably be known all over Asia Minor—they were written
between four and nine years previously, and Eph. was probably an encyclical to the Churches of Asia.

3. 16. The celebrated reference to the difficulty of St Paul's
Epistles.

(Third Group: The Epistles of St John)

(44–45)   THE FIRST EPISTLE OF
                  ST JOHN

"The same vein of divine love, and charity towards our
neighbour, which runs throughout the Gospel written by the
beloved disciple and evangelist, St John, is found also in his
Epistles": Dr Challoner in the heading to this Epistle.

That the author of this Epistle was the same person as the
author of the Fourth Gospel is obvious to any reader, apart
from the universal tradition which accepts John the Apostle
and Evangelist as its author. The tradition appears in writing
with Ireneus (c. A.D. 200), in his *Adversus Haereses*, III, 16
(Eusebius, V, 8), and probably already with Papias (c. A.D.
130) (Eusebius, III, 39 at the end). No reasonable doubts can
be cast on its authorship.

There is no exact indication of the time and place of writing. Some writers maintain that it was written as a preface to
the Gospel: others (I think more justifiably) hold that it was
written after the Gospel, for a knowledge of the Gospel is
almost essential to a sufficient understanding of the Epistle.
It is probably more or less contemporary with the Gospel,
i.e. from the time when John, released from his exile at
Patmos, was governing the Church of Ephesus, after A.D. 96

(the accession of the Emperor Nerva and revocation of Domitian's decrees of banishment: see Eusebius, III, 20 end). The readers seem to be well known to the writer, and one supposes them to be the Christian communities in Asia Minor. A date at the end of the first century also suggests itself from the presence of heretics who denied the divinity of Christ (e.g. I Jn. 3, 22), especially the Cerinthians (Ireneus, *Adv. Haer.*, I, 26 and see Eusebius, III, 27–29).

Argument. Although the main lines of the argument are clear enough, it is not easy to make hard and fast divisions. The themes recur and the thought passes lightly from one to another. In this the Epistle is unlike the Gospel, where, although there are frequently recurring themes, yet the plan is easy enough. This very fact perhaps suggests that the Epistle was written in its rather vague way to people who already knew the clear teaching of the Gospel. The story is told how St John in his very old age reduced Christian ethics to the command, "Little children, love one another":[1] perhaps St John, looking down the years of his long life, now saw the message of Christ to the world in all its simplicity. He had told the story in detail. Now in this letter he sums up the Christian message in its essentials. He is speaking "to them that know the truth" (2. 21), and he is warning them, as an affectionate father warns his children, against the dangers of falsehood. In this treasure of Christian teaching we have (together with the brief Second and Third Epistles) the last voice of an Apostle, still speaking to the world 100 years after the birth of Christ.

A notable (Johannine) characteristic is the argument by contrast. At each stage John speaks in terms of contrasts (light and darkness, truth and falsehood, etc.) and each pair finds its counterpart in the teaching of his Gospel.

---

[1] St Jerome's story (commentary on Gal. 6. 10), to be read in the Breviary on the Feast of St John, Dec. 27th, lectio vi.

I. The main theme: the Word of Life[1] (1. 1–4).

(Note that the Gospel begins with the same idea: 1. 4, "In him was life, and the life was the light of men"; 14. 6, "I am the way, and the truth, and the life"[2]).

II. God is *light*—to have fellowship with him we must not walk in *darkness* (sin) (1. 5–2. 17).

(Gospel 1. 5, "The light shineth in darkness, etc."; 8. 12, "I am the light of the world").

Sin is the only obstacle, and for sin we have a remedy: "We have an advocate, Jesus Christ" (2. 1).

We know whether we belong to him, if we keep his commandments (2. 3, Gospel 14. 15, "If you love me, keep my commandments").

And sins are forgiven through Christ (2. 12).

Therefore "love not the world" (2. 15), for "the *world* passeth away—but he that doth the *will of God*, abideth for ever" (2. 17).

III. Warning against the Antichrist (2. 18–29).

"There are many become *Antichrists*—but you have the *unction of the Holy One*" (2. 18, 20): "they went out from us, but they were not of us" (2. 19), the heretics. The essence of the Antichrist: "he who denieth that Jesus is the Christ" (2. 22), he is a *liar*—you know the *truth* (cf. Gospel 8. 44, "[The Devil] stood not in the truth, because truth is not in him . . . for he is a liar").

IV. The Christian vocation (c. 3).

We are called to be "*sons of God*"—not "*children of the devil*" (3. 1, 10) (cf. Gospel 1. 12, "But as many as received him, he gave them power to be made the sons of God, to them that believe in his name").

---

[1] The opening verses, enunciating the main theme, are beautifully rendered by Dr Wand: see below on 1. 1.

[2] We are choosing simply well-known Gospel parallels at random: a glance at a concordance under the key-words will show how often they come in St John's Gospel.

"This is the declaration . . . that you should love one another" (2. 11) (cf. Gospel 13. 34, 15. 12, "This is my commandment, that you love one another").

In this "we know that we have passed from *death* to *life* (3. 14); because of these principles they are not to wonder "if the world hate you" (3. 13) (cf. Gospel 15. 18, "If the world hate you, know you that it hath hated me before you").

Confidence in prayer: "whatsoever we shall ask, we shall receive" (3. 22) (cf. Gospel 16. 23, "If you shall ask the Father anything in my name, he will give it you").

V. Distinguish the *spirit of truth*—and the *spirit of error*, for "false prophets are gone out into the world" (4. 1) (4. 1–6).

"Every spirit that confesseth that Jesus Christ is come in the flesh, is *of God*—every spirit that dissolveth Jesus, is *not of God*" (4. 2–3): "you are of *God*—they are of *the world* (4. 4–5).

VI. "He who loveth God, love also his brother" (4. 21) (4. 7–5. 12).

In this section John returns to his principal themes: God's love for us: "By this hath the charity of God appeared towards us, because God hath sent his only begotten Son into the world, that we may live by him" (4. 9) (cf. Gospel 3. 16, usually considered to be not the words of Christ, but a reflection of the evangelist, "God so loved the world, as to give his only begotten Son; that whosoever believeth in him, may not perish, but may have life everlasting"). God is the source of life. Because God loves us, we are to love him, and because we love him, we are to love our neighbour. Here he says: "God *is* love (Rh, charity)" (4. 8). Further he here explains how for the lover of God, "God abideth in him" (4. 15) (cf. Gospel 14. 23, "If anyone love me, he will keep my word, and my

Father will love him, and we will come to him, and will make our abode with him"). Again he brings in the idea of our sonship of God (5. 1).

"Whatsoever is born of God, overcometh the world" (5. 4): the victory of Christ over the world is the central theme of the Apocalypse, and cf. Gospel 16. 33 (the end of Christ's discourse, before his prayer), "I have overcome the world".

The verses 5. 7–8, known as the text of the Heavenly Witnesses, will receive comment below.

VII. Epilogue: confidence in prayer is again urged, and warnings are given about sin and idolatry (5. 13–21).

Short exegesis

1. 1–4. The main theme of the Epistle. The sense and the manner of St John are so perfectly captured in the version of Dr Wand that we give it in its entirety:

"I am going to write to you about the Word of Life. He existed from the beginning, before time was; yet I have listened to Him; I have seen Him with my own eyes; I have really looked at Him, and have touched Him with my own hands. What that Word revealed to us was Life. I have really seen Eternal Life. And now I am testifying to it and announcing it to you. That Life was with the Father, and yet it was revealed to us. I am telling you about something that I have actually seen and heard, in order that you, too, may share our comradeship in this knowledge. And that comradeship of ours is with the Father and with His Son, Jesus Christ. The reason why I am writing to you on this subject is that I want your joy to be complete."

1. 9. "If we confess our sins," God in his faithfulness and justice forgives us. Taken alone this text would not prove the existence of sacramental confession of particular sins, but, being written at the very end of New Testament times, it must be taken together with other passages and it then

becomes itself very convincing evidence. Of particular importance is John's own witness (which he here would take for granted) about the power of forgiving sins given to the Apostles (Jn. 20. 23), "Whose sins you shall forgive, they are forgiven them; and whose sins you shall retain, they are retained". The famous text from James (5. 16), coming in the context of calling in the priests, "Confess therefore your sins one to another," must also be taken into account.

2. 1. Jesus is our "advocate": παράκλητος, a Johannine word, used elsewhere in the New Testament only in the Gospel of St John, and then always of the "other Paraclete", the Holy Ghost, whom the Father will send (Jn. 14. 16, 26, 15. 26, 16. 7). The word properly means an advocate (one called to someone's side), and this is the translation of all the versions in the Epistle. In the Gospel, Rh simply uses the Greek word (as the Latin also does[1]), while WV and USA (on the principle of consistent translation) have "advocate" in the Gospel also. The older versions generally use "comforter" in the Gospel (e.g. AV). RAK in the Gospel has "he who is to befriend you" or something similar.

2. 2. Christ is the "propitiation" for our sins: an idea treated at length by St Paul in Romans (e.g. 3. 25).

2. 7–8. The commandment that is both old and new: "That you love one another as I have loved you" (Jn. 13. 34). The commandment to love one's neighbour is already in the Old Testament (Leviticus 19. 18), and St Paul had already said (Rom. 13. 8), "He that loveth his neighbour hath fulfilled the Law". St John comes back to this idea in his Second Epistle (v. 5). We have had this commandment "from the beginning"; but it is new, because the motive is new. We are to love one another as Christ has loved us: and Christ, after repeating this in Jn. 15. 12, adds, "Greater love than this no man hath,

[1] The Rheims often preserved a Greek or Latin word in English, claiming that it is a theological technical term. Many such words from Rheims (like the present word) have in fact remained in the English language.

that a man lay down his life for his friends" (Jn. 15. 13). If we have such love for one another, this is verified "both in him (Christ) and in you (Christians)". Now, since Christ has come, "darkness is passed, and the true light shineth", and (2. 10) "he that loveth his brother, abideth in the light".

2. 12–14. "I write unto you, little children—fathers—young men—babes (παιδία Rh infants, USA little ones, RAK sons)": this is either addressed first to all Christians, under St John's frequent title "little children", and then to various categories; or else (as RAK holds) written to all under the various titles, "fathers" because they have long possessed the knowledge, "young men" because they are strong and have "gained the victory over the evil one". There is something touching in these words to "young men", written by one aged over ninety.

2. 16. Of the world is "the lust of the flesh, and the lust of the eyes, and the pride of life": these have become classical expressions.

2. 18. "Antichrist": St John's word (ἀντί properly means "opposite to", and so "in the place of"). It is probably to be understood in a wider sense than Paul's "man of sin, son of perdition" who is to come before the end, for here the Antichrist is he "who denieth the Father and the Son" (2. 22). "The last hour": the present age between the Redemption and Christ's return, what St Peter (I Pet. 1. 5 and 20) calls "these last times". St Paul had already warned Christians that there will be many signs before the end (II Thess. 2. 2 sq.) and St Peter that the end may be still be very far away (II Pet. 3. 8, "One day is as a thousand years").

2. 20. "You have an anointing from the Holy One" (USA): usually understood to refer to the grace of the Holy Spirit. The Holy One is Christ, in whose name the Father sends the Paraclete (Jn. 14. 26), or who himself sends the Paraclete (Jn. 15. 26, 16. 7).

2. 27. It is this "anointing" ("unction") that "teacheth

you of all things": cf. Gospel 15. 26, "The Paraclete . . . will teach you all things".

3. 2. In the next life, which will begin with the Second Coming of Christ, we shall see God "as he is", not as now "through a glass in a dark manner: but face to face" (I Cor. 13. 12). "We shall be like to him", or as St Peter put it (II Pet. 1. 4), "made partakers of the divine nature". It is an article of Faith that the blessed in Heaven see the very Essence of God, not through any medium, nor by the light of their created human intellect, but "lumine gloriae, ipsam (*sc.* the soul) elevante ad Deum videndum et eo beate fruendum" ("by the 'Light of Glory', i.e. divine illumination of the intellect, raising the soul to the vision of God and the blessed enjoyment of him") (Council of Vienne, A.D. 1311, Denz., 475, and cf. the famous Constitution *Benedictus Deus* of Pope Benedict XII, Denz., 530). It is by the elevation of our intellect to the vision of God that we become "like unto him". St Thomas treats of this matter at length in I 12. 2 and adjacent articles.

3. 9. For the idea of spiritual rebirth, cf. Jn. 3. 3–7 (Nicodemus), "Unless a man be born again . . ." It is obvious from what St John has said before that it is possible for one "reborn" by Baptism to fall into sin (and the opposite teaching has been condemned by the Church—Trent, session vi, canon 23, Denz., 833), and this passage can therefore only mean that a man, in so far as he has in him "the seed of God", cannot sin. St John writes the Epistle (2. 1) to keep them from sin, saying (1. 8–9) that we must admit the existence of sin in ourselves, and also confess our sins: the possibility is clearly envisaged. There is difficulty about the meaning of the "seed". The commoner interpretation is "the seed of grace" in the soul, though RAK and Wand in their translations suggest "seed" in the sense of "parentage" or "inheritance" from God.

3. 15. "Whosoever hateth his brother is a murderer": Our

Lord's principle, enunciated in the Sermon on the Mount, that evil lies in the intention of the will rather than in the deed itself (Mt. 5. 21–28), for the commandment not to kill forbids also hatred, and the commandment against adultery includes also lust.

3. 16. Once more (cf. 2. 7–8 with notes) our love for one another is to be like Christ's love for us.

3. 20. "If our heart reprehend us": RAK "our consciences", and Dr Wand introduces the word "scruples".

4. 3. "Every spirit that dissolveth Jesus . . . is Antichrist": "dissolveth" is the Vulgate reading here, having support in many early quotations in the Fathers, though the ancient MSS all read "that confesseth not". The sense of "dissolveth" is, of course, the separation of Christ's Divinity and Humanity, and the negation of one or the other, the two oldest heresies in Christendom (Cerinthians denying his Divinity, Docetists his Humanity[1]).

4. 8. "God is love": almost all the versions translate ἀγάπη by "love", though Rh keeps "charity", following the Vulgate, and linking the phrase with the Theological Virtue of Charity (friendship with God) planted in us by God himself, so that we thus participate in God's own love (St Thomas I–II 23. 2 *ad* 1). Love is the first movement of the Will, but in God, Love, like Being, Goodness, Wisdom, etc., is not merely a quality in God, but is the Divine Essence Itself (St Thomas I 3. 6, cf. I 20. 1), so that the words "God is his own Love" is theologically very accurate.

5. 6. "He that came by water and blood, Jesus Christ":[2] there are two principal interpretations of this difficult verse. (i) (traceable to Tertullian, and the commonest) That Christ's mission began with this Baptism, but was not merely a mission of preaching to the world. It ended with the shedding of

---

[1] "Docetist" is actually a nickname: they held that Christ is truly God, but only *appears* (δοκεῖ) to be a man.

[2] Codices ℵ and A have "by water and blood and spirit", which probably arose through the three being mentioned together in v. 8.

his Blood on the Cross for the Redemption of mankind. "And the Spirit testifieth" to this work: "he shall give testimony of me" (Jn. 15. 26). (ii) (traceable to St Augustine) That the passage is linked with the account (given by John alone, in 19. 34) that "one of the soldiers with a spear opened his side, and immediately there came out blood and water". This was apparently done by way of proving the reality of his death (for "they saw that he was already dead", v. 33). Here it would therefore be a proof of Christ's true humanity. But the blood and water at Christ's death receive also a symbolical meaning: the blood represents our redemption, and the water our entrance into that redemption by baptism. But water is also used in St John's Gospel as a symbol of grace, e.g. in Jn. 4. 14 (Christ to the Samaritan woman), "The water that I will give him, shall become in him a fountain of water, springing up into life everlasting."

5. 7–8. These verses contain a section which is not found in any of the ancient Greek codices, but which seems always to have been accepted by the Latin tradition, and appears in the Vulgate. This section we print here in italics: "And there are three who give testimony *in heaven: the Father, the Word, and the Holy Ghost. And these three are one. And there are three that give testimony on earth*: the spirit, and the water, and the blood, and these three are one". First of all it should be observed that the passage reads equally well with or without the disputed section, although the fuller version provides a valuable Trinitarian text. The constant absence in the East (and it would have been a useful text in the early trinitarian controversies) and the equally constant presence in the West make it impossible at present to decide whether the passage is genuine and got lost in the East, or is spurious and got inserted in the West.

Meanwhile, the Holy Office has regulated the position for practical purposes: in 1897 they were asked, "Can the authenticity of the text in I Jn. 5. 7 be safely denied or held in doubt?" They answered "No"; but in 1927 the same Congregation declared that the decree of 1897 was only made to restrain teachers from too boldly rejecting or doubting the authenticity, and by no means intends to prevent scholars from making further investigations, provided they are prepared to accept a decision of the Church, should one be made. (Denz., 2198 for both decrees.)

The disputed passage is known as "the text of the Heavenly Witnesses" or the "Comma Joanneum",[1] and is at present found in all Catholic versions, and had been put into the Greek printed texts of the sixteenth to seventeenth centuries, and so is also in the AV.

5. 16. "A sin not unto death"—we are to pray for such a sinner. But there is "a sin unto death"—we are not commanded to pray for such a case, though such prayer cannot of course be excluded, or forbidden. The intended distinction of sin is "hard to determine" (Dr Challoner's note in Rh: a very good note). Since "life shall be given" to the sinner converted from a sin not unto death, it would seem that both sins are mortal sins. The probability is that the sin unto death refers to wilful apostasy with final impenitence, when a man has become so hardened and obstinate in sin that he becomes quite unapproachable on the matter. It is the constant teaching of the Church that there is no sin that cannot be forgiven if the sinner repents before his death, as Pope Gelasius I wrote (c. A.D. 495), "Nullum est quippe peccatum, pro quo aut non oret Ecclesia remittendo, aut quod, data sibi divinitus potestate, desistentibus ab eodem non possit absolvere" (Denz., 167). It is only the unrepentant, or those who die in mortal sin without repentance (final impenitence), that the Church is powerless to help.

With regard to prayer for obstinate sinners, Dr Challoner writes: "Though we must pray for all sinners whatsoever,

---

[1] The Latin word Comma (gen. commatis) means a clause, or member of a sentence, and so came to be used of that which marks off a clause.

yet men cannot pray for such sinners with such a confidence
of obtaining always their petitions."

5. 21. One sentence at the very end is considered sufficient
by St John to give a warning against idolatry to those whom
he has been schooling in the Love of God.

THE SECOND EPISTLE OF ST JOHN

This is the shortest "book" in the whole Bible. The teaching
is so akin to that in I Jn., that little reasonable doubt is left
that the author is the same.

There are, however, two problems to be mentioned.

(i) The description of the author as ὁ πρεσβύτερος (Rh
"Senior", Challoner "Ancient", AV "Elder", WV "Priest",
USA, RAK "Presbyter") (and see note on this word in
I Pet. 5. 1), which caused some writers to hold that John the
Presbyter was not the same person as John the Apostle. We
have seen that this opinion persisted even till the Decree of
Pope Damasus in 382 (see p. 225). Let us observe first of all
that the Gospel and the First Epistle are anonymous, the
Second and Third Epistles are from the "Presbyter", and
the Apocalypse (1. 1, 4, 9) gives the writer's name. Eusebius
quotes Dionysius of Alexandria, who held that John, the
author of the Apocalypse, was not the same John who wrote
the Gospel and the First Epistle, and gives the report that
there are two tombs of Johns venerated at Ephesus, which, he
maintains, helps his thesis about the two authors (VII, 25).
Eusebius in III, 39 seems to incline to this view himself,
again quoting the report of the two tombs at Ephesus, and
supporting himself on the text of Papias (said by Ireneus in
Adv. Haer. V, 33, 4 to have been a "hearer" of John), which
he quotes as follows: "But if I met with anyone who had been
a follower of the presbyters anywhere, I made it a point to
inquire what were the declarations of the presbyters: what
Andrew or Peter said (εἶπεν), or Thomas or James or John
or Matthew or any other of the disciples of the Lord, also

what Aristion and the Presbyter John, disciples of the Lord, are saying (λέγουσιν)". Now Eusebius (having an "axe to grind", i.e. to maintain the distinct authorship of the Gospel and the Apocalypse) proceeds to observe with joy that John is listed twice, which, he says, proves the truth of the admittedly unconfirmed report about the two tombs. But an unbiased study of Papias' words shows that the first list refers to second-hand declarations ("said" in aorist), while Aristion and John the Presbyter are given as first-hand sources ("are saying" in present), with which Papias himself has had contact. So of John he has both had reports from others, and first-hand experience, he, therefore, is mentioned in both categories. Yet it is remarkable what theories have been built since Eusebius on a misunderstanding of this passage of Papias. Fr Hugh Pope calls John the Presbyter as a distinct person a "fiction".[1]

(ii) The question of the identity of ἐκλεκτή κυρία to whom the letter is addressed (Rh "the lady Elect", other versions "the elect Lady", RAK (translating and paraphrasing) "that sovereign lady whom God has chosen"). She has children (vv. 1, 4), she has a sister also with children (v. 13). Sometimes the singular is used (to her), sometimes the plural (to the family). He hopes soon to come and see them (v. 12), so they are probably also in Asia Minor.

It is impossible to say whether the ladies are individuals (III Jn. is clearly to an individual, but with a clear name) or represent Christian communities. Authors are divided. It is unlikely that the address represents a proper name, especially in view of the sister having the same title. The advice given to "walk in truth", to love one another, to persevere, to guard against heretics, seems rather to be intended for a local Church and her children, the faithful.

[1] The matter is fully treated (including the Greek text of Papias) in Höpfl's *Introductio* III, 13 sq., and briefly in WV, IV, Intro. to II–III Jn., and in Pope, V, 333.

THE THIRD EPISTLE OF ST JOHN

This short Epistle is also sent by "the Presbyter", this time to a certain Gaius. This is such a common name that it is hopeless to try and identify him.[1] Gaius is much commended for his good works, especially towards the travelling missionaries (vv. 6–8). John refers to a previous letter to the Church: the Greek text reads "I wrote something" (WV, v. 9), perhaps a short note like the present, which apparently has not come down to us. The proud Diotrephes has been trying to undermine John's authority (v. 9–10) (one thinks of II Cor. 10), but John will come soon himself and they will talk it over (v. 14). Demetrius is obviously a trusted friend of both John and Gaius (v. 12). The letter ends with anonymous greetings from friends to friends (v. 15).

[1] The *Apostolic Constitutions* (fourth-century traditional material)(VII, 46) say that this Gaius was Bishop of Pergamus.

PART V.

(46–50) THE APOCALYPSE OF ST JOHN

Note. The special nature of this very difficult book calls for a special treatment. We shall begin by noticing the problems connected with its authorship, and then go on to the main principles of interpretation. Next we shall give a general plan of the book, and finally we shall work rapidly through the text, amplifying the plan. Owing to the extreme difficulty it would be useless in a course like the present to attempt a detailed exegesis, or to set out to identify the various symbols in any detail or record their many interpretations. It will be much more useful to have a general impression of the visions, related to the dominant idea of the whole.

Authorship. From the beginning of the Christian tradition it has been generally held that the John who received the vision on the island of Patmos (Apoc. 1. 9) was indeed none other than John the Apostle and Evangelist. The earliest witness is Justin (in his Dialogue, 81, written *c.* A.D. 150) who clearly refers the work to "a man amongst us, by name John, one of Christ's Apostles". A hundred years later, however, this view had come to be doubted in certain circles in the East, beginning with Dionysius of Alexandria. This was on account of the use made of Apoc. 20. 1–7 by the adherents of Millenarianism or Chiliasm (mille, $\chi i\lambda\iota o\iota = 1000$), a belief which is found in various forms as early as Papias and as late as the time of St Jerome and St Augustine (*c.* 400).[1] When these ideas waned, the Apocalypse was restored to its rightful position in the East, and St Jerome says that in his time it was universally accepted in the East, and apparently had always been so in the West (Ep. 129,3 and cf. *De Vir. Illustr.*, 9).

Eusebius quotes Dionysius of Alexandria at length (VII, 25), and inclines to the view himself, supporting himself with

[1] The main idea of Chiliasm or Millenarianism is that after 1000 years Christ would come again to earth ("the first resurrection" of Apoc. 20. 5) and the just would reign with him on earth for a further 1000 years, while Satan would be bound. After this would come the "second resurrection", and the just would go to heaven with Christ and wicked to hell with Satan (cf. *Cath. Encycl.*, art. Millennium).

the theory of John the Presbyter, distinct from the Evangelist, who might be the author of the Apocalypse (III, 39). This matter was discussed in our study of St John's Second Epistle.

There are, however, reasons for hesitation apart from Chiliast associations. The style is most noticeably different: the Gospel and the Epistles are anonymous, while in Apoc. John names himself three times; the ideas are very different (though there are most striking similarities also, e.g. especially with regard to Christ, who is the "Word" and the "Lamb" in Apoc. also); Apoc. has many remarkable instances of patently wrong Greek grammar and syntax—errors that certainly do not occur in the other writings of John. (Examples of elementary grammatical mistakes are the nominative after ἀπό in 1. 4, or the masculine plural participle after πάντα in 5. 13.) In view of the strong tradition in favour of the Johannine authorship, one must attribute these differences to the very different circumstances of writing. The Apocalypse was written there and then, while John was rapt "in the spirit" (1. 10–11, etc.), and in hard conditions of banishment, while the Gospel and the Epistles were written in the friendly and meditative atmosphere of Ephesus after his release. Furthermore, the whole scope of the other writings is so different: John's own record of events and the teaching of Christ, his own moral advice, while the Apocalypse is the account made on the spot of a vision that transcends human understanding. These things fully suffice to explain a difference of style: in fact it would almost be remarkable if it were not so. The grammatical errors of the Apocalypse can be put down to the excitement of the moment (and he was writing in a foreign tongue, with no care at that moment for earthly grammar), and of course he would not wish afterwards to touch up what he had written during the trance. When writing his Gospel and Epistles he had every opportunity of writing deliberately and carefully.

There is no doubt that the vision occurred during the last years of the reign of Domitian, the Emperor who had banished St John to Patmos during his persecution of Christians (the Second Persecution, A.D. 91–93), after he had failed to kill him in Rome by placing him in boiling oil.[1] John was released at the accession of the Emperor Nerva in 96 (Eusebius, III, 20), which marks the latest date for the Apocalypse. Eusebius, followed by Jerome (*De Vir. Illustr.*, 9), places the vision in the fourteenth year of Domitian (A.D. 95).

It is sometimes suggested that the vision dates from the reign of Nero, who died in A.D 68, or just after this reign, for in Apoc. 17. 10 we read that five kings are fallen (Nero was the fifth Emperor of Rome), and the number 666 (in 13. 18) is usually interpreted to spell the name of Nero, and 11. 1 suggests that the Temple of Jerusalem was still standing (it was destroyed in 70). But these symbolic texts need not be taken so literally, since Nero may well stand for the type of the persecutor, and the Temple could easily indicate Jewish worship in general. The clear statement about Patmos in 1. 9 is a much surer guide to the date.

The main principles of interpretation. The title of the book is the 'Αποκάλυψις (from ἀπο-καλύπτω to un-cover, Latin "re-velare"), meaning therefore the "Revelation". The Latin text simply took over the original Greek word, which has continued to be preserved in our Catholic texts. The Protestant texts have all translated the word, so that the title in the AV is "The Revelation".

The whole book is an account of a revelation granted to John on a certain Sunday (1. 9), when he was rapt "in spirit", in a sort of trance. The writings of the mystics have always

---

[1] This event is commemorated in the Feast of St John before the Latin Gate (May 6th), for the ordeal took place near the Porta Latina in Rome, where the church of St John "in oleo" now stands. Tertullian says that John, "missus in ferventis olei dolium, purior et vegetior exiverit qvam intraverit". See St Jerome in the Breviary for May 6th (lectio v, OP iii); Tertullian, *De Praescriptionibus*, 36 (Rouët de Journel, n. 297).

shown that human diction is incapable of describing sublime mystical experience: recourse has to be had to symbols; and these symbols, presented in hard print, seem to our dull human ears fantastic and frequently impossible of clear imagination. St Paul said (II Cor. 12. 3–4): "I know such a man (whether in the body, or out of the body, I cannot tell: God knoweth): that he was caught up into paradise; and heard secret words, *which it is not granted to man to utter.*" Yet at the very beginning John was ordered :"What thou seest, write in a book" (1. 11), and he wrote as well as human words would allow. At one point, however, he is commanded not to write (10. 4): "And when the seven thunders had uttered their voices, I was about to write. And I heard a voice from heaven, saying to me: 'Seal up the things which the seven thunders have spoken; and write them not'." ("Seal up", i.e. so that no one may read them.) But at the end (22. 10): "Seal not the words of the prophecy of this book." So in general St John is writing, under obedience, things which normally "it is not granted to man to utter".

If these things are borne in mind, we shall not so easily stagger as we read, nor attempt laboriously to picture the scenes to ourselves and piece together the mysterious details.

In our own everynight experience of dreams we are often faced with strange symbols in no apparently consequent series, but while we are witnessing them we are never puzzled by the inconsequence; it is only by hard daylight that they seem fantastic. It may be that the vision seen by John in his trance partakes to some extent of dream-structure, especially when the events seem inconsequent or the scene incoherent. Yet, as so often in our own dreams, the dominant idea penetrates the symbols and is in itself plain enough.

It is this dominant idea that we shall study in its various aspects, leaving aside to a great extent the interpretation of the symbols singly, a matter on which there has been the widest divergence of opinion. In this way we shall take up the posi-

K

tion of the dreamer dreaming, who is not concerned at the time with the hidden meaning of what he is witnessing, rather than that of the psychologist attempting to interpret each symbol by scientific method. (Let it be said in passing that in the sphere of dream-interpretation there can also be much divergence of opinion.) By taking up the position of the dreamer dreaming, to whom the main issue is plain enough, we shall surely be more closely sharing the experience of the visionary himself, who described the scenes as he saw them, usually with hardly any explanation or clue to the meaning of the particular symbols. Such explanations would not enter his mind at the time. And let us remember all the time that the symbols represent a supernatural experience which exceeds the capacity of human expression.

The Dominant Idea. The plain central theme is THE VIC-TORY OF CHRIST OVER THE FORCES OF EVIL. There will be, are, and have been indeed great battles between Christ and his Angels and the dragons and beasts which symbolize the forces of evil which are constantly corrupting the world. But the victory will always eventually be with Christ. Many men will be seduced, and accept the "mark" of the beast, and the followers of Christ will be tormented and killed, but the just, who refuse to accept the mark of the beast, will pass into the heavenly glory, and especially those who have suffered for Christ will be for ever before the throne of God. This dominant idea of the victory of Christ in spite of all tribulations and all the attacks of evil appears in every scene and under many different symbols.

With this central idea in view it becomes obvious that the particular function of this book in the life of the Church is to bring *consolation* and *hope* to the faithful in times of persecution, trial and unbelief, with the assurance that, come what may, Christ and his Church will triumph, and that "the sufferings of this time are not worthy to be compared with the glory to come" (as St Paul said, Rom. 8. 18), or that "the trial of your faith . . . may be found unto praise and glory and honour at the appearing of Jesus Christ" (as St Peter said, I, 1. 7). The seer himself was under sentence of banishment for the faith as he wrote, a sentence following upon his ordeal under Domitian only a year or two previously. Only thirty years before had been the Great Persecution of Nero, when Peter and Paul had perished, and the next two centuries were going to bring the bitterest trials at the hands of the pagan Roman Emperors when the cruelty of Nero was to be repeated with added horrors, so that his name became the archetype of the enemy of Christ. Throughout Christian history the Apocalypse has held out consolation to the faithful, and indeed many of our images of the after life are taken from its pages. In the ordinary Mass of Requiem the Church consoles her mourners with the words from 14. 13, "Blessed are the dead who die in the Lord. From henceforth now, saith the Spirit, that they may rest from their labours, for their works follow them."

Methods of interpretation of particular symbols. Although in this course we are going to confine ourselves principally to the working out of the dominant idea in the various stages of the vision, yet we should take notice of the main schools of interpretation which seek to identify the various symbols which appear in the vision.[1]

(i) The "preterists" who identify events in the vision with historical events either past (Latin: praeteritum) or actually being enacted at the time of writing. This is the view of most of the rationalist critics of the last century, and has as its object the exclusion of any supernatural prophetic element, and is therefore rejected by Catholic writers.

(ii) The "futurists" who maintain that the symbols refer entirely to the end of the world, to Christ's last battle with

[1] Good classifications of methods are to be found in Pope, Sales and Höpfl. The titles of the schools are partly taken from Fr Hugh Pope and are partly my own.

Satan and ultimate victory. (Exception is made for the first three chapters, which contain the letters written to the Churches of Asia of the time.) This is the traditional view, and was held by most of the Fathers, beginning with Ireneus. It is reflected in the introductory note of Dr Challoner in the ordinary text.

(iii) The "continuists" who see in the stages of the vision a hidden representation of the continuous history of the Church, opening with the contemporary state of the Asian Churches, continuing through the various persecutions, and concluding with the end of the world. According to this view, which became popular in medieval times, beginning with the Abbot Joachim (†1202), it should be possible to identify particular events in the Church's history with particular symbols in the vision and so even to arrive at some knowledge of the future. It is obvious that on these lines it is very easy to fall into grave error. Abbot Joachim himself fell thereby into heresy, and Luther developed a theory of this kind to support his own anti-Catholic teaching.

(iv) A modification of the above "continuous history" theory is that which was propounded especially by Cardinal Bossuet (in 1689), according to which the vision represents the history of the Church in the first ages only, with Christ's gradual victory over those who set themselves against him: the Jews, the pagans and the heretics. Bossuet saw the dénouement in the sack of Rome by Alaric in A.D. 410.

(v) The "symbolists" see indeed the history of the Church in the Apocalypse, from the Incarnation to the end of the world, but not as a chronological account. The battle began at the Incarnation, and will go on to the end of the world. The various crises in the history of the Church are fundamentally the same: Christ *versus* Antichrist. "Whenever a great world crisis has arisen, men have come forward with the Apocalypse and have endeavoured to show—often with great reason—that it exactly fits the present situation" (Fr Hugh Pope, V,

348). Many of the symbols, for instance, are easily identified with the pagan Empire of Rome which persecuted the faithful, but it is just as easy to see therein the present-day tyranny of injustice, violence and mammon. Does not the following passage about the "beast coming up out of the earth" in 13. 16–17 fit the present situation? "He shall make all, both little and great, rich and poor, free men and bondmen to have a character in their right hand, or on their foreheads. And that no man might buy or sell, but he that hath the character, or the name of the beast, or the number of his name." Of course, the passage is enigmatic, but it expresses the age-long and universal concept of the opposition between Christ, his truth and freedom, and the power of evil, falsehood and oppression. The battle is the same battle, but THE VICTORY WILL BE CHRIST'S. According to this view, therefore, the many symbols are each to be identified with the many forms of the conflict which has raged round Christ's Church from the beginning, and will continue to do so until the end.

Some form of "symbolist" interpretation is the most usual among Catholic writers today, and its origin may be found in St Augustine (*De Civitate Dei*, lib. xx, written *c.* A.D. 425) and worked out in particular by the English writers, St Bede (†735) and Alcuin (†804).[1]

What is the story?[2] For it is indeed a story, but a story without a time-element (although at one stage there was "silence in heaven, as it were for half and hour", 8. 1); the seer is mysteriously transported from one stage to another, when the heavenly view somehow changes.

On a certain Sunday, during his exile on Patmos, John was "in the spirit" (1. 10) and suddenly heard behind him "a

[1] The outstanding modern commentator on the Apocalypse is undoubtedly the Dominican Père Allo (†1945), who takes a view of this kind. Various authors have slightly different explanations, but a general idea of a symbolist standpoint may be read in Fr Hugh Pope's *Aids*, and with a slightly different emphasis in Fr Gigot's introduction in WV.

[2] A quick reading of this section should give the student a general acquaintance with the contents of the book.

great voice as of a trumpet", which commands him to write
what he sees. He looks round and sees "one like to the Son of
man" (apparently Christ) standing among seven golden
lamps,[1] who proceeds to dictate letters of warning or encouragement (as necessity required) to the seven Churches of
Asia Minor (c. 2–3).

Thereupon the same voice bids John come up through "the
door opened in heaven" (4. 1), and he finds himself in the
presence of a throne, "and upon the throne one sitting" (4. 2).
He is in the court of heaven. Round the throne, seated upon
thrones also, are the twenty-four elders,[2] and in front of the
throne stand the four living creatures, who "rested not day
and night, saying, 'Holy, holy, holy, Lord God Almighty,
who was, and who is, and who is to come' " (4. 8). John then
becomes conscious of the presence between the throne and
the living creatures of a Lamb "as it were sacrificed" (5. 6),
and only the Lamb could open the seven seals on the scroll
which was in the hand of him that sat on the throne. At the
opening of each seal there are remarkable signs and portents.
After the last seal is opened "there was silence in heaven, as
it were for half an hour" (8. 1). John then realises that there
is a golden altar before the throne (8. 3). (Let us not bother
our heads to wonder why he did not notice it before, or
exactly where it stood.) Before the altar stands an Angel with
a thurible; seven other Angels with trumpets stand "in the
presence of God".

Now John is given a view down upon earth, and he witnesses the various manifestations upon earth that follow upon
the sounding of the trumpets (c. 8–11). After the seventh
trumpet "God's sanctuary in heaven was opened, and the ark
of his covenant was seen in his temple" (11. 19 WV).

Next he witnesses a series of seven mysterious signs in

---

[1] WV, rather than Rh "candlesticks".
[2] So all the modern translations. The word is "presbyters": see note on
I Pet. 5. 1 (p. 247).

heaven and on earth (c. 12–15. 4). These seven scenes make the most wonderful reading: they are the most fantastic and dream-like figures in the whole vision. They are easy to read, provided one does not pause to inquire into the meaning of the details or to imagine the scenes too exactly, but allows the dominant idea to penetrate their mystery.

At the end of this the veil is still further withdrawn: "the sanctuary of the tent of witness in heaven was opened" (15. 5 WV). Now once more John has a view down upon the earth, and he watches the effects of the pouring out of the seven vials (USA bowls, RAK cups) of God's wrath upon the earth (c. 15–16).

John is then transported "in spirit" into the desert, where he is shown the horrible symbol of the drunken woman who stands for the Great Babylon: "the woman which thou sawest, is the great city which hath kingdom over the kings of the earth" (17. 18). This ghastly vision does not of course take place in heaven, for he immediately sees "another Angel come down from heaven" and announce the fall of Babylon the great (18. 1–2). He then hears the lament of people on earth and the distant rejoicing of the people in heaven over the fall of Babylon (c. 18–19).

Still apparently in the desert, upon earth, he now sees the heavens opened, and a white horse is revealed with its Rider, whose name is THE WORD OF GOD, THE KING OF KINGS AND THE LORD OF LORDS. This, of course, is Christ himself who comes in this closing scene to do battle with Satan and defeat him for the last time. The present world passes away, and John sees the New Jerusalem "coming down out of heaven from God" (21. 2). This will be the everlasting abode: "the throne of God and of the Lamb shall be in it, and his servants shall serve him. And they shall see his face: and his name shall be on their foreheads . . . and they shall reign for ever and for ever" (22. 3–5).

So the vision fades. It is the end of the story. The voice of the Angel who had been his guide in the desert and who had shown him the New Jerusalem is still speaking: "These words are most faithful and true . . . Blessed is he that keepeth the words of the prophecy of this book" (22. 6–7). John bows low before the Angel, but the voice bids him rise and be ready to give Christ's message to the world: "Behold I come quickly, and my reward is with me . . . surely I come quickly. Amen."

The voice fades away. John can only stammer out his response, "COME, LORD JESUS."

This is the end. He simply writes on the last line the conventional Christian salutation so often used by St Paul: "The grace of our Lord Jesus Christ be with you all. Amen."

The Plan. The above outline gives briefly the story, chiefly from the aspect of John's own viewpoint, i.e. where John is ("in spirit", for he is actually busily writing it all down at the same time), when he sees the various things.

Yet at certain stages a deliberate plan and sequence is clearly discernible. There seem to be 7 clearly marked stages in the vision, and of these the first five have within themselves 7 clear elements. It is therefore tempting to try and see in the last two stages also 7 elements. This would mean that there are 7 × 7 or 49 distinct episodes of the vision. Add to these the last admonitions of the Angel as the vision fades, and we have 50 episodes in all.

The study of Apocalyptic literature in general (see next Section) reveals a special interest in the significance of *numbers*.[1] The number 7 seems to have some sacred character (and the Hebrew word for "to swear an oath" is perhaps from the same root), but the origin of this sacredness is shrouded in mystery—the days of the week, the days of the moon's quarters, the 7 planets,[2] the "7 stars in the sky" = the

---

[1] Allo, pp. xxxiii sq.

[2] i.e. the heavenly bodies not among the fixed stars: Sun, Moon, Mercury, Venus, Mars, Jupiter, Saturn. Uranus and Neptune are visible only through a telescope, and of Pluto so far only the position is known.

Great Bear, are all suggestions. The number 7, however, seems to represent a certain perfection and plenitude (not too much and not too little). Multiples, and especially the square, will share this perfection in a special way. 12 and its multiples (cf. the 144,000 in c. 7) seem to stand also for a certain plenitude. On the other hand, numbers which fall short of this perfection are regarded as essentially imperfect. Such is 6, and more than ever so would be its reiteration in 666 (which is a likely explanation of the number in 13. 18).[1] 10 and its multiples seem to stand for multitude, with 1000 for an indefinite multitude. Both 49 and 50, then, the number of episodes in the Apocalypse, contain a certain idea of completion.

The Apocalypse has been divided in many different ways, on the basis of 7 and otherwise. Fr Gigot's division in the introduction to WV, although the sevenfold division of the last two stages is questionable, provides at any rate a convenient working basis. The following plan is adapted from this.

The book opens with a short prologue, and dedication from John on the island of Patmos (about thirty-five miles off the coast of Asia Minor) to the Churches or Christian communities in Asia Minor. Ephesus, the chief Christian centre, was the residence of John before and after his exile. 1. 7–8 provides a summary of Christ's message, repeated again in the epilogue (c. 1. 1–19).

I. CHRIST DICTATES SEVEN LETTERS

A vision of Christ, standing among 7 lamps, with 7 stars in his right hand and with a sword issuing from his mouth (c. 1).

The letters
1. To Ephesus (c. 2).
2. To Smyrna.
3. To Pergamus.

[1] More about this when studying the text.

4. To Thyatira.
5. To Sardis (c. 3).
6. To Philadelphia.
7. To Laodicea.

II. THE SEVEN SEALS ON THE SCROLL

A vision of God upon the heavenly throne, holding the scroll with 7 seals, and surrounded by the 24 elders and 4 living creatures. Only the Lamb will be able to break the seals on the scroll (c. 4–5).

The Lamb opens the seals one by one, and each time there is a new vision:

1. Rider on white horse with bow (c. 6).
2. „ „ red „ „ sword.
3. „ „ black „ „ scales.
4. „ „ pale „ called "Death".
5. Under the altar the souls of the martyrs.
6. The earthquake—followed by the branding of the 144,000 of the faithful of Israel, and the sight of the great multitude of all nations, standing before the throne (c. 7).
7. Silence. Then the 7 Angels appear (c. 8).

III. THE SEVEN TRUMPETS

A vision of 7 Angels with trumpets, and of another Angel standing before the altar and offering incense, which is the prayers of saints. This Angel casts the censer full of fire down upon the earth, and then one by one the trumpets are sounded. Each time there is a cataclysm on earth, and one third of that particular part is destroyed:

1. The earth with its trees and grass (c. 8).
2. The sea with its creatures and ships.
3. The rivers and springs (which become bitter).
4. The sun, moon and stars.
5. The bottomless pit is opened and its smoke darkens the

sky: a plague of locusts torments men, but does not kill them (c. 9).

6. One third of mankind is killed by the four Angels, by means of 200,000,000 horsemen—whereupon another Angel appears and the seven thunders uttered their voices, but John is forbidden to write what they said. The Angel gives to John a book and orders him to eat it, which he does. He is then told to measure the temple, and is told of "the two witnesses" (9. 13, c. 10–11).

7. The court of heaven cries out a prayer of praise.

IV. The Seven Mysterious Signs

1. The Woman and the Dragon (c. 12).
2. The Beast from the sea (c. 13).
3. The Beast from the earth.
4. The Lamb and the 144,000 virgins (c. 14).
5. The Three Angels, and their warnings to the world—followed by the order to write "Blessed are the dead who die in the Lord".
6. Christ in heaven, assisted by two Angels, gather the harvest and the vintage upon earth.
7. Seven Angels appear (who afterwards have the 7 vials), and the conquerors of the beast, standing on the sea of glass, sing a song of triumph (c. 15).

V. The Seven Vials of the Wrath of God

One of the 4 living creatures gives to the 7 Angels the 7 vials, which they are to pour out upon the earth. Each time will occur a new calamity (15. 7):

1. Men are wounded, who had followed the beast (c. 16).
2. Creatures in the sea die.
3. Water is turned to blood.
4. The sun scorches men.
5. The throne of the beast is darkened.

6. The river Euphrates is dried up—three devils, looking like frogs, issue from the mouths of the dragon, the beast and the false prophet, to seduce the kings of the earth.

7. Storms and earthquakes ruin Babylon and the cities of the Gentiles.

VI. The Fall of Babylon

The seer is taken away to the desert to see the symbol of Babylon the Great.

1. He sees the drunken harlot (c. 17).
2. An Angel explains the symbol.
3. Another Angel comes and announces the fall of Babylon (c. 18).
4. The kings and the merchants of the earth mourn.
5. An Angel announces her final ruin.
6. The Song of Triumph in heaven (c. 19).
7. The Marriage feast of the Lamb.

VII. The End of the World

1. The Horseman on the white horse (19. 11).
2. The Defeat of the beast.
3. Satan is chained for 1000 years (c. 20).
4. The General Judgement.
5. The New Jerusalem, who is the bride (c. 21).
6. An Angel shows John the City.
7. He shows him Paradise, with river and the tree of life, whose leaves are "for the healing of the nations; and there shall be no more curse" (c. 22).

The vision fades and the book ends with an Epilogue, which is the voice of the guiding Angel repeating the message of Christ with which the book begins: "Behold I come quickly."

A note on the literary background. This is a complicated question, and we cannot go into it here. But it is important to know that St John's Apocalypse does not stand alone.

During the two centuries before Christ and the two centuries after there appeared in Palestine several Jewish apocryphal (i.e. not inspired, not scriptural) writings in the apocalyptic style. For the most part they were deliberate attempts to develop the apocalyptic matter in the Old Testament, to be found principally in the Books of Daniel, Ezechiel and Zacharias. The figures are in many cases taken or developed from those of the Old Testament. Some of the titles show that these works were imaginary continuations into the next life of the lives of men of the Old Testament whose passing out of this life was mysterious (such are Enoch in Gen. 5. 24, Moses in Deut. 34. 6, and Elias in IV Kings 2. 11). Well-known titles of apocalyptic books of this period are *The Book of Enoch* and *The Assumption of Moses* (both of which are quoted by St Jude in his Epistle), *The Ascension of Isaias, The Fourth* (apocryphal) *Book of Esdras,* and *The Apocalypse of Abraham.* The last three are probably contemporary with our Apocalypse. Now it must be observed at once that none of these apocryphal books rise to the stature and sublimity of the prophets of the Old Testament: it is only the inspired writing of John that does so. Nevertheless it is important to know that many of the figures of John's Apocalypse were current images in contemporary apocalyptic literature, and further, that the greater number of these are traceable to the Old Testament itself (the number of these has been estimated as no less than three hundred in the Apocalypse of St John[1]), and that when John had to attempt to describe in human language his heavenly experience, it was quite natural that he should adopt to some extent current apocalyptic terminology. P. Ignace Beaufays quotes an interesting modern example of a description of the war of 1914–1918 entirely in apocalyptic symbols of the first century A.D.[2] Without the key of contem-

[1] According to P. Ignace Beaufays, o.f.m., *St Jean*, Brussels, 1944, p. 139.
[2] Ibid.

porary history it would read like pure fantasy. Now the
Christians of Asia Minor would have had the key to some of
the symbols of the Apocalypse (especially, of course, in the
Seven Letters, and some of the symbols applicable to the
Roman Empire), but already to the writers of the second
century (Justin and Ireneus) the precise meaning of the
symbols was in great part lost: if ever indeed there had been
a precise one; for on a "symbolist" interpretation the types
are of permanent value to the whole history of the Redemption, from the beginning, to the end of time.

It should be added that apocalyptic literature was not confined to Palestine and to the Jews. We have referred before
(pp. 13 sq.) to the Messianism of Virgil. The poet is looking
into the future of the messianic age in his Fourth Eclogue,
and the Sixth Book of the Aeneid is a portrayal of life-after-
death. The latter idea was already familiar to the Greek-
speaking world in the Eleventh Book of Homer's Odyssey.
Of course these are but shadows, but it is important to bear
them in mind, since it was in a Graeco-Roman world that the
Apocalypse of John was first read.

Lastly, the Christian tradition itself did not neglect the
apocalyptic manner, building upon all these elements: in the
early ages we have the *Pastor of Hermas* (*c.* A.D. 150) and the
Gnostic *Pistis Sophia* (*c.* A.D. 250), and on through the early
medieval legends to arrive at the crown of Christian apocalyptic writing in the *Divina Commedia* of Dante (1265–1321),
which draws largely upon the images of St John.[1]

Some exegetical notes. These notes are intended to accom-
pany a quick reading of the text. They do not set out to
identify the hidden meaning of the various figures, on which
there are so many opinions, and which on a "symbolist"
interpretation are not to be identified exclusively with fixed

[1] P. Allo on the literary background in great detail: Introduction to his
Commentary, c. IV–V, pp. xviii–lviii.

historical events or persons. (Where identifications are traditional and obvious, they will be noted in small type.) The
notes are simply intended to elucidate the literal meaning of
the text, i.e. to make more precise, where necessary, John's
description of what he saw. The Apocalypse is not difficult
to read, and with the studies we have already made, it should
be easy to notice the emergence of the dominant idea of
Christ's victory over evil, and to understand the message of
hope and consolation which the book brings to troubled
Christians, together with the stern *warning* against compro-
mising with Satan and forgetting that Christ will indeed come
again soon to judge the living and the dead.

THE PROLOGUE

1. 4. An address not unlike the beginning of Paul's Epistles.

1. 6. "Hath made us a kingdom and priests": cf. I Pet. 2. 5
and 9: "Be you also a holy priesthood ... a chosen generation, a kingly priesthood" with notes there (pp. 242-3) on the
"priesthood of the laity".

I. THE SEVEN LETTERS (1.10-c. 3)

1. 17–18. "I am the first and the last" (cf. alpha and omega,
v. 8). This and the other phrases here, "alive and was dead
... living for ever, and have the keys," show clearly that the
person is Christ himself. This is the *first type of Christ* in the
Apocalypse.

2. 1 (and beginnings of each letter). "The angel of the
Church of ..." This is almost universally understood to
mean the bishop of the Church.

2. 4–5. The famous accusation, "Thou hast left thy first
charity." They are therefore to "repent and do the former
works" (WV, USA), "go back to the old ways" (RAK).

2. 6. The Nicolaites, again in the letter to Pergamus (2. 15),
where, however, there is further explanation in the likeness

to Balaam, the prophet, who gave his services to Balac, king of Moab, but being asked by the king to curse Israel, blessed them instead (to the great annoyance of the king) (Numbers 22–24). The point is, however, that immediately after this (Num. 25) the Israelites took part in Moabite pagan worship, partook of their sacrifices, and committed fornication with their women. This occurrence was afterwards attributed by Moses (Num. 31. 16) to Balaam's incitation of the Moabite women to seduce the Israelites. This is the "doctrine of Balaam" of Apoc. 2. 15. The Nicolaites were therefore apparently teaching the faithful to partake in local pagan worship, including the eating of εἰδωλόθυτα (cf. St Paul in I Cor. 8 and 10 saying that in itself this was meaningless, but is undesirable if it should give scandal, see notes pp. 92 sq.), and probably ritual fornication. It was probably an attempt to work Christianity into a system of "Syncretism" or synthesis of the various religions to be found in the Empire (see Intro. *d.*, Religion in the Roman Empire, p. 25). The attribution of this heresy to one of the first seven deacons, Nicolas, a proselyte of Antioch (Acts 6. 5), seems gratuitous, though it was already believed as early as Ireneus (*Adv. Haer.*, I, 36, *c.* A.D. 200).[1]

2. 13. "Where the seat of Satan is" (at Pergamus) probably refers to the great centre there of pagan cult, which would give special opportunity to the Nicolaite heresy.

2. 17. "Hidden manna": i.e. a God-given means of sustenance, but perhaps referring to the manna that was preserved in the ark.

Tradition since Origen has seen in this a reference to the Eucharist, and it is used in the office of Corpus Christi (Ant. 5 at Lauds).

"A white counter," lit. "pebble" (USA), as used in Greece for voting, so that to "cast the pebble" became the usual

[1] Cf. Allo, Excursus xi, p. 46. It might be added that a modern manifestation of the Nicolaite heresy is the false Oecumenism of the present day, which looks forward to a World-Church arising from a syncretism of the various existing forms of Christianity.

word for voting by secret ballot ("the name which no man knoweth"), and is used by St Paul in Acts 26. 10 of his vote cast against the Christians.

2. 20. Jezabel, the wicked queen of Israel, a type of wickedness.

3. 14. "The Amen" reads as strangely in Greek as it does in English. But of course the Hebrew word means "true".

3. 15–16. The famous accusation of lukewarmness.

3. 19. "Such as I love, I rebuke and chastise": cf. Proverbs 3. 12, "For whom the Lord loveth, he chastiseth."

3. 20. "Behold I stand at the gate, and knock": another famous figure from this letter, so often quoted by the spiritual writers, and known to so many through Holman Hunt's picture "The Light of the World".

II. THE COURT OF HEAVEN AND THE SEVEN SEALS (c. 4-8. 1)

4. 3. "Jasper and Sardine": two precious stones, with names more or less transliterated. Modern Jasper is opaque, while in 21. 11 it is transparent ("as crystal"), so the matter is not clear. Sard or Sardian is a red stone. (All the old versions wrote "Sardine".)

4. 4–6. The twenty-four elders and the four living creatures in the court of heaven: in Isaias 24. 23 we find the "elders" in the sight of God, and there are twenty-four orders of priests in I Par. 24. 6–19; the four living creatures are in Ezechiel's vision (Ez. 1. 5–14).

Their significance is very difficult to determine. The living creatures seem to be angelic beings, while the elders seem to represent in some way humanity. The living creatures, lion, bull, man, eagle, were already by Ireneus taken as types of the evangelists (Mt. man, Mk. lion, Lk. bull, Jn. eagle) (*Adv. Haer.*, III, 11).

5. 1. The outside edge of the scroll was sealed to the rolled part.

5. 6. The Lamb: this, the *second type of Christ* in the Apocalypse, is a name also used in John's Gospel: "Behold the

Lamb of God" (Jn. 1. 29, 36). Note the contrasts: the Lion of Juda—the Lamb; the Lamb is as it were slain—but standing up (symbol of the Resurrection). Similarly in v. 12: the Lamb that was slain—is worthy to receive power. . . . (This latter text is the Introit for the Feast of Christ the King.)

6. 2. sq. The four horses.

Their significance is very much disputed.

6. 6. "A measure of wheat for a denarius" (USA): a denarius was a day's pay. "These are famine prices, at which a labourer would have to spend the whole of his day's wages to provide bread for himself alone" (RAK's note).

7. 5–8. Note that the tribe of Dan is omitted. (The number 12 is achieved by Joseph and his son Manasses being mentioned.) Ireneus (*Adv. Haer.* V, 30) states that the Antichrist was to come from the tribe of Dan, probably preserving a Jewish tradition, and that this is the reason for its omission here. Most commentators have followed this opinion, though the evidence for such a tradition is very faint.

III. THE SEVEN TRUMPETS (8.2–c. 11)

8. 4. The smoke of incense as a symbol of prayer occurs already in Ps. 140 (Heb. 141) 2, in the verse used as the versicle at Vespers on Sunday.

8. 11. "Wormwood": this word (nothing to do with worms or wood) is a corruption of "weremod" or (as Wyclif wrote) "wermed", which gives the German Wermut and French Vermout: it is the name of a bitter-tasting plant, in Latin "absinthius" (corresponding to the Greek word here), used in the preparation of the liqueurs Vermouth and Absinthe, which preserve the Germanic and Latin names. Vermouth is flavoured with wormwood, while Absinthe is a distillation of pure wormwood and is a very dangerous drug.

9. 1. "given to him"—to the Angel, or to the fallen star?

Most versions preserve the ambiguity of the Greek, though RAK deliberately refers it to the star, and P. Allo interprets it so. But Dr Challoner's note specially says it refers to the Angel.

9. 11. Abaddon = destruction; Greek and Latin = destroyer.

9. 15. "prepared for *the* hour and day, etc.": i.e. the appointed hour, etc.

10. 2. "A little book": βιβλαρίδιον a diminutive of a diminutive not hitherto found elsewhere except in the *Pastor of Hermas*, vision ii, 1 and 3, and iv, 3.

11. 2. "42 months" = $3\frac{1}{2}$ years, which being half of the perfect number 7, is an expression of evil and calamity.

11. 3. "1260 days" = 42 months.

11. 3-4. The two witnesses, as two olive trees and two candlesticks, occur in the vision in c. 4 of Zacharias, where they refer fairly obviously to the two leaders of the restored Jerusalem after the captivity, the spiritual, Jesus the High Priest, and the temporal, Zorobabel the civil governor.

The words of vv. 5-6 suggest that they stand here for Moses and Elias (the plagues, and the shutting of the heavens), and they were witnesses of the Transfiguration. Both men passed mysteriously out of this world (cf. above p. 283 on apocalyptic literature), which is perhaps why they have not yet "finished their testimony", but the identification is quite obscure.

IV. THE SEVEN SIGNS (c. 12-15. 4)

12. 1. The vision of the Woman and the Dragon is central to the whole of the Apocalypse. One thing is quite clear: that the Woman is on the side of Christ, and that the Dragon is Christ's enemy in the world. In v. 9 the Dragon is expressly called "that old serpent, who is called the devil and Satan". The Woman stands for the followers of Christ, the Church personified, who is to enjoy God's protection in her tribulations.

Devotional tradition since the early seventeenth century has connected the Woman of this chapter with Our Lady Immaculate. Apparently the first pictures of her standing upon the moon and with a crown of twelve stars (obvious references to here) were painted by Guido Reni (1575-1642) in Italy about the time of Paul V's decree (in 1617) forbidding anyone to teach that Mary was conceived in original sin.[1] Guido Reni was at the time painter to the papal court. In the same year the dogma of the Immaculate Conception was promulgated for Spain, and this was also the year of the birth of the Spanish painter, Murillo (†1682). Murillo painted Our Lady Immaculate at least twenty-five times, usually with the apocalyptic symbols, sometimes even including the dragon. Minute regulations for the painting of Our Lady Immaculate were laid down by the painter Pacheco (who was apparently artistic adviser to the Inquisition) in 1649. She is to be represented "with all the beauty painting can express", with golden hair, with hands folded on her bosom or joined in prayer; her robe is to be white and her mantle or scarf blue; under her feet is to be the moon, with its horns pointing downwards (which detail rarely appears in pictures), round her head twelve stars, and her being "clothed with the sun" is to be represented by a flood of light all round her. These instructions were issued when Guido Reni had already set the style and Murillo's paintings were becoming well known. So it has happened that in popular devotion the symbols of this chapter have been permanently linked with Our Lady.[2] The office of the Immaculate Conception includes this verse (Capitulum at None), as does also that of Our Lady of Lourdes (February 11th) (in the Epistle at Mass, and in the 2nd Antiphon at Lauds). An obvious connexion is the text in Gen. 3. 15 about "enmities between thee (the serpent) and the woman".

The exegetes, however, seem to favour the interpretation of the Woman as the Church, or else as Israel which gave birth to Christ. The connexion with Our Lady is traceable as far back as St Augustine, though it can be no more than an "appropriation", since the details of the symbol do not fit (see note in WV).

12. 6. "1260 days", again, = 42 months = $3\frac{1}{2}$ years, half of 7.

12. 7. Michael, the Archangel, is mentioned in Scripture only here, in Daniel 10. 13, 21 and 12. 1 (where "he shall rise up, the great prince, who standeth for the children of thy people") and in Jude 9 (when "disputing with the devil" he "contended about the body of Moses": the passage borrowed from the apocryphal *Assumption of Moses*). But it is our passage here that has made for us our popular idea of St Michael and inspired the prayer we say after Mass: "Holy Michael, Archangel, defend us in the day of battle . . . thrust down into hell Satan and all wicked spirits who wander through the world for the ruin of souls", the prayer that has

[1] There, is, however, an earlier Madonna, plainly dated 1588, by Francesco Vanni of Siena, which includes the moon and crown of stars.
[2] Mrs Jameson, *Legends of the Madonna, as represented in the Fine Arts*, 1852, and *Cath. Encycl.* art. Immaculate (p. 680*b*), and Murillo.

rightly been called the "Little Exorcism", so needful in our days.

12. 14. The "desert" here is the same word as the "wilderness" in v. 6, and the period is probably the same: a time, 2 times, and half a time, i.e. $3\frac{1}{2}$.

12. 18. "And he stood upon the sand of the sea": a wonderful picture of the desperate and disappointed dragon, pausing before undertaking his next baleful pursuit. The verse also serves to introduce the next vision.

13. 1. The beast rising out of the sea, who received his power from the dragon (v. 2 and 4) and was admired by all the earth (v. 3 and 8).

13. 11. The beast rising out of the earth, with horns like a lamb but with the voice of a dragon—a symbol of hypocrisy.

13. 12. The second beast merely carries out the orders of the first beast, and orders men to make an image of the first beast which they are then to adore. He receives power to make this image speak.

13. 16. He takes away men's freedom.

13. 18. The beast's number is 666.

The great symbols of evil on the earth, powers opposed to Christ, be they (as is most usually supposed) the Roman Emperor (= 1st beast) and his minions who make men adore him (= 2nd beast), or else any other such evil power at any other time, such as the hidden power of mammon (= 1st beast) and his minions the politicians who serve him (= 2nd beast) (especially if under the guise of welfare), or any other such application in history. The figures are, on a symbolist interpretation, perennial.

The commonest interpretation of the number 666 is by "gematria" (a Hebrew corruption of the word "geometry"), by which the letters of the alphabet, used by the Greeks and Hebrews as numerals also, are taken in their numerical value to make a name. Many names, especially of Emperors, have been thus worked out from St Ireneus onwards. The most well known of these is Nerōn Qesar (Caesar) in Hebrew נרון קסר, i.e.
Nero. (One of the ancient codices, Codex C, reads "616", from which the same result may be obtained by omitting the second n from Nerōn, which is the Greek form, giving the Latin form Nero. The letter n in Hebrew has the value 50.) St John's words do indeed suggest such a riddle, and a Hebrew riddle would undoubtedly require one who "hath understanding". The application to Nero and the emperor-worship exacted by his minions is, of course, very plausible, owing to its aptness at the time: Nero as the type of the persecutor.

But the symbolic meaning of the number 666, as being that which for ever fails to reach 7, is also a likely possibility.[1] As P. Allo remarks, St Ireneus' solution (although he mentions some attempts) is much the best: not to attempt a solution—and he was writing only 100 years after St John.[2]

14. 20. "Up to the horses' bridles, for 1600 furlongs": the imagery is obscure. Sales thinks of a vast lake. Some sort of universal cataclysm is intended: 1600 being probably connected with "the four corners of the earth".

V. THE SEVEN VIALS (15. 5–c. 16)

15. 5. "The tabernacle of the testimony" ("tent of witness" WV or "tent of meeting" RV): St John uses the words of the LXX for the portable tabernacle of the desert in Exodus 40. 34–35 (Vulg. 32–33).

15. 8. "Smoke from the majesty of God": cf. in Isaias' vision of God in heaven (Is. 6. 4).

16. 7. "Just are thy judgements": for the men adored the image of the beast (v. 2) and refused to do penance (v. 9).

16. 12. The kings from the east probably mean the Parthians, who are a symbol of destruction and terror, for at the time this was the chief danger-point on the borders of the Roman Empire.

16. 13. "Unclean spirits like frogs" issue from the mouths of the three symbols of evil: the dragon, the first beast, and the false prophet, who is probably to be identified with the second beast, which typified hypocrisy (cf. 13. 11).

16. 16. "Armagedon" probably stands for "Har-Megiddon" (הר־מגדון) the Mount of Megiddo (Vulg. Mageddo). Mageddo (which, however, is in the plain of Esdraelon and not on a mountain) was the site of the disastrous battle in which Juda (under the good king Josias) was allied to the Assyrians and they were defeated by the Egyptians and Josias was

[1] 666 is an interesting number anyway: it is a multiple (×18) of the prime number 37, which includes in its table 111, 222, etc. to 999. 777 is 37 × 7 × 3.
[2] P. Allo, Excursus xxxi, p. 210, for the whole problem.

killed (IV Kings 23. 29). The name has simply come to be a symbol of disaster, and it is a place where the last battle for the defence of Jerusalem from the north would be fought.

VI. THE FALL OF BABYLON (c. 17-19. 10)

This horrible vision is largely explained by the guiding Angel. The harlot (v. 1), Babylon (v. 5) is the great city (v. 18). She is seated upon a scarlet beast with seven heads (v. 3), which stand for seven hills (v. 9), or again for seven kings of whom five are fallen (v. 10). Its ten horns are ten kings who will come after the beast is dead (v. 12), and who will betray the woman (v. 16). She rules many waters, i.e. nations (v. 15), and is drunk with the blood of the martyrs (v. 6).

All this seems to indicate pagan Rome fairly clearly, but pagan Rome itself is only a symbol of the world that hates Christ.

18. 3. When Babylon falls, those who have committed fornication with the harlot shall lament: kings or tyrants (who rule by power) and merchants or profiteers (who rule by money), such as compromised themselves with her and so got enriched, they will lament.

18. 4. But the faithful are to get out.

18. 12–14. These wicked merchants enriched themselves by trafficking in various commodities. The list ends with the sinister words "and souls of men". Again not applicable only to ancient Rome.

19. 7. "The marriage of the Lamb": the bride is named only later: "the New Jerusalem, prepared as a bride adorned for her husband" (21. 2). The marriage of the Lamb is forcibly contrasted with the fornication of the world. And one thinks of the Christian interpretation of the Canticle of Canticles, the marriage of Christ to his Spouse the Church.

VII. THE END (19. 11-22. 5)

19. 11. The *third figure of Christ* in the Apocalypse: the rider on the white horse, whose name is THE WORD OF GOD,

and KING OF KINGS AND LORD OF LORDS (vv. 13, 16). This last title, together with the cry of the heavenly voices after the seventh Trumpet in 11. 15, "The kingdom of this world is become the Kingdom of our Lord and of his Christ, and he shall reign for ever and ever" is the burden of the great Hallelujah Chorus in Handel's Messiah.[1]

19. 19–20. 2. The triumphal emergence of the great theme: CHRIST'S FINAL COMPLETE VICTORY. As in the very first vision (1. 16) "out of his mouth proceedeth a sharp two-edged sword" (19. 15), and now he defeats for ever the beast and the false prophet (= the second beast) (19. 19–20), and finally the dragon also (20. 2). The three great symbols of evil have been overcome.

20. 2–5. Satan is bound for 1000 years (after which he is loosed for a little time); during these 1000 years the souls of the just live and reign with Christ—this is "the first resurrection". The error of the Chiliasts or Millenarians (see note, p. 268 above) was to take these figures literally (a theory finally disproved when nothing happened in A.D. 1000), and to separate the 1000 years of Satan's incarceration from the 1000 years' reign of the just with Christ. The "first resurrection" can only mean the entry into heaven of the *souls* (20. 4) of the just, which takes place straight after their death on earth, according to the teaching of the Church.[2] The 1000 years (a symbol of an indefinitely long time) is the period from Christ's First Coming (at the Incarnation) to his Second Coming (at the Parousia). During this period the souls of the just will reign in heaven and await the end of the world, when the great battle with Satan, now loosed, will take place, followed by the second resurrection at the General Judgement.[3]

---

[1] Handel's text, as often, departs from any usual biblical text. It was drawn up by his friend Charles Jennens, a wealthy and eccentric littérateur and amateur musician (see DNB).

[2] "Mox post mortem suam": the constitution *Benedictus Deus* of Pope Benedict XII in 1336 (Denz., 530).

[3] For all this, Allo, Excursus xxxviii, p. 292.

20. 7. The great final battle (which was already described before in different terms in c. 19). Gog and Magog are names taken from Ezechiel's prophecy (c. 38–39) of the tribulation that shall overcome Israel. Gog dwells in "the land of Magog" (38. 2) and will invade with a mighty army from "the northern parts" (38. 15, 39. 2). Cuneiform inscriptions have yielded the names Gugu, Gaga and Gagi connected with barbarous tribes to the north, so that Ezechiel may well have had historical foundation for his names. But here the northern tribes, like the eastern kings of Apoc. 16. 12, are simply a symbol of destruction.[1]

20. 12–15. The second resurrection (of the bodies of the dead, including those in the sea) and the Last Judgement.

21. 12 sq. In the description of the heavenly Jerusalem note the recurrence of the perfect number twelve: twelve gates and foundations, the length, height and breadth (all equal, forming a cube) 12,000 furlongs (v. 16), and the height of the wall 144 cubits. The cubical shape is probably no more than a symbol of perfection.

21. 17. "By man's measure, which is angel's measure" (WV), i.e. although the measurements were taken by an Angel (v. 15), yet they are ordinary human measures.

22. 1. "Water of life": cf. Jn. 4. 14 (to the Samaritan woman), "Water springing up into life everlasting", and the significance of water in I Jn. 5. 6 (where see note).

22. 2. Again the number twelve: twelve fruits of the tree of life.

The significance of the various details of the New Jerusalem must perforce remain obscure. What is plain, however, is that the city stands for the Church triumphant, the company of the faithful in the everlasting light of God's presence, and that in that heavenly city all will be entirely perfect.

THE EPILOGUE

22. 11. Men will continue in their ways of vice or of virtue, and will receive their reward accordingly. Christ is

[1] Allo, Excursus xxxv, p. 290.

sending his warning through John that the time will come quickly.

22. 20. The Angel's voice reiterates its warning at the very end: "Surely I come quickly. Amen."

John's answer is the answer that all the saints have made with a clear conscience. Because they have loved him and served him on earth they have nothing to fear at his Coming. It is our constant Christian prayer that we also may be able to have always ready on our lips the same answer: COME, LORD JESUS.

APPENDIX A

A TABLE OF THE LITURGICAL USE OF THE EPISTLES AND APOCALYPSE FOR THE "EPISTLE" AT MASS

Days of obligation are shown in italics

ROMANS
1. 1–6. Christmas Eve
5. 1–5. Pent. Ember Sat., Mark and Marcellinus
6. 3–11. *6 Pent.*
6. 19–23. *7 Pent.*
7. 22–25. Vot. Forgiveness
8. 12–17. *8 Pent.*
8. 18–23. *4 Pent.*, Marcellus, etc., Trypho, etc.
8. 35–39. Ignatius Ant.
10. 10–18. Andrew
11. 23–29. *Corpus Christi*
11. 33–36. *Trinity*
12. 1–5. *1 Epiph.*[1]
12. 6–15. *2 Epiph.*
12. 16–21. *3 Epiph.*
13. 8–10. *4 Epiph.*
13. 11–14. *1 Advent*
14. 7–12. Vot. Good Death
15. 4–13. *2 Advent*

I CORINTHIANS
1. 4–9. *18 Pent.*
1. 17–25. Paul of Cross
   18–25, 30 Justin
1. 26–31. Agatha
4. 1–5. *4 Advent*
4. 9–14. Conf. not Bp, Vig. Simon and Jude
   9–15. James the Gt
5. 7–9. *Easter*
7. 25–34. Virgins
9. 24–10. 5. *Septuagesima*
10. 6–14. *9 Pent.*
11. 20–32. Maundy Thurs.
12. 2–11. *10 Pent.*

12. 27–31. Bartholomew
13. 1–13. *Quinquagesima*, Joseph of Cup.
15. 1–10. *11 Pent.*
15. 51–57. All Souls

II CORINTHIANS
1. 3–7. Martyr Bishop
3. 4–9. *12 Pent.*
4. 5–14. Athanasius
6. 1–10. *1 Lent.*
   4–10. Abdon, etc., Chrysanthus, etc.
8. 9–15. Paulinus
8. 16–24. Luke
9. 6–10. Laurence
10. 17–11. 2. Virgins
11. 19–12. 9. *Sexagesima*
13. 11, 13. Vot. Trinity

GALATIANS
1. 11–20. Comm. St Paul
3. 16–22. *13 Pent.*
4. 1–7. *Sun. after Christmas*
4. 22–31. *4 Lent*
5. 16–24. *14 Pent.*
5. 25–6. 11. *15 Pent.*
6. 14–18. Francis (and Stigmata)

EPHESIANS
2. 19–22. Thomas Apostle
3. 8–19. Sacred Heart
3. 13–21. *16 Pent.*
4. 1–6. *17 Pent.*
4. 7–13. Vig. Ascension, Simon and Jude, Vot. Apostles
4. 1–7, 13–21. Vot. Unity

[1] Sunday eclipsed by the Feast of the Holy Family.

4. 23–28. *19 Pent.*
5. 1–9. *3 Lent*
5. 15–21. *20 Pent.*
5. 22–33. Wedding
6. 10–17. *21 Pent.*

PHILIPPIANS
1. 6–11. *22 Pent.*
2. 5–11. *Palm Sunday*
          Feasts of Cross
    8–11. Vot. of Cross
3. 7–12. Paul hermit, Francis of
          Paula and Peter Alc.
3. 17–4. 3. *23 Pent.*
          Clement
4. 4–7. *3 Advent*

COLOSSIANS
1. 9–14. *24 Pent.*
1. 12–20. *Christ the King*
3. 1–4. Holy Saturday
3. 12–17. *5 Epiph.*
   12–18. *Holy Family* (1 Epiph.)

I THESSALONIANS
1. 2–10. *6 Epiph.*
2. 2–9. Augustine Cantuar.
2. 13–16. Cyriac, etc.
4. 1–7. *2 Lent.*
4. 13–18. Funeral
5. 14–23. Lent Ember Sat.

II THESSALONIANS
2. 1–8. Advent Ember Sat.

I TIMOTHY
4. 8–16. Anthony M. Zacc.
5. 3–10. Monica
6. 6–12. Alexius

II TIMOTHY
2. 1–7. Alphonsus
2. 8–10. } Mart. not Bp
3. 10–12. }
3. 14–4. 5. Ireneus
4. 1–8. Doctor

TITUS
2. 11–15. *Christmas I*
          Circumcision
3. 4–7. *Christmas II*
          Vot. B.V.M.

PHILEMON

HEBREWS
1. 1–12. *Christmas III*
4. 16–5. 7. Vot. Elect. Pope
5. 1–10. Vot. Christ the Priest
    1–6. Thomas Cantuar.
          Josaphat Martyr
    1–4. Callistus
7. 23–27. Conf. Bishop
9. 2–12. Sept. Ember Sat.
9. 11–15. *Passion Sunday*,
          Precious Blood
10. 32–38. Many Martyrs
11. 33–39. Fabian and Sebastian,
          40 Mart., Symphorosa,
          etc.
13. 7–17. Nicholas

JAMES
1. 2–12. Donatus
1. 12–18. Martyr Bishop
1. 17–21. *4 Easter*
1. 22–27. *5 Easter*
2. 12–17. John Cantius
5. 13–16. Vot. for Sick
5. 16–20. Rogations

I PETER
1. 1–7. Peter's Chair
    3–7. Many Martyrs
    4–7. Vot. Creation Pope
2. 1–10. Sat. after Easter
2. 11–19. *3 Easter*
2. 21–25. *2 Easter*
3. 8–15. *5 Pent.*
3. 18–22. Fri. after Easter
4. 7–11. *Sun. after Asc.*
4. 13–19. Nereus, etc., Gervase,
          etc., Martin I
5. 1–11. Apollinaris
    1–4. Creation of Bp
    1–4, 10–11. Common of Popes
5. 6–11. *3 Pent.*

II PETER
1. 16–19. Transfiguration

I JOHN
1. 10–16. Polycarp
3. 13–18. *2 Pent.*
          Camillus

4.	18–21.	1 Pent.[1]	5.	6–12.	Vig. All Saints
5.	4–10.	*Low Sunday*	5.	11–14.	Vot. Angels
			7.	2–12.	*All Saints*
II JOHN			7.	13–17.	Maurice
III JOHN			11.	19–12. 1, 10.	B.V.M. Lourdes
JUDE			14.	1–5.	Innocents
			14.	13.	Daily Requiem
APOCALYPSE			19.	1–9.	Soter and Caius
1.	1–5.	Michael	21.	2–5.	Dedication

---

[1] This Sunday is always eclipsed by the Feast of the Trinity, but the Mass remains in the Roman Missal.

APPENDIX B

A LIST OF ST PAUL'S FRIENDS

to whom, or from whom he sends greetings in the course of his Epistles

Note.—The letter P after an Epistle indicates that the person was at St Paul's end of the correspondence. If we remember that I Cor. was written from Ephesus, Rom. from Corinth, and the Epp. of the Captivity from Rome, the residence of such people becomes obvious; but on the other hand, it is the mention of these people that sometimes helps us to understand where the letter was written from.   k = Paul's "kinsman" in Rom. 16.

	Epistle	Residence	Date in Mart.	Further news, if any, chiefly in the Roman Martyrology[1] (m. = martyred d. = died.)
Achaicus	I Cor.	Corinth		
Ampliatus	Rom.	Rome	Oct. 31	m. Rome w. Urbanus and Narcissus
Andronicus (k)	Rom.	Rome		
Apelles	Rom.	Rome		
Apollo	I Cor. P, Tit.	travels		
Appia	Philem.	Colossae	Nov. 22	m. Col. w. Philemon (see. p. 55)
Aquila	I Cor. P, II Tim, Rom.	Ephesus ⎫ Rome ⎭	July 8	d. Asia Minor w. Prisca
Archippus	Col., Philem.	Colossae	Mar. 20	m. Asia (a priest?) (see p. 55)
Aristarchus	Col., Philem. P	Rome	Aug. 4	Bp of Thessalonica, m. there (his home town, Acts 20. 4)
Artemas	Tit. P	travels		
Asyncritus	Rom.	Rome	Apr. 8	m. Rome w. Herodian and Phlegon

[1] The traditional data, even of the Roman Martyrology, are not to be given credence too readily. Apparently a number of names from the Epistles were not inserted until the ninth century by one Ado. The more unlikely identifications we have bracketed and queried. We have ignored the legendary sixth century "Lists of the seventy disciples" of Ps.–Dorotheus and Ps.–Hippolytus, which put most of St Paul's friends among the seventy (cf. Lk. 10) and assigned to them bishoprics.

The Martyrology-dates will guide the inquirer to further legends in the *Acta Sanctorum*, or (in the few cases treated of) to the Butler-Thurston *Lives of the Saints*.

	Epistle	*Residence*	*Date in Mart.*	*Further news, if any, chiefly in the Roman Martyrology (m. =martyred d. =died.)*
Caius	I Cor., Rom. P	Corinth	Oct. 4	m. Corinth w. Crispus
Carpus	II Tim.	Troas	Oct. 13	d. Troas
Chloe	I Cor.	Corinth		
Claudia	II Tim. P	Rome		dau. of Caractacus, wife of Pudens? (see p. 223)
Clement	Phil.	Philippi	Nov. 23	4th Pope, m. Crimea, relics at his church in Rome
Crescens	II Tim.	Rome and Galatia	June 27 and Dec. 29 }	Bp of Vienne (Gaul), then back to Galatia where m. as Bp
Crispus	I Cor.	Corinth	Oct. 4	m. Corinth w. Caius
Demas	Col., Philem. P, II Tim.	Rome and Thess.		
Epaphras	Col., Philem. P	Colossae	July 19	Bp of Col., m. there, relics at St Mary Major in Rome
Epaphroditus	Phil. P	Philippi and Rome		(=? Bp of Terracina, ordained by Peter, d. there Mar. 22?)
Epenetus	Rom.	Rome		
Erastus	Rom. P, II Tim.	Corinth	July 26	Bp of Philippi, m. there
Eubulus	II Tim. P	Rome		
Evodia	Phil.	Philippi		(unlike Syntyche, not in Mart., so perhaps did not mend her ways)
Fortunatus	I Cor.	Corinth		
Hermas	Rom.	Rome	May 9	m. Rome
Hermes	Rom.	Rome		
Herodian (k)	Rom.	Rome	Apr. 8	m. Rome w. Asyncritus and Phlegon
Jason (k)	Rom. P	Corinth	July 12	d. Cyprus (or in prison w. Sosipater in Corfu?) (=?Paul's host at Thess. in Acts 17?) (? Bp of Tarsus)
Jesus Justus	Col. P	Rome		
Julia	Rom.	Rome		(wife or sister of Philologus?)
Junias (k)	Rom.	Rome		
Linus	II Tim. P	Rome	Sept. 3	2nd Pope, m. Rome, buried in St Peter's

	Epistle	Residence	Date in Mart.	Further news, if any, chiefly in the Roman Martyrology (m. =martyred d. =died)
Lucius (k)	Rom. P	Corinth		
Luke	Col., Philem., II Tim. P	Rome	Oct. 18	d. Asia Minor, after preaching in Italy, Gaul and Greece, relics at Padua
Mark	Col., Philem. P, II Tim.	Rome and travels	Apr. 25	Bp of Alexandria, m. there, relics at Venice
Mary	Rom.	Rome		
Nereus and sister	Rom.	Rome		(=? bro. of Achilles, both bapt. by Peter and martyrs in Rome May 12, relics in own church)
Narcissus	Rom.	Rome	Oct. 31	m. Rome w. Amplia-tus and Urbanus
Nymphas	Col.	Laodicea		
Olympias	Rom.	Rome		
Onesimus	Philem.	Colossae	Feb. 16	Bp of Ephesus after Timothy, m. in Rome (=?Bp of Ephesus met by Ignatius in 107?)
Onesiphorus	II Tim.	Ephesus	Sept. 6	m. (wild horses) in Hellespont with one Porphyrius
Patrobas	Rom.	Rome	Nov. 4	m. Rome w. Philo-gus (=? freedman in time of Nero in Tacitus, Hist., 1. 49, 2. 95?)
Persis	Rom.	Rome		
Phebe	Rom. P	Cenchrae	Sept. 3	
Philemon	Philem.	Colossae	Nov. 22	m. Col. w. Appia (see p. 55)
Philologus	Rom.	Rome	Nov. 4	m. Rome w. Patrobas
Phlegon	Rom.	Rome	Apr. 8	m. Rome w. Asycri-tus and Herodian
Prisca	as for Aquila		July 8	(her church in Rome?)
Pudens	II Tim. P	Rome	May 19	senator (see p. 223)
Quartus	Rom. P	Corinth	Nov. 3	
Rufus and mother	Rom.	Rome	Nov. 21	
Silvanus	I–II Th., II Cor.	travels	July 13	d. Macedonia

	Epistle	Residence	Date in Mart.	Further news, if any, chiefly in the Roman Martyrology (m. = martyred d. = died)
Sosipater (k)	Rom. P	Corinth	June 25	d. Berea (his home town if = Sopater of Acts 20. 4) (or ? as Bp of Iconium d. in prison at Corfu w. Jason?)
Sosthenes	I Cor. P	Ephesus	Nov. 28	d. Corinth, where beaten as pres. of synagogue, Acts 18. 17
Stachys	Rom.	Rome		(= ? 1st Bp of Byzantium, cons. by St Andrew ? Oct. 31)
Stephanas	I Cor.	Corinth		
Syntyche	Phil.	Philippi	July 22	(cf. Evodia above)
Tertius	Rom. P	Corinth		the scribe
Timothy	all Epp. exc. Eph., Col. Philem.	with St Paul	Jan. 24	Bp of Ephesus, m. there (stoning)
Titus	II Cor., Tit., II Tim.	Crete Dalmatia }	Jan. 4 and Feb. 6 }	d. Crete
Trophimus	II Tim.	Ephesus (Miletus)		(prob. not = 1st Bp of Arles in France, Dec. 29) Ephesus home town, Acts 21. 29
Tryphena Tryphosa }	Rom.	Rome	Nov. 10	d. Iconium
Tychicus	Eph., Col., Tit., II Tim. }	travels	Apr. 29	d. Paphos (Crete), in every ref. he is messenger
Urbanus	Rom.	Rome	Oct. 31	m. Rome w. Ampliatus and Narcissus
Zenas	Tit.	travels		a lawyer

APPENDIX C

A SHORT ESSAY ON SLAVERY

in the Roman world at the time of the Apostles, with special reference to the case of Onesimus[1]

Slavery was an accepted system in Roman society and centuries of laws defined clearly the conditions. First of all, a slave had no rights whatever in law ("servile caput nullum jus habet", *Digest*, IV, 5). Consequently, he had no legitimate marriage or paternity—he would be allowed cohabitation with no legal status. It followed that he was incapable of legal adultery: a situation which of course led to the possibility of hideous abuses on the part of masters and mistresses—probably one of the chief causes of Roman degeneracy in the later Empire. He could not legally acquire property: anything he acquired belonged to his master. He was therefore incapable of theft, and if he took anything, he was technically merely moving his master's property. His master could, however, allow him "pocket money" (*peculium*) and permit him to accumulate some savings. No contract could exist between master and slave, and the master had a complete right to "direct" (as one says nowadays) the labour of the slave to whatever task he willed. The slave had no claim to choose work, or any right to enter military or public service. If a slave committed any crime against his master, such as theft or flight or any independent action of which he was legally incapable, the master had complete freedom to punish him any way he wished, even by death—crucifixion was a slave's death—and the slave had no redress whatever.

[1] Good sources are: art. Slavery in the *Cath. Encycl.* by no less an authority than Paul Allard, author of the classical work, *Les esclaves chrétiens* (1900); art. in *Encycl. Britt.*; and Bp Lightfoot's commentary on Col. and Philem., especially pp. 308–10, 318 sq.

A result of this legal condition was, as Bp Lightfoot points out (p. 309), a complete moral irresponsibility on the part of the slave. He knew he was regarded as a mere talking implement (Varro had said only a century before in *De re rustica*, I, 17: "Instrumenti genus vocale, semivocale et mutum: vocale, in quo sunt servi; semivocale, in quo boves; mutum, in quo plaustra, i.e. carts"). If therefore there was a chance, he would take the law at its word, and without responsibility or conscience, strike for liberty, murder if necessary, rob and flee. If he could evade capture, he had after all only done what was reasonable. This attitude is of course directly opposed to every moral and ethical code, but was the natural outcome of the system. And if it is true, as it seems, that three quarters of the inhabitants of the Roman world in the first century were slaves, it is obvious that an utter subversion of morality must have ensued.

Although in point of fact very many masters treated their slaves with kindliness and even affection (Seneca said they should be looked upon as "humble friends"), and although they were often given positions of responsibility and even honour, yet their degraded legal status remained, and examples of cruelty and oppression continue to be found, as the writings of Latin authors round the beginning of the Christian era show, such as Ovid, Horace, Martial and Juvenal. Seneca (*Ep. Moral.*, 47) mentions the current proverb, "Totidem hostes esse quot servos," which shows the way things were going. It was only about three years (at most) after Paul had written to Philemon about Onesimus that the frightful incident of the murder of Pedanius Secundus by one of his slaves occurred in Rome (A.D. 61: Tacitus, *Annales*, 14, 42). If this happened, the law directed that all slaves of the household should be put to death. In this case 400 came under the sentence. There was a popular rising to prevent the execution. But the Senate decided that the law must be obeyed, the tumult was quelled and the prisoners marched to their death under heavy military guard.

All this throws much light on the case of Onesimus. When he robbed Philemon and fled, he was only acting according to the slaves' code. He was a slave, and his mentality was that which had been thrust upon him by the very system itself. We can understand something of what conversion to the Christian life must have meant to him. We can appreciate the earnestness of Paul's pleading with his master, when we realise the master's power over his slave. We marvel at Paul's daring in suggesting that a slave should make restitution to his master in the only form he could, by offering his further service.

A Christian inheritance from Judaism, especially through the preaching and example of St Paul, was the idea of the dignity of human labour, a notion which modern industrial slavery is abolishing in our own day. In the early times of Israel slavery had existed, but in post-exilic times the idea of one Israelite being the slave of another had already become abominable (II Esdras, 5. 1–13). The Rabbis considered that every man should be able to work for his living. Our Lord himself and most of his Apostles were honourable "working men". St Paul himself plied his trade of tent-making "lest we should be chargeable to any of you" (II Thess. 3. 8), and he intended this to be a pattern to his followers, recording also his own saying, "If any man will not work, neither let him eat" (ibid. v. 10).

In the Roman world manual labour, because performed by slaves, had come to be looked upon as low and degrading. (The words *opus servile* in the legislation about Sunday rest is a relic of this state of affairs.) This attitude towards work produced the notorious cult of luxury and idleness which characterized the degenerate times of the later Empire.

"Primitive Christianity", says Paul Allard, "did not attack slavery directly; but it acted as though slavery did not exist."

St Paul wrote (I Cor. 12. 13): "For in one Spirit were we all baptized into one body . . . whether bond or free," and (Gal. 3. 28), "There is neither bond nor free . . . for you are all one in Christ." Yet so much was slavery part of the social system that nowhere do the Apostles urge emancipation of slaves, and still less do they advocate slaves throwing off the yoke. Paul advises Onesimus to go back. Both Peter (I Pet. 2. 18) and Paul (Eph. 6. 5, Col. 3. 22) recommend humble submission of slaves to masters. Yet Christianity was quite incompatible with the principle of slavery, for as Bp Lightfoot says, once that "the Apostolic precept that in Christ Jesus is neither bond nor free was not only recognised but acted upon, then slavery was doomed. Henceforward it was only a question of time" (p. 323).

The religious equality proclaimed by Christianity for slaves and free was something new to Rome, for in pagan Rome slaves were excluded from participation in the national religion. Among Christians all received the same sacraments and the same burial (as the catacombs show). The sacrament of Matrimony open to all made the marriage of slaves legal in the eyes of the Church. This was a most fundamental emancipation. Slaves and free alike could occupy offices in the Church, and as early as the middle of the second century we find Pope Pius I who is said to have been a slave. Tradition says that Onesimus became Bishop of Ephesus after the death of Timothy. Very many of St Paul's friends bear names usually associated with slaves.

As Christianity developed, the freeing of slaves in Christian households became more general. Instead of requiring slaves to buy their liberty out of their own savings or *peculium* (as e.g. Seneca, *Ep.* 80, describes), Christian masters gave it to them as an alms. Sometimes, it appears, slaves were redeemed by money collected by the Christian community, though Ignatius of Antioch, writing to Polycarp, discourages slaves from expecting this to happen: "Let them not desire to be set free at the public cost" (*Ep. to Polycarp*, 4; A.D. 107). The most remarkable example occurs around the year A.D. 400, when the Roman millionaire St Melania the Younger (Martyrology-date Dec. 31) gave away all her possessions, including all her slaves. By the year 406, when her fortune was by no means yet exhausted, she had already freed 8000 slaves.

But freeing of slaves (*manumissio*) already existed in pagan times. Either the slave could buy his freedom out of his own *peculium*, as we have already said (and this was very natural since the purchase of a slave often involved considerable capital outlay—as we can understand if we think of it as a working lifetime's wages), or he could be granted his freedom by his master. In the latter case, it was apparently more frequently by the master's will or testament, so that the slave obtained his freedom at his master's death. When a slave was granted his freedom by his master, and so became a *libertus* or freedman, there were usually certain conditions attached, such as a contract for continued employment. Usually a freedman could only bequeath half of his property, the other half returning to his patron. But a freedman's grandson could attain to full free citizenship.

From the first century onwards the number of freedmen increased very greatly and they entered into the professions, the army and political life. Since, in common with most slaves, they were of foreign origin, a considerable alien influence began in this way to make itself felt in Roman society. Some freedmen reached positions of the highest influence, and amassed the most fabulous wealth. Famous among these were Narcissus and Pallas, both freedmen of the Emperor Claudius, and in his time great favourites at court. Their intrigues brought death to both of them in the time of Nero, first Narcissus (Tacitus, *Ann.*, 13, 1), and later Pallas (14, 65, where Tacitus also records his "immensam pecuniam").

Another of Claudius' freedmen is of particular interest to

us. This is the brother of Pallas, who was none other than Felix who rose to be procurator of Judea (an unprecedented honour for a freedman), and of whom we read so much in Acts 23–24. Suetonius (*Claudius*, 28) says that his successes included being "trium reginarum maritus", i.e. his three marriages were all with royal blood: Drusilla (Acts 24. 24) was the daughter of King Herod Agrippa I, and another wife was the granddaughter of Antony and Cleopatra according to Tacitus (*Hist.*, 5, 9), although Tacitus here mistakenly identifies these two wives—see Josephus, *Ant.*, XX, 7, who would have known more about it. Tacitus (ibi) speaks of Felix's "servile ingenium" (slave's cunning). Felix was suddenly removed from office in 57 when complaints had been made by the Jews about his cruelty. It was only the fact that his brother Pallas was still in favour at court that saved him from punishment (Josephus, *Ant.*, XX, 8, 9).

The vulgarity and pride of some of these *nouveaux riches* is recounted by many of the Latin writers (e.g. Tacitus, *Ann.*, 11, 29; 13, 23, of Narcissus), and it may well be that the decadent and cruel entertainments and the debased luxuries of the later Empire were the pursuits primarily of this multitude of alien upstarts, rather than of the race of the real Romans themselves.

Thus the system of slavery, so integral to Roman society, brought ruin to that very society by the moral irresponsibility of the slave, by the degradation of the idea of work, and by the birth of a vulgar new aristocracy. But meanwhile Christian Rome was growing amid the moral wreckage and preaching the brotherhood of all men in Christ.

APPENDIX D

A NOTE ON THE TOMBS OF THE APOSTLES PETER AND PAUL IN ROME

A broadcast of the present Holy Father, Pope Pius XII, on May 13th, 1942, raised wide interest in the excavations which had been begun under the High Altar of the Basilica of St Peter in Rome. These works will be concluded before the Holy Year of 1950, and before then complete results will probably not be published. But the Holy Father mentioned some important preliminary discoveries, notably of the pagan cemetery on the site. The tomb of St Peter itself is very difficult of access, because of the several early rebuildings and the fact that it is surrounded by vital foundations of the present basilica. Furthermore, it probably lies more than forty feet below the present floor-level. Work must be careful and slow, but there is no doubt that exciting discoveries will be made on a site untouched for 1100 or even 1600 years.

In this brief note we shall not attempt to give historical or archaeological detail, but only a summary of the history of the two tombs. Further information may be read in the sources mentioned at the end.

THE FIRST BURIAL

In the year 67, during the persecution of Nero, Peter was killed (by crucifixion head downwards) in the Circus of Nero, which lay to the south (or left) of the present Basilica; and Paul was beheaded at the place now known as the "Tre Fontane" (the three fountains which sprang up at the spots where the Apostle's head bounded as it fell), about three miles from the gates of the City on the Via Ostiense.

Both were immediately buried in cemeteries nearby, St

Peter in that along the Via Cornelia adjoining the Circus, and St Paul in that along the Via Ostiense about 1¼ miles outside the City. The traces of these cemeteries were discovered under St Paul's Basilica during the restorations of 1850 and under St Peter's in 1942, thus confirming the traditions about the burial.

Immediately, the two tombs, just as they were, became the objects of veneration. Already about A.D. 80 Cletus (or Anacletus), second successor of Peter, built some sort of vault over each tomb. Eusebius (II, 25) quotes a certain Caius, who was "born about the time of Zephyrinus Bishop of Rome" (i.e. about 200), as having written, "If you will go to the Vatican, or to the Ostian Road, you will find the *trophaea* of those who have laid the foundations of this Church." The discoveries of 1942 include a wall within the pagan cemetery, on which are many *graffiti* (or scribblings scratched into the surface) in the form of Christian invocations, dating from long before 300. The Holy Father in his broadcast said that these evidences of popular veneration at this spot "which take us back to the times of persecution, provide us with historical certainty that we have here the remains of that *trophaeum* of which Caius spoke".

IN THE CATACOMBS

Beneath the church of St Sebastian, about 1½ miles from the City gates, along the Via Appia, and still now in the open country, there are many catacombs, and remains have been found of complete pagan cemeteries dating from the first century A.D. In the earliest Christian guide-books to Rome (the "*Notitia ecclesiarum Urbis Romae*" of the early seventh century, for instance) we find it stated that here, at St Sebastian's, are to be found "the sepulchres of the apostles Peter and Paul, in which they rested forty years". In the Philocalian Calendar (fourth century) we find the reference to their bodies being there "Tusco et Basso consulibus", which gives the year 258, the date of the persecution of Valerian. The discovery in 1915 of a wall in these catacombs covered with *graffiti* invoking the intercession of Peter and Paul, and to be dated in the third century, strongly confirmed the tradition that the Apostles were buried here for a time.

It is therefore generally held nowadays that in 258 the danger became too great to allow the sacred relics to remain in the city, and that this remote spot on the Via Appia was chosen as a suitable hiding-place. The holy Martyr Sebastian, the courageous Roman officer who was first shot with arrows and then clubbed to death for his faith, died in the persecution of Diocletian about A.D. 298 and was buried at the same place. Now Diocletian's reign came to an end in 305, and it was probably then considered safe to restore the bodies of the Apostles to their own resting-places. This would give very little over forty years in the catacombs, as the old guides stated.

After the removal of the Apostles the catacomb came to be known by the name of the popular hero of the time, St Sebastian; but the thrillingly spontaneous *graffiti* (in their popular mis-spelt Latin and Greek, or sometimes a mixture of both), there for all to see, are a witness to the sojourn there of the bones of the Apostles.

CONSTANTINE

In 312 the Emperor Constantine succeeded, and the story of his conversion is well known. He immediately set about adorning the tombs of the Princes of the Apostles. It is said that he personally assisted in digging and laying the foundations of the Basilica that was to crown the tomb of St Peter. It was not completed until after his death in 337. He also raised a small basilica over the tomb of St Paul on the Via Ostiense. This, however, was rebuilt and greatly enlarged by the Emperors Theodosius, Honorius and Valentinian (the "Basilica of the Three Emperors", begun in 384).

Constantine is said to have adorned the sarcophagi of the Apostles in the most splendid manner, including for each a massive gold cross.

Subsequent History of St Paul's

The Basilica of the Three Emperors remained intact until the terrible fire of 1823 which wrecked the whole building. But the tomb of St Paul under the high altar remained untouched, and has never been opened since the time of Constantine. In 1838, however, in the course of rebuilding, the vault was accidentally pierced, and the architect and Abbot of St Paul's peeped through the crack. It was immediately sealed and the happening remained a secret for many years. It appears that they did glimpse the stone sarcophagus of the Apostle, but evidence of what exactly they saw is obscure. The restoration also involved the clearing of a slab below the high altar inscribed in lettering of the time of Constantine PAVLO APOSTOLO MART. The Basilica was rebuilt on the original pattern and solemnly re-opened by Pope Pius IX on the occasion of the definition of the Dogma of the Immaculate Conception in 1854.

Subsequent History of St Peter's

Although work was begun in 1450, the Constantinian Basilica remained substantially intact until it was pulled down in 1505. After nearly 1200 years the structure had become unsafe. It was in connexion with indulgences being attached to the good work of contributing money to the rebuilding of St Peter's that trouble began with Martin Luther in 1517. Four of the greatest architects the world has known were employed on the new Basilica: Bramante, Michelangelo, Maderna and Bernini. All contributed substantially to the design of the building, and Raphael was also consulted. The new Basilica, the greatest and most glorious church in Christendom, was opened by Pope Urban VIII in 1626.

A new high altar had been built over the tomb of St Peter (known as the *confessio*), but the tomb itself was not touched. It had not, however, remained unscathed, like St Paul's. In 846 the old basilica had been pillaged during a raid on Rome by the Saracens. They had bent the iron bars that surrounded the tomb and stolen the golden ornaments placed there by Constantine. The Pope of the time, Leo IV, restored the shrine. He regretted that he could not replace the splendour of Constantine, but he apparently strengthened its defences against further intrusion by solid masonry (as he also did the Vatican territory, whence it is still called the Città Leonina).

So it is that the tomb of St Peter is covered first by the vault of Cletus, decorated and enclosed by Constantine, fortified by Pope Leo IV, and finally had its whole superstructure rebuilt in the sixteenth to seventeenth century. Yet, well below the floor of the present Basilica, and probably directly above the tomb itself, is the little altar called *Ad Caput*, dating probably from the time of St Gregory (*c*. 600), and it is the joy of every priest who has had the privilege to do so, to have said Mass on the altar whose relics are the bones, far below, of St Peter himself.

SUMMARY

67 Peter martyred in Circus of Nero Buried at Vatican	67 Paul martyred at "Tre Fontane" Buried near Via Ostiense

258–305
at catacombs of St Sebastian

305 Restored to Vatican	305 Restored to Via Ostiense

c. 314	Constantine's Basilica	*c.* 314	Constantine's Basilica
		384	Basilica of the Three Emperors
864	Rebuilding by Leo IV		
1505	New Basilica begun		
1626	New Basilica opened		
		1823	Basilica burnt down
		1854	Restored
1942	Excavations		

Some sources: Noële M. Denis and R. Boulet, *Romée, ou le pèlerin moderne à Rome*, 1935, pp. 7 sq., 89 sq., 173 sq. (detailed); Butler-Thurston, *Lives of the Saints* for Nov. 18 (Ded. of SS Peter and Paul), cf. Breviary for same date; *Cath. Encycl.*, art. Saint Peter, Tomb of, by Mgr A. S. Barnes, and Basilica of, and Saint Paul (all under letter S); Mgr Barnes' books, *St Peter in Rome*, and *The Martyrdom of St Peter and St Paul*; T. Livius, C. SS. R., *St Peter Bishop of Rome*, 1888; H. V. Morton, *In the Steps of St Paul*, pp. 409 sq. (especially for 1838 episode); and finally the radio address (in Italian) of Pope Pius XII, May 13th, 1942 (to be found in the *Acta Apostolicae Sedis* for 1942).

INDICES

I.—GENERAL INDEX

Jerusalem 11 (refs), 117, 121, 126, 134, 154, 166, 226, 249 (Jude)

Jerusalem, Council of 41, 123*n*., 150, 155sqq.

"Jerusalem, the New" 277, 282, 293, 295

Jesus, Holy Name of
in Epp. 59, 106
in Apoc. 278, 296

Jesus Justus 182, 186, App. B

Jesus (high priest) 289

Jews, Paul and the 74, 124, 132, 137sq., esp. 146–149, 155sqq., 176, 199
conversion of the 148

Jezabel 287

Joachim, Abbot 274

Joanna, wife of Chusa 97

Job 236

Johanan ben-Zakkai, Rabbi 30

John the Evangelist, St
Epistles of 3, **254–267**
authorship of 254sq., 265sq.
Gospel parallels in 256sq.
vocabulary of 256sqq.
Apocalypse **268–296**, q.v.
at Jerusalem 155
ordeal of 270
the Presbyter 5, 225, 265sq.
tomb of 265
witness of Transfiguration 253, 258

"John the Presbyter" 5, 225, 265sqq., 268sq.

Joseph (in OT) 288

Josephus, historian 21sqq., 33sq. (life), 130, 201, 229, 309

Josias, king 292

Judaizers 79, 123, 155sqq., 196, 199

Judas Iscariot 4, 248

Jude, St 3sq., 95, 228, 248sq.
Epistle of **248–250**

Judgement-Day, v.s. Parousia.

Jus gladii 20

Justification 80, 132, esp. 135–146, 157, 164, 200, 233sqq.

Justin, St 202, 268

Juvenal 305

Keating, Fr Joseph, S.J. xii

Kenotic passage in Phil. 190sq.

Kent, Fr W. H., O.S.C. xii, 226*n*.

Kenyon, Sir Frederick 31*n*.

Keogh, Fr A., S.J. xii, 154*n*.

"King, honour the" (I Pet. 2. 17) 244

King, A. A. 105*n*.

Kissane, Dr Edward 81

Knabenbauer, Fr J., S.J. xiii, xiv, 171

Knox, Mgr R. A. passim

Konia (Iconium) 10sq.

"Lady Elect, the" (II Jn 1) 266

Lagrange, Fr M. J., O.P. xiv, 21*n*., 135, 144, 154*n*., 156*n*., 158, 160*n*., 163

Lamb in Apoc. 276sq., 280, 282, 287sq., 293

Laodicea 9, 10, 170sq., 280

"Laodiceans, Ep. to the" 170sq., 182

Lateran, IV Council of the 245

Lattey, Fr Cuthbert, S.J., xii, and passim

Law
Canon, s.v.
Roman, v.s. Roman Empire

Law, the Old 126, 160sqq., 183, 213sq.

Leaven (I Cor. 5.6–8) 86

Lechaeum 7

Leo I, St, Pope 128, 194*n*., 215

Leo IV, Pope 314

Leo XIII, Pope 90, 194*n*.

Letter-form, Roman 55, 77

Martyrology
  Christmas 13
  Narcissus 151n.
  Melania 308
  Philemon 55, 183
  Pudens 223
  Sosthenes 77
  Timothy 196
  Titus 199
  and Appendix B
Mary, the Blessed Virgin, v.s.
  Our Lady
Mary Magdalen 96, 228
Mary, mother of James 96,
  228sq.
Mass, v.s. Eucharistic teaching
  Epistle at, v.s. Liturgy and
  App. A
Matthew, St
  parallels in Thess. 68
  parallels in I Cor. 107n.
  wrote in Aramaic 12
Mediator 164, 209
  Christ as 205sqq.
Mediatrix, Our Lady as 210
Megiddo 292
Melania, St 308
Melchisedech 205, 211
Menander of Athens 114n.
Messengers, St Paul's 49, 51
  Epaphroditus 192
  Phebe 151
  Stephanas 117
  Tychicus 52sqq., 167, 181,
    218, 222
  Zenas 200
Messiah, Handel's 113, 116, 143,
  294
Messianic prophecies 14
Michael, Archangel 290
Micheas 15
Michelangelo 16, 313
Midrash 30
Miletus 169
Millenarianism 268, 294
Mishnah 29sqq.

Monro, Miss Margaret xiii, 48,
  151
Montefiore, C. G. 29
Monumentum Ancyranum 27
Mortification 98, 197sq.
Morton, H. V. xiii, 9, 12, 73, 75,
  223n., 237n., 315
Moses 164, 221, 249, 289
  v.s. Assumption of
Muratori, L. A. 224
Muratorian Canon 5, 194n.,
  202, esp. 224, 226
Murillo 290
Musical instruments 110, 221n.
Mynster 160
Mystical Body 81 (refs), 89, 99,
  108, 178sq., 183sqq.

Names, Saul and Silas, meaning
  of 64
Narcissus 151, 308, App. B
Neapolis 60
Nero, emperor 20, 36, 149, 201,
  217, 237, 239, 244, 252,
  270, 273, 291, 310
Nerva, emperor 20, 36, 255, 270
Newman 143
Nicodemus 28, 261
Nicolaites (heretics) 285sq.
Nicopolis 8, 42, 193, 199, 222
Noe 246
Novatus, s. of Pudens 223
Novatians (heretics) 202, 215
Numbers (in Apoc.), signifi-
  cance of 278sq., 289sqq.
Nymphas 182, App. B

Oecumenism, false 286
"Old man—new man" 143sq.,
  175, 179
Onesimus 52sqq., 167, 181,
  305sqq., App. B
Onesiphorus 220, App. B
Onqelos, his Targum 28
Orchard, Dom Bernard 68sq.
Ordination rite 219

II.—INDEX OF GREEK WORDS COMMENTED

332

III.—INDEX OF SCRIPTURAL PASSAGES

Note.—In the Epistles and Apocalypse passages which are the subject of formal commentary in their own context are *not* listed here. They will easily be found in the body of the book.

IV.—AN INDEX OF A HUNDRED CLASSICAL PASSAGES FROM THE EPISTLES[1]

There is no respect of persons with God: Rom. 2.11 (137).

God is true; and every man a liar: Rom. 3.4 (138).

Being justified therefore by faith: Rom. 5.1 (140).

For I do not that good which I will: Rom. 7.15 (144).

You have received the spirit of adoption of sons, whereby we cry: Abba (Father): Rom. 8.15 (145).

I reckon that the sufferings of this time are not worthy to be compared with the glory to come: Rom. 8.18 (145).

Every creature groaneth and travaileth . . . even till now: Rom. 8.22 (17).

O the depth of the riches of the wisdom and the knowledge of God: Rom. 11.33 (149).

We being many, are one body in Christ: Rom. 12.5 (149).

He that loveth his neighbour hath fulfilled the law: Rom. 13.8 (150).

We preach Christ crucified, unto the Jews a stumbling-block, and unto the Gentiles foolishness: I Cor. 1.23 (80).

Eye hath not seen . . . what things God hath prepared for them that love him: I Cor. 2.9 (81).

We have the mind of Christ: I Cor. 2.16 (81).

I have planted, Apollo watered, but God gave the increase: I Cor. 3.6 (82).

Shall I come to you with a rod?: I Cor. 4.21 (84, 125).

Purge out the old leaven: I Cor. 5.7 (86).

"All things are lawful to me, but not all are expedient": I Cor. 6.12 (88).

Your bodies are the members of Christ: I Cor. 6.15 (89).

As God hath called every one, so let him walk: I Cor. 7.17 (91).

Am I not an apostle, have I not seen Christ?: I Cor. 9.1 (95).

Doth God take care for oxen?: I Cor. 9.9 (96).

I became all things to all men: I Cor. 9.22 (97).

I chastise my body and bring it into subjection: lest perhaps, when I have preached to others, I myself should become a castaway: I Cor. 9.27 (98).

He that thinketh himself to stand, let him take heed lest he fall: I Cor. 10.12 (99).

[1] Doubtless any reader would have chosen a different hundred, but most of these texts are on the tip of the tongue of most of us, though our memory often fails to guide us to the place, and this index may help us. The passages are arranged as they stand in the Bible, for it is easier to glance through the list than to decide which word should be sought alphabetically. The bracketed numbers refer to pages of this book.

The chalice . . . is it not . . . the blood of Christ?: I Cor. 10.16 (99).

For we, being many, are one bread, one body: I Cor. 10.17 (99).

No man can say the Lord Jesus, but by the Holy Ghost: I Cor. 12.3 (106).

If I speak with the tongues of men, and of angels, and have not charity . . .: I Cor. 13.1 (109).

We see now through a glass in a dark manner: I Cor. 13.12 (109).

There remain faith, hope and charity, these three, but the greatest of these is charity: I Cor. 13.13 (109).

If the trumpet give an uncertain sound, who shall prepare himself to the battle?: I Cor. 14.8 (110).

I am the least of the apostles . . . but by the grace of God I am what I am: I Cor. 15.9–10 (112).

If Christ be not risen again, . . . your faith is vain: I Cor. 15.14 (112).

In a moment, in the twinkling of an eye, at the last trumpet: I Cor. 15.52 (115).

O death, where is thy victory? O death, where is thy sting?: I Cor. 15.55 (116).

The letter killeth: but the spirit quickeneth: II Cor. 3.6 (126).

As dying, and behold we live . . . as having nothing, and possessing all things: II Cor. 6.9–10 (38).

"His bodily presence is weak, and his speech contemptible": II Cor. 10.10 (121, 124).

I know a man . . . rapt even to the third heaven: II Cor. 12.2 (128).

I live, now not I; but Christ liveth in me: Gal. 2.20 (38, 161).

O senseless Galatians, who hath bewitched you?: Gal. 3.1 (161).

A little leaven corrupteth the whole lump: Gal. 5.9

The fruit of the spirit is charity, joy . . . &c.: Gal. 5.22.

I bear the marks of the Lord Jesus in my body: Gal. 6.17 (166).

To re-establish all things in Christ: Eph. 1.10 (173).

The church, which is his body, and the fullness of him who is filled all in all: Eph. 1.23 (174).

Built upon the foundation of the apostles and prophets, Jesus Christ himself being the chief corner stone: Eph. 2.20 (176).

That Christ may dwell by faith in your hearts . . . that you may comprehend . . . what is the breadth, and length . . . , the charity of Christ, which surpasseth all knowledge: Eph. 3.18–19 (178).

Careful to keep the unity of the Spirit in the bond of peace: Eph. 4.3 (178).

For to me, to live is Christ, and to die is gain: Phil. 1.21 (190).

Having a desire to be dissolved and to be with Christ: Phil. 1.23 (190).

Who . . . emptied himself, taking the form of a servant: Phil. 2.6–7 (190).

I count all things to be but loss for the excellent knowledge of Jesus Christ my Lord: Phil. 3.8 (192).

But our conversation is in heaven: Phil. 3.20 (192).

Rejoice in the Lord always: Phil. 4.4 (192).

The peace of God, which surpasseth all understanding: Phil. 4.7.

I . . . fill up those things that are wanting of the sufferings of Christ: Col. 1.24 (184).

Rooted and built up in him: Col. 2.7 (183).

Blotting out the handwriting of the decree . . . fastening it to the cross: Col. 2.14 (185).

Luke, the most dear physician: Col. 4.14 (59).

This is the will of God, your sanctification: I Thess. 4.3 **(65)**.

Pray without ceasing: I Thess. 5.17.

The man of sin, the son of perdition: II Thess. 2.3 (69).

"If a man will not work, neither let him eat": II Thess. 3.10 (71).

Not greedy of filthy lucre: I Tim. 3.8, Tit. 1.7 (199).

Neglect not the grace that is in thee: I Tim. 4.14 (198).

The desire of money is the root of all evils: I Tim. 6.10 (198).

But thou, O man of God, fly these things: I Tim. 6.11.

Labour as a good soldier of Christ Jesus: II Tim. 2.3 (220).

All Scripture, inspired of God, is profitable: II Tim. 3.16 (221).

For I am even now ready to be sacrificed: and the time of my dissolution is at hand. I have fought a good fight, I have finished my course, I have kept the faith: II Tim. 4.6–7 (38, 216, 222).

The cloak that I left at Troas: II Tim. 4.13 (222).

All things are clean to the clean: Tit. 1.15 (199).

Christ . . . an high priest of the good things to come: Heb. 9.11 (212).

Entered once into the Holies, having obtained eternal redemption: Heb. 9.13 (212).

It is a fearful thing to fall into the hands of the living God: Heb. 10.31.

We have here no abiding city: Heb. 13.14 (WV) (208).

Patience hath a perfect work: James 1.4 (231).

From the Father of lights, with whom there is no change, nor shadow of alteration: James 1.17 (232).

Let every man be swift to hear, but slow to speak, and slow to anger: James 1.19 (232).

Be ye doers of the word, and not hearers only: James 1.22 (232).

Religion clean and undefiled . . . is this: . . .: James 1.27 (232).

Fulfil the royal law: Thou shalt love thy neighbour: James 2.8 (233).

Faith, if it have not works, is dead: James 2.17 (234).

If any man offend not in word, the same is a perfect man: James 3.2 (234).

The fruit of justice is sown in peace: James 3.18.

Draw nigh to God, and he will draw nigh to you: James 4.8 (235).

As new-born babes, desire the rational milk without guile: I Pet. 2.2 (242).

You are a chosen generation, a kingly priesthood: I Pet. 2.9 (242).

Honour all men. Love the brotherhood. Fear God. Honour the king: I Pet. 2.17 (244).

Charity covereth a multitude of sins: I Pet. 4.8 (247).

Partakers of the divine nature: II Pet. 1.4 (253).

One day with the Lord is as a thousand years, and a thousand years as one day: II Pet. 3.8 (253).

As also our most dear brother Paul . . . hath written: II Pet. 3.15 (vii, 44, 254).

The concupiscence of the flesh, and the concupiscence of the eyes, and the pride of life: I Jn 2.16 (260).

He that doth the will of God, abideth for ever: I Jn 2.17 (256).

Whosoever hateth his brother is a murderer: I Jn 3.15 (261).

Antichrist is now already in the world: I Jn 4.3 (70, 262).

God is love: I Jn 4.8 (WV) (262).

The victory which overcometh the world, our faith: I Jn 5.4.

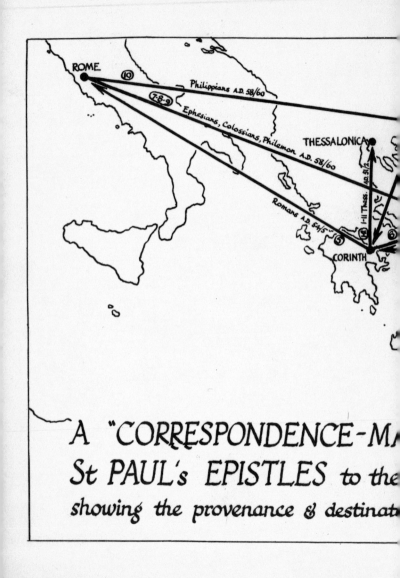

A "CORRESPONDENCE-M~
St PAUL's EPISTLES to the
showing the provenance & destinat~